UNBREAKABLE
JELENA DOKIC
WITH JESSICA HALLORAN

PENGUIN BOOKS

PENGUIN BOOKS

UK | USA | Canada | Ireland | Australia
India | New Zealand | South Africa | China

Penguin Books is part of the Penguin Random House group of companies
whose addresses can be found at global.penguinrandomhouse.com.

First published by Ebury Press in 2017
This edition published by Penguin in 2024

Cover image courtesy of Roadshow Films
Typeset in Janson Text by Midland Typesetters, Australia

Printed and bound in Australia by Griffin Press, an accredited
ISO AS/NZS 14001 Environmental Management Systems printer

 A catalogue record for this
book is available from the
NATIONAL LIBRARY OF AUSTRALIA — National Library of Australia

ISBN 978 1 76135 432 8

penguin.com.au

MIX
Paper | Supporting
responsible forestry
FSC® C018684

We at Penguin Random House Australia acknowledge that Aboriginal and Torres Strait
Islander peoples are the Traditional Custodians and the first storytellers of the lands
on which we live and work. We honour Aboriginal and Torres Strait Islander peoples'
continuous connection to Country, waters, skies and communities. We celebrate Aboriginal
and Torres Strait Islander stories, traditions and living cultures; and we pay our respects to
Elders past and present.

Contents

To my family, Tin and Savo.

Thank you both for loving me and supporting me unconditionally. Words can't explain what you mean to me.

Tin, my rock, thank you for being there for the last fourteen years and for loving me the same way no matter what. I am so grateful to have you. Whenever life got hard you stood by me and our relationship became even stronger. I love you with my heart and soul.

Savo, my dear baby brother. I have loved you from the first time I saw you. I couldn't have asked for a better brother. I wish I could have the years we spent apart back but know that you were in my heart every second. Thank you for your understanding, kindness, love, patience and support. I am so proud of you.

Prologue, July 2000

I don't know where my dad is. I'm standing in the plush Wimbledon players' lounge waiting, looking around for him: we're due to go out for a nice dinner with my managers, Ivan and John. I am seventeen years old and I have just played in the semi-finals. Of Wimbledon.

Surely, you'd think, he would be okay that I got this far at the All England Club. You would think. At the end of the match, as I shook Lindsay's hand, I looked up to the stands and saw my father bolt out of his green seat, nothing but the back of his burly frame rushing from Wimbledon's Centre Court. Usually after my matches, he stands around somewhere near the players' lounge and I have to find him. But today there's neither sight nor sound of him. I called his mobile after I finished my press duties and he didn't pick up.

This has been my greatest run ever in a grand slam and I want to know what he'll say, and to organise how we will get to dinner with Ivan and John. So I call him again, and this time, finally, he picks up.

The dull slur in his slow, loud voice tells me he is drunk. I know this tone; it's the tone of white wine and probably a few glasses of whisky.

He is angry. Furious that I lost. His voice booms down the phone. 'You are pathetic, you are a hopeless cow, you are not to come home. You are an embarrassment. You can't stay at our hotel.'

'But, Dad ...' I say quietly, trying to plead with him.

'You need to go and find somewhere else to sleep,' he yells at the top of his voice. 'Stay at Wimbledon and sleep there somewhere ... Or wherever else. I don't care.'

He hangs up.

I have just made the semi-finals of Wimbledon. But in my father's eyes I am not good enough to come home.

Players around me are getting on with life, chatting, eating dinner, winding down with their coaches. I am alone and shattered. I have no money – well, no access to it – no credit card. It is Dad who has all that. He controls everything in my life.

Emotion starts to overwhelm me. *Failure – I'm a failure*. Minutes tick by, and then hours. I tuck myself away on a small couch in the corner of the players' lounge, hoping no one notices me, and eventually the place is empty.

At around 11 pm the cleaner arrives. She sees me in the corner and comes over. 'You can't stay here,' she says softly.

I make the confession: 'I have nowhere to sleep tonight.' As I say it, the reality hits me. The tears prick in the corner of my eyes.

'I have to let the tournament authorities know,' she says.

Wimbledon's referee, Alan Mills, arrives. 'What happened?' he asks gently.

'I have nowhere to go,' I say. 'I have nowhere to sleep.'

Hot tears are running down my face, but I don't let on that my own father has banished me: as always I must protect him. Alan, however, seems to know what's going on. My management agency, Advantage, has rented a beautiful house in Wimbledon village; Alan calls my managers and they say they will take me in. He arranges for a tournament car to take me to the house.

I arrive sobbing and Ivan and John look concerned when they see me. They explain they'd called my dad earlier in the evening trying to locate us, and my nine-year-old brother, Savo, answered. John says he could hear my father's voice in the background. Apparently Savo said simply, 'My dad isn't here.'

I am both heartbroken by my father's rejection and embarrassed by it.

I'm shown to the spare room. *At least I didn't get a beating from him.*

As I wait for sleep, through the shock and hurt I start to realise that I might never make my father happy. That I might never be good enough in his eyes.

1

Yugoslavia, 1991–94

I am eight years old when I see my first dead body.

It's a foggy morning in our Croatian city, Osijek, when my father and I push out from the bank in our little wooden boat to go fishing on the River Drava. And suddenly I see a man, his hair matted, bobbing face down in the water. His body looks bloated and his hands are blue.

'Papa,' I say, pointing.

'Don't look,' he says, nervous. Our weekly fishing trip is over. He turns the boat back and rows quickly to shore.

War is brewing here; the dead body is a sign – not that I understand this till long afterwards. After the Second World War, Croatia was bundled up with Serbia, Slovenia, Montenegro, Macedonia and Bosnia-Herzegovina to become Yugoslavia, a federation of states. It was inevitable that the nationalism of each country would boil over at some point. Croatia wanted its independence from Serbia, but Serbia didn't want Croatia to have its independence.

In the preceding weeks there have been indications close to home that the Balkans is about to erupt in battle again. Angry Croatian neighbours have threatened my proudly Serbian father straight to his face. 'Get out or die,' they say. There have been phone calls to our family home, men threatening to throw me and my baby brother out the window of our eleventh-floor apartment.

The country is fractured. Dad is worried. Mum is frightened. And now this body – tensions are rising.

A few weeks after the incident of the floating corpse on the river, our lives radically change. It is a hot summer's night. The twenty-first of June 1991, to be exact. It is night-time when my usually stoic truck-driving father arrives home anxious. Another threat has been made.

'Pack tonight – you are leaving tomorrow morning,' he tells us. Mum and I are in shock.

My father is staying behind in Osijek. I think he wants to stay and fight for the life he knows; and he can continue his work as a truck driver here, which would be harder in a new place. He says we are to leave town only for a few weeks, to be out of the way of danger for now. Until the tensions in our city settle.

The next morning we wave goodbye to my dad and leave. We take just a small bag each, a baby bag for three-month-old Savo, and my two treasured tennis racquets. We don't plan to be gone for long. Five of us pile into a small car: Uncle Pavle, Dad's brother, is driving us there, and my paternal grandmother, Ana, a surly old woman, sits in the front. My grandfather is deaf to the arguments of Dad and Uncle Pavle and refuses to come with us. 'They can come here and kill me today or tomorrow, but I'm not leaving,' he says.

My mother and I take our places in the back seat; I hold my restless, tiny baby brother on my lap. Already the heat is intense. The car is stuffy. The air is pungent with sweat. Nobody speaks at first, and the mood is low. I am scared. For five hours, the car winds across beautiful Croatian countryside. From time to time, my mum talks in quiet, concerned tones to my uncle and grandmother.

Our destination is the northern city of Sombor in Serbia; we are refugees running from conflict, looking for a safe place. And we will be safer in Sombor. Everything feels strange when we arrive. But I realise the place looks similar to my home town – the cityscape consists of old architecture and streets lined with beautiful trees. The scenery may look familiar but I'm frightened of what is to come. Our overnight move is still sinking in. I never had the chance to say goodbye to my school friends, my teachers, even my grandfather; I am already homesick and wondering when we will be back in Osijek.

Families are taking in people who are escaping the conflict in Croatia. A Serbian family is hosting us, generous people who have opened their small, cosy home to us until we get on our feet. They live on the outskirts of the city and are willing to look after us for a few weeks until we find our own accommodation. They cook us meals and are kind and well-meaning.

In that first week, our main priority is Savo. He has a condition called hip dysplasia. A cast is required to help move his bones into the correct position, so he needs to see a doctor every week. Mum and I find ourselves walking the three-hour round trip into the city, with trucks screaming perilously close by, to take Savo to a doctor. There is no doctor closer. There are no buses. My mother and I alternate carrying my precious baby brother, his little frame making my arms and hers ache. When driving rain makes the footpath muddy and slippery, we have to be extra careful.

For several weeks we make this journey every third day. It's exhausting and taxing. Then a few weeks into our stay Dad contacts us with welcome news: he's got hold of his friend who has a place in town, closer to the doctor.

This 'place' turns out to be a storage shed – a shabby structure, beside their house, that reeks of dust, rats and melancholy.

A day after arriving there, my uncle and grandmother pack up their things. 'We're going back to Osijek,' my grandmother announces coolly.

It's obvious to me that Mum is angry, but hiding it.

Unable to hold back my sadness and worry, I plead with them: 'You can't leave us behind; you need to stay and help.' They go anyway.

Their departure makes me feel betrayed and angry.

War has broken out, and it's become clear that we are refugees; in fact, the Serbian government has granted us refugee status. Within weeks of arriving, I am enrolled in the local primary school, though I'm still holding out hope that soon we'll be going back to Osijek. But after a few months, I begin to realise we are not going home anytime soon. The group of giggling kids in my apartment block; my friends at school, of whom I was the ring leader; my friends at tennis school, my tennis coaches, my teachers – I will not see them again.

My reality is that I live in a storage shed.

In the shed we have water, electricity, an old double bed and a bassinette for Savo. We wash our clothes by hand. There is a tiny bathroom. It's space we share with a bunch of rodents: mice scurry along the floor in the night; rats lurk in corners. There is no stove but the family lets us use their oven in the main house to bake bread every few days. Mum often makes bread in the evening for the next day. She covers the dough with a cotton cloth and leaves it on a high shelf in the 'warm' corner of the room, away from the vermin. Or so she hopes. Too often in the morning there are rats stuck in the dough, and I have to help her start all over again.

Still, there is a roof over our heads. Plus we have water and a little heat: two small electric heaters in the main room work hard to take the sting out of the cold. Soon I stop wishing for my old life. I know I have different priorities now. We just need to survive.

Although I love Dad, I don't miss the chaos and tension he can create in our home. I don't miss his negativity. The stress he puts my mum and me under. She and I can laugh freely now; it's liberating being able to express my emotions without care, and we don't walk on eggshells here. We don't live with the worry he is going to scream at my mother that lunch was rubbish. Cutlery and dinnerware remain on the table – he's not here to throw it in anger. It's not just food that sets him off – any innocuous thing can trigger one of his outbursts. At least in Sombor we don't live in fear and worry. But we are concerned for his safety.

Once a week my parents talk on the phone in the main house. Not for long, and Mum always looks grave afterwards. The pain on her face speaks volumes about what is happening at home – there is fighting and killing in Osijek.

She hasn't found work yet – her time is spent caring for Savo. When I'm not at school, I spend all my spare time helping out to give her a break. My baby brother is gorgeous. I help bathe him in the sink of the small kitchenette. I feed him and change him. I help get him to sleep, rocking him, walking circles around our small space. In the night, when fatigue gets the better of Mum, I resettle him, help him to sleep. I feel an incredible connection to and love for him. After my mum gave birth to him and it was time to leave the hospital and go home, I insisted on carrying him, wouldn't allow anyone to touch him. From the moment he arrived I felt like his protector.

It's a relief that Mum has such a short walk now to the doctor's for Savo's regular check-ups. That hip problem is tough on us all. Twice a day we go through the ordeal of putting the leather cast on him. Savo always cries and flaps and flails around. He detests it. The mere sight of it makes him wail – obviously it causes him terrible discomfort. So I try to distract him while Mum battles to get it back on to his squirming frame. I sing to him and wave things in front of him, like a picture of Minnie Mouse I have cut out from a magazine. Minnie really calms him down for some reason.

Meanwhile, Dad remains in our apartment in Osijek, holding his ground, earning what he can and sending us money to live. But it's hard for him to send us much: tensions continue to rise in Yugoslavia and incomes are becoming erratic. As a family we are starting to really struggle financially, we are only just managing to feed ourselves – we have hardly a cent by the end of some weeks and are eating bread and margarine.

Fortunately, however, I have been born with a talent that might get us all out of this hell.

⊖

Dad spied the adult-sized deep-grey tennis racquet in the front window of an Osijek sports store on a summer's day in 1989. A Yugoslav girl – Monica Seles – has become hugely successful in this sport. Thinking, *if she can do it* … he forks out some of his hard-earned cash to buy the racquet. With this shiny racquet he has a quiet plan to change my six-year-old life, and his.

Brandishing the treasure, he strides through the front door of our Osijek apartment, an apartment so small you can barely swing this beautiful grey racquet in it. He hands the object to me. It glistens in the afternoon light.

'Let's go and try it out,' he says. It's an order; my father is not asking, he never asks.

Down the stairs we go. The old courtyard of our apartment block is all grey and beige walls, barely a trace of greenery, and he sends me to one end with my new racquet.

I take a few air swings, testing it, getting used to it.

Dad stands a few metres away and feeds a tennis ball my way. I aim my racquet at that very first tennis ball and I smack it back to my father. It makes an efficient soft thud and lands directly in his hands. He delivers another ball. Again I smack it straight back into his hands. And again. Five times I do it. I don't falter.

My father takes me around to the big grey brick wall at the bottom of our apartment block. Against that wall I hit the ball over and over again with precision. The air pops with the sound of me working the ball. Immediately I feel an affinity for the basics of the game. I'm accurate. I have excellent hand–eye co-ordination, a feel for the ball. From that moment I love tennis. A calmness washes over me as I fall into the rhythm of practice. I know this sport will come easily to me. I just love to hit that ball.

Within days of being given the racquet I am here at the wall before and after school. When the sun comes up and as the sun goes down I thump the ball at the wall.

Dad calls up Tennis Club Osijek, which is nestled in a small park in the middle of the city. He asks when and how I can start playing. It's a sunny day when we walk into the small, neat clubrooms. My father finds the head coach and announces I am a talent and can I join the tennis school.

The coach takes a look at me. He frowns. 'She is too small.'

But this coach doesn't know my father – he is always right. He pesters the coach to take a look at my hitting and eventually the man

7

surrenders to his persistence and we go out to a court. Readying themselves for a drill on the clay are ten children who are part of the beginners' tennis school. All are around four years older and much bigger than me. The coach says I can take part.

This is the first time I've ever seen a tennis court, let alone been on one. I stand quietly on the red clay, at attention. The practice begins and several members of the tennis school miss the ball completely or flounder. Some connect with it but don't deliver it back over the net. It's my turn and I take to the service line. The coach feeds me a ball. I connect it to the middle of my racquet and slam it back at him. I nail the shot. Over and over again. I might be six years old but I have a powerful hit.

The coach turns to my father. It's obvious he's gobsmacked by my power and precision. 'She can stay. She is good.'

Within a few weeks I am having one-on-one sessions twice a week.

Dad starts to read up on this game of tennis. He watches the grand slams on TV, focuses on the best players and absorbs their methods. From the stands at the Tennis Club Osijek, he intently studies – and memorises – my coach's methods. After a while my private coach becomes Drago Zorić, and as well as training at Tennis Club Osijek, I also attend Tennis Club Olympia.

Although my father drives trucks for a living, delivering goods around the countryside, he is a fiercely intelligent man. He finished school and did well there, but his parents were too poor to send him to university. Perhaps as an outlet for his frustrated hopes of further education, he is now inhaling every fact and nuance about this game he can.

My dad becomes friendly with the other tennis parents, and likes to cook for us and my friends when they come over. On these occasions he's filled with bonhomie and makes sure that everyone is well fed. He cooks up big hunks of meat, and he loves cooking fish. Fish goulash. Fish soup. He's a proud man but he's also sensitive. Sensitive to the fact that he could have been more than a truck driver. He didn't have a chance, though: he grew up in the small country town of Čepin, a few kilometres south-west of Osijek. His parents weren't well off at all. His father, Strahinja, a kind man, struggled with alcoholism, which meant his mother had to bring up her two sons with no help. But my dad adored his father and had a difficult relationship with his mother. Although my grandfather had a problem with alcohol, he would never have hurt Dad. My grandmother, Ana, however, used to beat him all the time, and made him feel worthless. Yet she treated his brother, my Uncle Pavle, with tenderness and care. My dad could never understand why she picked on him, why he always came second to Pavle. He felt rejected by his mother. When my grandparents saved enough to put one child through school, they decided to give the chance to their first-born – Pavle – who eventually became an architect.

That disappointment and sadness from his childhood is something my father carries around with him. But too easily that frustration is taken out on my mum, and soon I will feel it as well. Because my father, who didn't have a chance, is about to start channelling everything through me. Yes, if things go well with me he could have an opportunity for a different life. He becomes my teacher, my unofficial coach, my conduit – he hopes – to sporting glory.

Dad buys a big laundry bucket, fills it with 30 or so tennis balls, and takes it to the courts to feed them to me, to warm me up before my lessons or to do more after the private training sessions with my coach. The laundry bucket of tennis balls remains by his side while we're at the courts. He's always ready to throw me some balls if there is ever a spare moment.

As I practise with my private coach, my father watches to see where I can improve. Over and over, he says, 'Hard work will make you a champion, Jelena.' In his view, I can never hit too many balls, never do too much practice. I am only six but I practise every day after school.

It's soon clear to me that in Dad's world there are no limits when it comes to this game.

Winter descends on Osijek, and snow falls, but at my father's insistence my hitting continues. One freezing day there's a thin layer of snow on the Osijek roads as we take the tram to the courts. The temperature is around −5°C. Snow forms a shiny, icy armour on the trees near the tennis club, on the wire fence surrounding the court and even on the clay. The cold air stings my cheeks. My father throws his plastic laundry bucket of balls on the ground and we begin my practice. No one else is around, no one else would play in these difficult conditions, no one else is committed to the game like my dad and me. With our gloves and coats on we play. I am cold to my bones.

⊖

At six years of age, I have discovered a pastime that gives me enormous pleasure and satisfaction. I don't even think of tennis as a sport yet, more as a game of targeting and hitting those small yellow balls at the person across the net from me. However, for the first time I am also experiencing pressure from my father – and, much worse, pain.

Until now, Dad has never really yelled at me. I've never been in serious trouble. I was a content, carefree child until tennis entered my life. From the first day I start playing, this changes: with the arrival of tennis comes beatings and violence.

My dad can lash out at any time. But one of the first times comes after I have finished a practice session with my coach. It's been a lighter session than the others. My coach laughs and jokes with me, has me giggling through it. I'm working my heart out. I don't know any other way. But today I'm having fun.

When I get off the court my father's face is a picture of disapproval. As we leave, he tells me I have let him down. Tennis isn't for fun, he adds, and he orders me to do laps of the park as punishment. For fifteen minutes I run hard, then we take the tram home in silence. In the lift to our apartment he starts yelling at me, letting loose a diatribe. His yelling turns almost to screaming. Harsh words about everything I have done the wrong way in this session, that I am hopeless.

His rage peaks when we enter our apartment. My mother's at work so we're alone, and his screaming gets louder until it feels like the walls are shaking. Then he slaps me. His huge right hand strikes my six-year-old cheeks – once, twice, three times rapidly. The shock of the smack is more severe than the pain of his hand against my cheek. He has never done this. My father has never hit me. Hot tears run down my face. I am so confused. Sure, I have seen him overturn the family dinner table in a rage, screaming at my mum and throwing plates of her food against a wall, but he has never *hit* me.

'Go and study,' he thunders.

I nod and comply, unable to stop the tears. Thumping the door shut behind him, Dad leaves the apartment.

My hand shaking, I pick up the phone and call my mum at her work. I am crying so hard I can barely speak. 'He slapped me, Mama,' I manage to sob down the phone. All of a sudden the front door bursts open and he's back. He barrels towards me, grabs the phone and hangs up. I am steadying myself for another slap, but it doesn't come. Instead he chastises me for calling my mother and then saunters off.

When my mother gets home she doesn't confront him about the incident, doesn't call him out on his abuse. This is the point at which something shifts in me.

And from this moment, it's horribly clear: I am afraid of my father.

However, with this slap, my father has introduced me to something that will make me brilliant on the court: fear. Fear of him drives me to work harder to improve. Being average on the tennis court in my father's eyes is not an option; the consequences are too frightening.

From that moment on, tennis seems to prick his rage all the time. I know that if I fail in his eyes, if I don't work hard enough, if I miss that crucial shot, he will strike me. And it can happen anywhere. It happens one day at the bottom of our building, where I grind a ball against the wall. As usual, he is standing watching with total focus, and when I mess up, he takes the slipper off his foot and hits me. He strikes my head and whacks my back. Of course I turn into a miserable mess. But I soon learn to compose myself quickly and start again. To be better than before. I don't want to disappoint my father.

⊖

It is my fighting spirit and success on the tennis court that sees my mum, Savo and me move out of the rat-infested Sombor storage shed in the summer of 1992 and into a house – admittedly an old, abandoned one, but a house nonetheless.

Our move to Sombor hasn't halted my tennis rise. In fact I haven't missed a beat. As soon as we got here my mum and I found some local courts, and I started smashing my way around them and entering competitions in nearby towns. Word is soon out that I have arrived and that I am brilliant at this sport. The Sombor tennis officials see my potential, and they speak to important people in the Serbian Tennis Federation. Those men in turn get in touch with some local government officials, and suddenly we are moved to our new home. Our status as refugees and the fact that Savo is so young have also helped our cause.

In comparison to the storage shed we have been living in for months, our new place feels nicer. It's rundown but there is soft carpet inside. It has better heating so we no longer have to shiver in winter and as we bathe. And there is space, so much space, in comparison to the storage shed; it's also bigger than our apartment in Osijek, with two actual bedrooms – two! It's especially good to have that space because my father has by now arrived from Osijek to join us in Sombor and escape the war.

Within months of our move, my grandmother Ana and Uncle Pavle have returned from Osijek, despite the terrifying state of affairs there. Quietly I'm annoyed. I think to myself, *When we lived in an awful place with rats, you left us – a little girl and a mother with a baby to look after*. But I don't engage with them too much; instead I go about my business. Practise my tennis. Go to school.

In the Sombor primary school playground I am popular: outgoing, friendly, chatty. I make friends easily and have a large group of them. In the classroom my grades are excellent. While the language is basically the same, I have to learn to write and read in Serbian, and quickly, as our teachers write all the lessons on the blackboard in this script. Initially its letters look like a jumble of scribbles – it's a Cyrillic script – but I study it intensively before, during and after school, and with dedicated work I learn how to write and read it within a few weeks.

Soon I'm excelling at any subject that's maths-based. Numbers click in my head and I have an awesome recall for them. Also I excel at pretty much all the other subjects too, including geography. Arts-based lessons? Well, not so much. Facts and figures are more my cup of tea. And I like to be organised and neat. So much so that when the teacher dictates in class I write down the notes in draft form and then at night at home I rewrite them in my class book. I strive for perfection. I am obsessed with order – my pencils are always sharp – everything has a place. I love school and I continue to do well, just like I did in Osijek.

My mum starts working part-time as a store manager of a small supermarket while Dad takes on the care of my younger brother and me. Little love is shown in our house, though. Our parents never hold hands or kiss or hug each other. And my father gets impatient when things are not said or done the way he wants. Food not cooked the right way? The door shut too loudly? He blows up. My mother and I handle his moods with silence and submission. We all walk on eggshells around him, dance round trying to please him. Mum tries to make him the right food, and I try to do the right thing on the tennis court. When I get back from school I long for my mother's return from work. I keep out of my dad's way if we're not on the court – doing my school work, or playing with my little brother, whom I adore.

I feel guilt that sometimes I detest my father being around. That I would rather it just be me, Mum and Savo because then I know our days will be peaceful. When my dad is out, my mother pays more attention to the two of us kids. She becomes kinder, helps me do my homework. We cook together. When my father's at home she goes quiet and withdraws from us. It's like she can't or isn't allowed to show as much love and emotion towards us when he is home. Instead her focus is on pleasing him. She lets him take over. While we were only in Sombor, just the three of us, my mum, brother and I, life was calmer. Now he is here the tension is back in our home.

⊖

Dad gets his wish: aged nine, I'm the national champion in the under-10s and he no longer drives trucks; he devotes himself full-time to my tennis. We travel to the Serbian city of Novi Sad, where I take on kids several years older than me for the under-12 national title. I win the final 6–0, 6–2. It should be a moment of joy but my father is furious at me for dropping two games against an opponent who's three years older than me. Behind the club house he hits my cheeks with great force, away from the other parents and coaches. He berates me loudly for dropping the games and hits me a few more times for emphasis.

Quickly putting that behind me, I go on to win the under-14 national title and, at only twelve years old, to enter under-16 and 18 competitions – though even my ambitious father warns me these are 'mission impossible'. And I do find going up against giant, gangly teenagers challenging. My presence at these tournaments becomes national front-page news; journalists love photographing tiny me alongside tall teens. And I give a lot of them a run for their money, going to three sets against under-18 girls ranked in the top five in the country. They can't beat me easily; I am a little giant-killer.

Meanwhile, in our home town people we know are dying. My mother's obstetrician, the woman who delivered me and my brother, has been strangled to death, another body found floating down the River Drava. Money is scarce and we're living off my mother's meagre salary, supplementing it with a stall at the local market. Because of the war raging across the borders there are embargos and restrictions on Serbia, which means basic goods are becoming increasingly hard to buy. So every month Uncle Pavle makes a ten-hour trip to Hungary, where he stocks up on toiletries that we then on-sell. On weekends I help my family for hours selling soap, toilet paper and toothpaste.

At times there is no bread or milk available, and when deliveries do come in, the queues for these household staples are long. Hours of waiting. Sometimes my uncle or father will be up at 4 am to be one of the first in line.

My life is okay despite the difficulties we are enduring. I can see others are struggling more than us, some even going hungry. I really love school and my tennis is going very well. Tennis Club Zak, where I have become the star although I am still one of the youngest, feels like a second home.

My coach is Milan Lacko and he's a great guy, but I end up working with Josip Molnar, a man who my dad likes very much. Josip used to coach Monica Seles and my father loves this – one of his favourite grand slam matches is the one between Steffi Graf and Monica Seles at the French Open final in 1990, when sixteen-year-old Seles mercilessly took down top-seeded Graf. Dad often talks about this match in depth to me; he thinks I can do something like this – I could be like Monica.

Josip is a calm coach but if I mess up he is firm. Within a year of starting with him I am claiming all the national titles on offer. The three of us spend lots of time together going to tournaments; we take Josip's car and drive for hours to all the big towns across Serbia, where I continue my domination of the national junior ranks. Because we're broke we sleep in the car at tournaments and eat cheap sandwiches from local shops. Soon I have so many trophies that I have to store them in our small shed. The victories are incredibly exciting for me, and my father is pleased by my progress. With my spate of wins, I start to attract more attention in Serbia.

I also attract the attention of adidas. A German man comes to the tennis club and closely watches me train and play other children. In a low voice he talks to my coach, and of course to my father. Within a day a lucrative deal is on offer – an adidas sponsorship and an invitation to train at a world-class tennis academy in Germany.

This incredible news is broken to me and my father in a meeting in the clubrooms. I'm over the moon. This is our shot. I'm also given an invitation to play a tennis tournament in Germany so I can see the academy. My father, Josip and I drive for a day to get there. When we arrive, my father is fascinated by the complex – the beautiful courts, the slick-looking gym. It is a huge, luxurious facility and I have never seen anything like it. This is the next level; this place will take us closer to the dream. After the first day of the tournament, which goes by in a blur, we all stay the night in a cheap local hotel. I play the next day and I win. We haven't planned for this win financially, though, and we don't have enough money for another night in the hotel. So we sleep in the car. My dad and Josip take the front seats reclining them back to sleep; I am given the back seat so I can stretch out my tired legs and I cover myself in my sports jacket for warmth. The summer's night air means we don't get too cold. It's not that uncomfortable and I manage to get some rest. I am bundled out of the tournament the next day by a seasoned and older opponent. On the drive home, my dad talks about moving to Germany – we are both excited about the prospect. 'This is a big opportunity to move forward,' he says.

I nod, quietly elated. *This is what I have hoped for*, I think to myself as we wind our way back through the night to Sombor.

But this path to tennis glory starts to fall apart when it comes to visas. Germany is refusing to accept any more refugees or migrants from regions of the former Yugoslavia. Our hopes that my tennis talent would trump this are dashed when the authorities formally quash our application. There is no way out of this problem – we will not get to Germany.

The day we hear that news, my father's temper erupts in the kitchen of our Sombor house. 'We need to go,' he yells. 'We need to go. There is no future here.'

Mum and I fall silent. Of course, I'm bitterly disappointed. But I keep my thoughts and feelings to myself; we have to stay quiet so we don't upset him further.

Then, late one night, terrible news comes via a phone call. My kind and loving grandfather has been strangled. Nobody knows who killed him, and it's a devastating blow for Dad, Uncle Pavle and my grandmother. We can't believe the news and sit around our table in shocked silence. I am in tears, but it must be especially painful for Dad to lose the only parent who he felt truly loved him. Grief-stricken, I picture the last time I saw my grandfather – two years ago in Osijek, a few days before we left home, I visited him in Čepin. We all had a meal together. I helped my grandfather cook lunch for everyone. It haunts me that I never got the chance to say goodbye to him – I know he cared for me dearly and I loved him so much.

Not long after this, my father comes up with a new plan and that plan is Australia. Sydney, Australia. Where my grandmother's sister, Katica, lives in a suburb called Fairfield. Katica, my father has decided, is our guarantee to make a new life in Australia, a country that's turned out some of the best tennis players in the world – Rod Laver, Tony Roche, John Newcombe and Evonne Goolagong. The four of us will go; Uncle Pavle and my grandmother choose to stay in Sombor for now. My parents know a little about this country from my auntie via phone calls. I know absolutely nothing about it.

We apply for Australian visas and have our health checks. Auntie Katica sponsors us and pays for our flights. None of our friends know about any of this. Dad wants to keep it all a secret so our plan can't be sabotaged.

I am really sad we're leaving Sombor: I had started with zero here and made some sort of a life at school and at the tennis club, a good balance. What will it be like in this new country we're going to? The idea of it scares me. I don't want to leave my friends at school and the tennis club, who I'm really fond of, and move all over again. But nothing can stop my dad, who forges ahead with the application. My mum, as usual, obeys his every word. Whatever he says she does. Through my eyes she seems to think it's normal that he dictates everything, that he screams, hits her and throws a table full of food into the wall if it is 'no good'.

I will learn later on that despite his violent ways my mother has a determination that her children will be raised with a father. She didn't have much of relationship with her father. Her mother passed away from illness when she was fourteen. She was then raised by her three sisters, had a tough upbringing, and she wants Savo and me to be raised in a home with two parents.

Six months after the German tennis academy disaster, we are informed our Australian visas have come through. No hurdles remain; we'll be leaving Serbia soon. My father is glad the papers are finalised; however, he's not happy we have to leave. And I feel abject grief to be farewelling this new network of friends, this new home that I have come to love.

Dad decrees that we are not to say goodbye to anyone. Within 48 hours, he tells us, we'll be gone from Sombor, and ahead of us lies a big trip involving buses, long layovers and planes. Again he stresses that no one is to know, not even my tennis coach.

Above all, I dearly want to say goodbye to Josip, but Dad is insistent. 'No, don't,' he repeats. So I never get the chance to thank him – he has been incredibly supportive of me, my tennis and my family. It hurts that my father refuses to inform him in person we are leaving. To my relief, he softens 24 hours later and phones Josip to let him know we're leaving for Australia the next day, and thank him. It comes as a shock to Josip, he is very, very disappointed we are leaving. He pleads with us to stay but soon concedes and says he understands our situation. I never see him again.

Dad relents about one more thing at the last minute and allows me to tell my school friends and teachers I'm leaving. It's raining the morning I walk into the Sombor primary school for the final time, adding to my desolation when I stand up in front of the class to say I'm moving to Australia. Before me I see a wave of sad faces. Big goodbyes and hugs follow. With each farewell my mood dips further. Feeling completely miserable, I walk away from the rectangular school buildings, rain pouring off them. I am crying.

The four of us leave on the night of 21 June 1994 – spookily, it's the same date we had left Osijek three years earlier. I say goodbye to Pavle and my grandmother, though in honesty I feel no particular sadness leaving them.

With just three suitcases and my racquet bag between us, we catch a bus from Sombor to Belgrade, where we stay the night in a grotty hotel. The next morning we file onto a dirty, smelly old bus that barely looks like it will make the ten-hour trip to Romania's capital, Bucharest, from where our flight leaves. It's cramped, dank and stinking; there are people sitting in the aisle; and the trip is a nightmare. The heat is suffocating. There's no airconditioning. My toddler brother shuttles restlessly between my lap and Mum's. I sense my father's mood growing darker by the hour.

As we speed through the countryside, pushing north to Romania, I'm overcome again by the sadness of saying goodbye to my school friends.

Finally we cross the border to fly from Bucharest to Athens. In Athens we board an Olympic Air plane bound for Sydney. As the plane sits on the tarmac readying to leave I feel intense fear. Then we take off and I leave behind a life where I fitted in. In Osijek I was a content child. In Sombor I have grown into a more robust girl. A confident child, despite my father's moods and violence.

But in Australia that girl will quickly disappear.

2

Australia, 1994

All four of us sleep on an old double mattress on the hard, rough floor of our tiny two-bedroom apartment. My father, mother, Savo and I twist ourselves to fit in the small padded space and try to rest. Our only other possession is a fridge, which hums and clicks loudly through the night. Big cockroaches scurry around in the dark and cold. My great-aunt Katica, who lives around the corner, gave us the mattress and fridge as a parting gift. We stayed with her for the first week, but then she said that was long enough, so we found this place. We're classified as refugees, and on our Australian government benefits this rundown apartment is all we can afford.

This country has been a total culture shock for me. Since our arrival I have been walking around in a haze of homesickness, a miserable, dislocated eleven-year-old with no English. The concrete landscape of western Sydney, red-brick apartment blocks, the fierce sun – none of it is like home. But I am also aware there is no going back.

Our first four weeks in Sydney have been consumed by Dad's fruitless search to find tennis courts and a coach. There is infuriating barrier after infuriating barrier: none of us speaks a word of English; we have no car, little money. My two tennis racquets sit untouched in their sports bag in the corner of our sparse apartment.

As each day in Sydney's west passes, my father's mood worsens. He is brimming with frustration and has us all on edge more than ever before. With me unable to hit a single ball, his dream is dormant and this is causing dreadful tension in our new home. I can also sense he doesn't feel at home in this country, that he almost detests being here in Australia.

Finally, one day we are given a break. When Dad goes to get bread at a local bakery owned by Serbs he sees a man, also Serbian, opening the back of his car. His boot is peppered with tennis balls. It must look like a boot full of neon yellow diamonds to Dad. He excitedly approaches the man and they speak in Serbian.

'I have a daughter, she plays tennis. She is really good. I need a club, a coach, a contact. Can you help me?'

The man tells my father he will try to help. He asks for our home phone number and says he'll call us.

He sticks to his word: a day later he rings with the number for a man called John Will.

My father meets John; he likes him. I do a trial session and then start with my new coach immediately.

John is an incredibly nice, kind man – and extremely tall. Through my young girl's eyes he seems like a giant as he stands at two metres. He has two courts at the back of his house just a ten-minute bus ride from our Fairfield apartment, and from his manicured, green suburban yard he gives tennis lessons and hosts some afternoon competitions. This backyard is like an oasis to us. It gives my father hope.

We rise early, careful not to wake Savo and Mum sleeping beside us, and are on the local bus at 5.30 am to take John's six o'clock session. In my group are five other children. I whip through training like a robot but I notice there's an ease about the way they play as the sun comes up – they seem to practise with joy. I am on edge, of course, under my father's scrutiny. Just like at Tennis Club Zak, he prowls up and down behind the cyclone fencing inhaling my every move.

Dad approves of John to such an extent that before long I start taking private lessons with him twice a week after school. We pay him out of our social security money, after which we have just enough left over for food and bus fares. My mum is busy looking after Savo so she can't work. Also, as with my father, her English is poor, which is a huge barrier for finding work. My parents keep to themselves. We don't try to connect with the local Serbian community; my father is just obsessed with furthering my tennis talent.

Soon after our arrival I enrol in Fairfield Public School. My first day is unbelievably scary. I eat lunch alone in a quiet corner of the playground and I can't talk to anyone because I can't speak English. Along with other refugee kids, I am placed in a special class to pick up English. Thankfully this new language clicks in my head quickly and within weeks I'm taking part in the normal lessons.

But I know immediately that I don't fit in here. Where in Osijek and Sombor I made friends easily and was a popular girl, in western Sydney my confidence deserts me. In this country I feel intimidated and I withdraw, continue to spend recess by myself, eat lunch by myself. Being at my new primary school feels like social torture. Soon I'm being teased. Harassed. On my chin I have a distinct mole, and whenever I walk by certain kids, or sit anywhere near them, they call me 'mole face'. No way am I going to just take this – I answer back, tell them to piss off, grimace in their direction, ice them with a stare.

But it doesn't help. Despite the fortitude instilled in me since leaving Osijek, I start to dread school for the first time in my life. It makes me sad. I used to love going.

It's strange that I don't fit in – Fairfield is a multicultural mixing pot, with kids from Cambodia, Africa, Vietnam. Yet still I feel that no one accepts me and I drift on the edges, horribly lonely. But after I walk home from school to our little apartment and put down my school bag, I always reply brightly to Dad's rare questions about my day. 'Yes, school is fine,' I say.

Not that he cares much if I'm fitting in or not. All he wants is for me to get top marks. In the same way he wants me to succeed in tennis, he also wants me shine at school. So I never let on to either of my parents what I am going through. I feel like they have enough worries on their hands trying to work out life here. My situation at school doesn't feel good but I don't cry about it. Deep down, do I want friends? Yes, very much. But at the same time I have developed a tough mentality – when you have been forced to leave your family home twice and people you know have been murdered, girls and boys calling me names? I know it's not the worst thing that can happen to me.

⊘

In the early days of our private coaching sessions, John seems shocked by my talent. At the end of one of the sessions he turns to me and I translate his words for my father: 'Your daughter has great intensity. She can hit that ball.' John soon encourages me into a Saturday afternoon competition in which I take on the women of Sydney's west – I'm eleven and all my opponents are much older, in their late twenties, thirties, even their forties. Some have been playing for decades. But I win against some of these women quite easily. In moving countries at least I haven't lost my talent.

My first real sporting test on Australian soil comes two weeks after I begin training with John. He enters me and another Serbian girl I train with in the under-14s at the Australian Capital Territory junior tournament in Canberra. This girl is much older than me but I chat with her sometimes, despite my father's discouragement. Never keen on me having friends, he is becoming stricter here in Australia.

John, the Serbian girl and her mother, Dad and I do the three-hour road trip down to the nation's capital in the Serbian mother's old car. Within moments of arriving in Canberra, the car breaks down and it is freezing as we stand on the side of the road waiting for a mechanic.

At the tournament I play several rounds of matches in the morning and knock off my opponents without too much bother. My father yells out during the matches, shouting orders and advice at me like I'm a seasoned prize-fighter doing battle in a boxing ring, not a little girl wielding a racquet in a regional tennis tournament.

In the quarter-finals I play the No. 1 seed in this tournament, a fourteen-year-old named Bree Calderwood. She is an imposing figure to me – when I see her across the net she looks enormous, like an adult.

What I don't realise is that Bree is one of the top young talents in the country. As well as being the under-14 champion, she also holds the under-16 title. She is one of the best junior players around and has an air of quiet confidence. She is always smiling. So she should – no one in her age group can beat her. Then again, no one gathered around this quiet Canberra court really knows who the hell I am.

When the umpire says it is time to play the sun is low in the sky. The floodlights are on. The cold Canberra air is starting to sting. Bree doesn't give up anything as the match progresses, and neither do I – we play two sets and take one apiece.

Because my English is not great I can't understand exactly where I am in each game; for example, I don't know the English word for 'advantage' or scores like '40–15'. So I'm confused at times.

It's evolved into an unbelievable match. Rallies are long and fierce.

While every other tennis parent watches sitting composed and restrained, my father is pacing up and down the court. They politely clap; he bellows like a wild animal. He yells on good points and bad points. His booming foreign voice dishes out advice in Serbian. At Bree's end when she goes to serve, he rattles the cyclone fence. From the crowd come audible sighs of disapproval at the scene he's making. I keep my head down and keep fighting on.

When I look over between points, I can see that Dad is drinking a beer, too. This is an unfamiliar sight to me. I don't often see my father drinking, but here he is, at a junior tournament, having a beer. Not one beer, either – I see him down another and then another.

A call doesn't go my way and he loses it. He smashes a beer bottle against the fence then drops it on the ground. It's as though someone has set off a firecracker; the sound of shattering glass makes the crowd gasp. None of these spectators would have seen anything like this before at a junior tournament. I haven't seen this from my father before. Bree ignores the bottle smashing. I ignore it, too, and try to focus on Bree.

There are tenuous line calls, and I dispute quite a few, which doesn't go over well with some people in the crowd. But there's no way I'm making bad calls. We go through three umpires – fellow junior players – because of all this drama and eventually the tournament referee takes the chair.

Under the lights, I am pushing hard to return the giant teenager's powerful serve, compensating for my relative lack of strength with lots of effort. But it is Bree who eventually triumphs. She is a graceful and gracious winner of the three-and-a-half-hour fight, especially considering she's had to put up with my father's behaviour at both ends of the court. I am deeply embarrassed by him. I can see that she's a kind young girl. We embrace at the finish of the match.

Nervously I head over to see my dad, expecting him to yell at me, and steady myself for a verbal barrage. But to my relief his eyes are soft and so are his words. His breath smells of beer. 'I can't say anything. You fought so hard. You played unbelievably well. I have nothing to say.'

These are some of the nicest words of praise he will ever give me during my career, one of the only times he speaks positively to me about my tennis.

It doesn't take long before Dad decides that my early-morning group training with John, my private lessons twice a week and the competition on the weekend with the older ladies are not enough. By now he has discovered the Fairfield tennis club and we go there most evenings. As the sun sets he feeds me ball after ball, hundreds of them. We do all sorts of drills. I must hit at least three hundred balls a night. I practise serves and then I run laps around the local park for at least half an hour – this is after training. As I run I listen to the sound of other children laughing and having fun – they're playing tennis and soccer – goofing around, mucking about. No one else in Sydney's west seems to be sweating their heart and mind out like me. No one is doing the hours I am doing.

For hours a day, I am on the court in the searing, thick heat, the rain, the cold. My skin turns a deep caramel from the intense Australian sun. I work, and work some more. But I never resent it. Tennis is a break from my fraught school life. It's an escape. I love the game and the heavy training.

I am now winning tournaments all the time. Not many of my opponents look forward to playing me because they know I'm relentless and don't give up. Ever.

Quickly my ranking rises and I am the No. 1 player in the under-12s and under-14s in Australia. Whispers about me start among some tennis parents. I hear people questioning my age, overhear them murmuring to each other that I have arrived without papers, that I can't be eleven years old, that I must have lied. I know my father and I are not welcome on their conservative scene: I am too quiet, unfriendly, and my father is too loud.

At home, it is clear to my mum and me that my father's unhappy and feeling the pressure. He mutters every day, since the first day we arrived, that he feels it is shoved in his face that he's not welcome here. Admittedly he doesn't help matters with his embarrassingly loud outbursts and bad behaviour. But guess who cops it in the end? On courts everywhere – rural and city – he is made to feel he doesn't belong, and when he feels like he can't fit in and when the pressure piles on, he lashes out at me.

After yet another excruciating day at school, followed by a long training session, I love getting home and seeing my little brother, who is now three years old. But as much as I adore Savo, my delight in his is marred by the constant, enormous pressure I carry: the pressure of pleasing my dad.

As for my mother, I don't know how she feels about living here in Fairfield, Sydney, Australia. She's never allowed to have a say, to express her feelings. She carries on much as she did in Sombor: looking after Savo, doing laundry, cleaning and cooking. Nowadays she and I don't talk as much or confide in each other. All of us are just trying to survive our move here in our own way.

I go back to participate in another tournament in Canberra, and this time I play poorly and don't make it past the first round of the under-14s division of the nationals. Back at our budget hotel my father hits me in the face a few times, he pulls my hair and ears, and then sends me out to run. My face is red from his abuse. I am sobbing. It is a searing hot day but still he orders me to do laps for an hour around some Canberra bushland, and he stands there watching me. I run my heart out until finally he tells me to stop. I am sweaty, exhausted, my whole body is aching. Then he makes an announcement.

'I have entered you into the under-18s,' he says.

My heart sinks. There will be hell to pay if I don't win. The next day I turn up and all the girls are much taller than me and they look stronger too. Adding to my woes I have the worst draw ever – my opponents are ranked in the top echelon of Australian junior tennis. At the age of eleven I am taking on young national tennis stars. On court for my first match, I'm frightened. Not of my opponents but of my father. What kind of beating will I get if I lose? The hair- and ear-pulling and hitting from yesterday have me worried. The fear is so powerful that I go out and beat the No. 6, No. 4, No. 2 and No. 1 junior players in the country. I scrape through the matches and somehow prevail in the final. I win the under-18 national title.

It's crazy. It's a ridiculous feat.

It's early 1995 and I have arrived on the Australian national tennis scene.

Tennis New South Wales's head coach, Craig Miller, hears about me beating girls in this tournament who are six years older than I am. Like everyone else in the tennis community, he is astonished by an eleven-year-old winning an under-18 event. He hasn't seen me hit a ball but that result alone has made me eligible for the New South Wales state squad. Craig tracks me down and invites me to White City – the prestigious tennis club in Sydney's east – to train with the junior squad there. Within months I have a fully paid scholarship, courtesy of the New South Wales Institute of Sport (NSWIS). It's a sought-after program – every ambitious tennis parent wants their child to be part of it. Coaching and fitness training are covered.

Because of my tennis talent I am allowed to leave school at 1.15 pm. Three times a week I sprint home, with my heavy backpack smashing against my sweaty back, quickly eat lunch and then board the first train to the city. Of course, with my father. We are always the first to arrive at the perfectly kept Eastern Suburbs courts. Before formal practice begins, under his watchful eye I methodically hit tennis balls into a brick wall at the entrance of the White City courts for up to half an hour. I hit that ball with such ferocity and precision that often a small crowd of commuters to and from Edgecliff train station gathers to watch me as I work like a manic tennis robot with no off switch. They seem in awe of me. Craig, too, is amazed by the way I grind the ball against the wall – he says it's like I am trying to break the mortar with the tennis ball. Later I learn that he tells other coaches that he's never seen a child with a work ethic like mine.

It's obvious I'm not like the other girls at White City. Most of them arrive in nice family cars driven by their parents; some of the cars are worth more than the cockroach-infested apartment we live in. My father and I walk ten minutes to Fairfield station, catch two trains, then walk from Kings Cross to White City for the state squad sessions run by Craig.

As I rhythmically bash at that wall, those girls start arriving; they sit around chatting together in the shade, giggling, laughing, idly stretching, talking about the weekend, hair, clothes, school – topics that are alien to me. I know I look like a weirdo to them, smashing at this wall while they gossip. Eyes down, I might mutter a quiet 'hello' their way, but I don't do small talk with them. To be honest, I am torn. I want to. But I can't. Partly, I am paralysed by awkwardness and shyness. I'm still learning English and I speak with an accent. Compared to these effortlessly confident, happy girls, I seem like another, quite different species. Above all, my father has forbidden me from talking to anyone.

'You're not here to make friends, Jelena, to muck around or have fun. You are here to win,' he reminds me.

Dad is big on presentation so Mum makes sure I look sharp. Even if my clothes are sourced from bargain bins or sale racks or are old – stuff that I was wearing back in Sombor that's fraying at the edges – everything I put on for training is ironed perfectly. The other girls turn up in the latest Nike gear and have new shiny white shoes; my tennis shoes are dated and have holes in them. We simply don't have money to buy new ones.

The others saunter onto court; I straightaway get to work, firing balls their way even if they're not ready for them. While they might think I'm being impatient, I'm actually under pressure from my father to get cracking. Wasting time is strictly forbidden. Those girls don't like this. Plus I am too intense for them in all ways. On the court I show no emotion during practice. I don't grimace. I never throw my racquet, don't swear. Even when I expertly execute a shot, a serve, I don't smile like the other girls might.

There are two hours of tennis followed by an hour of fitness. Within weeks of starting with the state squad and because of my talent I also begin private lessons with Craig, two, sometimes three times a week – they're provided as part of my NSWIS scholarship. My father always lurks within earshot, and he never looks happy as Craig guides me through the intense two-hour sessions.

'How she is going?' he asks Craig afterwards. 'What do you think?' He's gruff, he just wants direct answers.

Craig sees that I have the potential to be a champion. My strength is my groundstrokes. My serve needs improvement. My intensity, fight and commitment are unquestionable.

Since we arrived in Sydney around six months ago, the open, content side of me has all but disappeared. I am no longer the girl I was in Yugoslavia – I don't laugh, I don't crack jokes like I used to. A sad shyness has completely gripped me. I force myself not to care that the other kids here – at school and in the squad – don't talk to me. That I don't fit in and that I haven't since I set foot in this country.

I don't care because I have a bigger problem – and that problem is my father.

$\ominus$

Every morning I wake at home and worries assail my mind before I have even lifted my head off the pillow. *How can I make sure he doesn't hurt me today? How can I make sure he doesn't explode?* These days that's hard – he's getting more aggressive.

It feels as though ever since we walked through the doors of Sydney Airport he has been panicked, fearful and miserable. His eyes are now never soft like they sometimes were in Serbia; he is still grieving the death of his father. Nor have my parents been able to get jobs. Once more, at times our main meals are bread and margarine with salt. On the day before we are due to receive our fortnightly government benefit we are usually down to our last eight dollars, and six of those must be spent on train and bus fares for Dad and me to get to White City.

Fortunately my work is paying off. At White City, on my hectic training regimen I am improving at a rapid rate. I've made the kind of gains in my tennis over three months that most other children would manage in three years. It's not normal, but it's impossible not to improve like this when you've got someone like my father behind you. There is no other option but to succeed.

He tells me I *must* succeed as this is our only way out from this situation here in Australia. He tells me this daily – in our Fairfield apartment, on the way to training: 'You are our way out.'

And I know that I am. Absolutely, I am our only chance of a better life in this new country.

I begin to feel that the stakes are so high for my family around my success or failure that every shot has to be perfect. Indeed, Dad tells me he wants me to be perfect on the tennis court. But even when I deliver perfection he wants more. When I reach No. 1 in the under-14s, he demands I should be No. 1 in the under-16 age group. It doesn't take much to set him off into a rage.

For a man who rarely even sipped alcohol in Yugoslavia he is drinking hard here in Australia. The beers at my match with Bree signal the start of a habit. My guess is that he starts to drink because of the pain he is feeling being away from his country. He drinks to cope with being an outsider. He drinks to cope with pressure. He starts downing cheap white wine mixed with soda water, a spritzer, from the early afternoon well into the night.

Things aren't all bad for our family. There are some good times – a few hours when we have a happy family dinner with Dad cooking up an old family favourite. But it never takes long for the misery to descend again. I spend less and less time with my mum – everything is tennis-related now; it's 24/7 – about the game and my dad making me successful.

As the months roll on it becomes more difficult to make him happy. Even if I have a good session, he picks on little things. He tears into me about some technicality of a shot, yells if my feet are not working hard enough. He verbally rips me apart if I am not intense enough. And he has become more violent.

⊖

The belt is brown, its leather thick and hard, it feels as sharp as a knife when it's whipped against my skin. A mediocre training session, a loss, a bad mood – any of these trigger him to bring out the belt. My losing particularly sends my father into a rage. I rarely lose but when I do the consequence is brutal. The consequence now is often a belt-whipping. I can see he has decided slapping and hitting me are not enough of a punishment.

Whenever I'm losing he paces up and down beside the court. Then, if he can sense the match is over, even before 'game, set, match' is called he will storm off. And after I've shaken hands with my opponent and the umpire, packed up my racquet bag and walked off the court, I have to play an awful game of finding him.

I have to find him even though I'm scared to my bones about what he is about to do to me.

Inevitably he will be skulking where no one can see him – behind tennis clubrooms, trees, outside courts, in the car park – and he will scowl at me as I approach having finally caught a glimpse of him. If no one is looking, there will be a verbal barrage – these have got nastier – and then he'll hit me a number of times, stinging my cheeks. He often spits in my face. He pulls my ears. But the punishment never ends at the courts. When I get home he screams that I am hopeless, a pathetic player. Over and over. He also screams at me that I am 'stupid cow', 'dumb', 'an embarrassment' and 'a whore'. And there, with only Mum and Savo looking on, he is able to strike me quite hard.

My mother never steps in to stop the beatings though sometimes she says in a sad, quiet voice, in a polite tone, 'Please stop.'

He always turns to her and yells 'Shut up and piss off' and resumes the beating.

She remains close by, witnessing this hell unfold. Savo sometimes sees me being beaten but usually they send him away to his room to play.

I am realising that my mother sees physical abuse as normal. I've cottoned on that not only has he yelled at her, emotionally abused her, for years, but also he's hit her.

After the hits, out comes the brown belt. At that point sometimes he orders my mother and little brother out of the apartment. I get to know that belt really well. He wears it all the time and when he whips it out of the belt holes, I start to shake. He orders me to be quiet and not to cry – to show no emotion. Then he tells me to take off my shirt. It hurts a lot less when you have your shirt on and that's why he makes me take it off. I stand in my bra, my back to him, and he orders me not to move as he hits me. Often he almost slices my skin with the belt. Sometimes the pain is just too much so I run away to a corner of the living room and he chases me. He grabs me, physically turns me around so my back is to him and he can whip me again. It hurts like hell. It is hell.

He divides up his abuse of me. He will emotionally abuse me, then whip me. I steel myself through the pain. He will stop but then will verbally berate me for ages. 'Jelena, you are hopeless' is the message.

When it is finally all over, he never shows remorse. It's as though he thinks hitting me is the right thing to do. Or he'll blame me: 'It's your own fault, you made me do it,' he'll sometimes say.

Somehow I can go to school or back on court the next day and act as if it never happened. I force myself to switch off and erase the pain from my mind. I use an enormous amount of energy to push the hellish episodes of abuse out of my head.

My father makes sure I wear long-sleeved t-shirts to school and training to try to cover up the marks: those deep-blue, purple bruises on the tops of my arms, all over my back that remind me of his anger. I don't want to see them but sometimes I dare myself to look in the mirror at what his beatings have done to me. And when I look, sometimes I can barely see a centimetre of unmarked skin. Almost my entire back is taken up by blue, red, purple bruises and welts. Sometimes my back is bleeding. It hurts to touch and aches.

No one asks about the bruises. I don't know if they see them but certainly nobody asks.

But some days I can't hide his abuse. One day he hits me, misses the side of my head and hits my left eye. It goes black, blue and purple. I miss training for three days. I miss school. My father hides me away so no one can question what has happened.

During training sessions when I am not doing things right for him and there are people around, or I am on the court with a coach, he will call me over to the side of the court. There he will pretend he is giving me a towel and twist my hand aggressively underneath the cloak of the towel. Sometimes he grips my arms so hard underneath it and makes sure his fingernails pierce my skin. 'You are practising like shit,' he sneers. 'You will see what you are getting afterwards.'

On the long runs he makes me do, after training for hours on the court – up to ten kilometres on the really bad days – I go into my own world and start talking to myself. I reassure myself I will be okay, that I can do this. That I can survive. I also talk to myself because I have reached a point where I feel like I am not talking enough. I will never reveal to anyone what happens to me because I am so afraid of my father. I will never say anything to anyone – I don't consider telling a single soul – there would be hell to pay if even one person were to find out.

⊖

My grandmother has now arrived in Australia and lives with us; my Uncle Pavle is still in Serbia but is considering coming as well. No doubt my parents know what is going on at home with our loved ones and the war. But I have no time to take notice of anything or anyone these days except tennis.

As my star starts to rise on the junior Australian circuit, Dad's behaviour worsens. It's weird but the better I play, the worse he seems to get. He continues to drink at tournaments. On rare occasions when I'm runner-up, he takes my 'losing trophy' and smashes it.

One day I lose in the final of a tournament in White City. This is seen as a failing in my father's eyes. He's in a mood, he's already hurled a truckload of verbal abuse at me on the walk to the station, and we are now standing on the platform at Edgecliff. He suddenly snatches my 'losing' crystal trophy out of my hand and pelts it into a nearby brick wall. The sound of glass breaking echoes around the station as it smashes, causing a bunch of commuters to turn to see what's happened. I crouch to try to pick up the fragments on the platform. I put them in a nearby trash can while everyone is sadly watching on. I felt utterly ashamed and miserable. Bitter tears stream down my face as I picked up the shards. Sometimes he throws the balls from our bucket all over the place and I have to pick them up. I am anxious that doesn't happen now. He's already made me carry all our kit to the station – another one of his punishments.

His drunken madness bubbles to the surface again one afternoon in a round-robin event at a suburban tennis club in Sydney. After an epic match against an older girl, the minute we are out of sight of other parents and coaches he sprays me with abuse as my mother and Savo, who have also been watching the match, stand helplessly to one side. On this occasion he thinks I won – he hasn't seen the scoreboard – and that I have just played terribly. He hurls a heap of verbal abuse my way.

Thank God he doesn't know I actually lost.

The rage still comes my way as we walk as a family to the station to go home to Fairfield. He spits at me as I cower, hoping for a miracle, for the abuse to end, though I know it won't. I am really concerned by the public humiliation as we make our way to the station. Then, for some reason completely beyond my comprehension, Mum suddenly decides to break the truth to him. 'No, she lost,' she says. I am horrified she has told the truth. Stunned.

He whips around, looks to see if anyone is watching, and fronts his big frame up to me. He's towering over me and I am bracing. 'You *lost?*' he yells. Spots of spittle land on my face. He takes off a shoe and hits me over the head several times. He wears a hard-soled dress shoe. It feels like a cricket bat against my head. The pain is intense.

I am cowering now. Trying to ease the blows by going with every strike. He whacks over and over again until all his anger is spent. We then continue to the station and board the train in silence. When I get home the abuse continues; the belt comes out and the barrage of verbal insults begins again. My head is throbbing from the thumps of his shoe, my back stinging from the strikes from his belt, and my heart is broken.

3
Outsider, 1995–98

'I wish they'd go back to where they came from,' a hard-looking blonde mother sneers over my shoulder at my father. She practically spits the words at him. My father knows a bit of English now, but you wouldn't have to speak English to know that we, the Dokics, are not welcome. There's palpable annoyance that a Serbian refugee has been awarded a state tennis scholarship. Even though I have won everything, beaten everyone, am No. 1 in Australia in multiple age groups, it's evident that some parents don't think a foreign kid with an erratic father who rattles the fence to distract their children from serving correctly should be getting help from the Institute.

'She arrived five minutes ago and she's getting all this,' I hear a father say to one of the top coaches. 'It's unfair.'

I am distressed that there seems to be so much animosity towards me – a two-time refugee who can barely afford to travel to training.

Why don't these people just focus on themselves and their own kids? I wonder if it is racism or jealousy.

While Dad struggles to adapt to the culture and language, he feels from the beginning we are up against this obstacle of discrimination. He knows other tennis parents think we have taken a place on the squad that should be their kids'. And this is made all the clearer when certain parents don't let their children practise with me at White City.

Amid the crop of hostile parents, however, are David and Maureen Calderwood, Bree's parents. Maureen Calderwood has raised her children with Christian values: 'Be kind to others and don't be jealous,' she tells them. And she does what none of the other parents do – Maureen ensures Bree practises with me every Saturday morning at White City. Bree, my biggest rival, has become an ally. She is nice to me, and I'm friendly back, but I have to behave according to Dad's rules so we can't be true friends. I wish we could be, she is so nice towards me, but I am not allowed. When we do get a small window to go away on a team trip, Bree and I talk and hang out a little, but when I return to Sydney and my father is around I go back to being introverted. I wish I could be a true friend to someone. I know she must find it difficult to practise with me when he is watching on at White City, but she persists. Kindness overrules her competitive instinct.

Maureen's two-year-old-daughter, Tyra, also befriends my mischievous four-year-old brother, Savo, who sometimes accompanies me to training with my mother on the weekends. On these Saturday mornings the children giggle and roll down the lush green grass embankment near the courts as we train. Sometimes I notice them as I change ends, but most of my focus is on tennis.

Maureen picks up Dad and me from Strathfield station when Bree and I have to go to Tennis World in Epping – it's the second home base for our NSWIS squad and very hard to get to on public transport – a taxi is involved, which is too expensive for us. If Maureen notices my dad and me walking home in the rain, she calls out for us to get in the car and gives us a lift. She has a big heart and has worked out we are living week to week. When we have matches out of Sydney, sometimes she gets my dad's permission to take me out for dinner.

'Yes, go with them ... go with them,' he will say, ushering me off. He likes the Calderwoods a lot and trusts them when he feels wary of so many other people he's come across at White City. During those dinners, for a few hours I pretend I am part of this happy family. We joke a little, I eat up the rich spaghetti bolognese they feed me at various suburban Italian restaurants. It is all a welcome break from silent dinners at home and the meals when he loses it and ends up throwing food, sometimes the kitchen table, across the room.

When Christmas 1995 is upon us, Maureen gives Savo a colouring book, which he is very pleased about. At home we have barely any money for a Christmas tree and presents, although at this stage I am winning small tournaments around Sydney, so I am sure to save the little prize money I earn to buy Savo a present myself.

As 1996 dawns, I'm playing tennis like no other young girl. I am harder and tougher than anyone else. Although I'm told by my coaches I have an immense amount of talent, at times I feel myself faltering under the strain of pleasing my father. And the first nasty symptom of this is a diminishment of my honesty on the court.

Under this mammoth pressure, and out of my growing fear of Dad, I do something terrible – I sometimes start to cheat in practice. I do this only when he isn't watching and I'm in a tight situation. I know if he caught me cheating he would lose his mind – the beating he'd dish out would be worse than ever; I wouldn't have any teeth left.

On this issue he is firm: he maintains I must always play fair in the match. Yet my fear of him is so intense that if he isn't court-side I call close line calls out because if he comes back and I am not winning I will be in the shit.

I am ashamed of my new bad habit. This is not who I am, I hate my newfound dishonesty. I hate who I am turning into; I know I shouldn't do it but in the end I will do whatever it takes to avoid a whipping from his brown belt.

My ways, of course, incense the other girls. They feel ripped off. Cheated. They have every right to. The general way I go about my tennis on the court isn't friendly in any way. I put on pressure; I don't give away points. If I do relax a little, let my opponent win a point, like they do with each other, I will be hit. My father continues to hit, scream abuse at me and spit in my face out of the sight and earshot of my competitors. My mother consistently stands by and wordlessly observes it all unfold. No matter what awful things he says to me, she doesn't intervene, ever. She doesn't tell him to stop emotionally abusing me. Sometimes the things he says to me hurt me as much as the physical abuse.

'You are bitch.'

'You are a whore.'

'You are a prostitute.'

'You are dumb.'

'You are hopeless.'

I am only twelve years old and words like these damage me every bit as much as the brutal force of his hand or the sting from his belt. And it feels like his abuse is growing more and more violent by the day.

None of my competitors know what I am going through. They don't know I could be beaten, slapped, spat at if I give up a measly point, so they see me simply as ruthless. And, you know what, I am ruthless. With my father watching on, I just can't afford to be any other way. While I might seem arrogant and rude to some of the kids, at the heart of it I am not – that's not who I am. But for sure I have a wall up. It's the only way I can manage the situation I'm in.

⊘

Eighteen months on from our first epic battle in Canberra, in February 1996 Bree and I compete again, this time in the Australian national under-16s championships. At fifteen, Bree is three years my senior. She takes the first set easily; I scrape through to win the second in a fight. In the third and final set I take the title and the trophy. Bree is gracious in defeat as always. She congratulates me and embraces me.

After the nationals Bree and I go to Canberra to do a stint at the Australian Institute of Sport (AIS). Another player named Alicia Molik joins us on this trip – she, Bree and I are the top junior girls in the country.

On the day I leave for Canberra Dad gives me a ten-dollar note. I know this is the last ten dollars that he has. 'In case you are thirsty or hungry,' he says. Giving it to me will leave my family short for the week. I know I won't spend any of it. I will make it my priority to bring back the money. I realise how much it will mean if I bring that note back to him. But certainly I am excited to get away. It's a relief.

Being at the AIS is fantastic. It's a terrific facility and I'm fascinated by the other athletes there, especially the small, muscly gymnasts. I am so interested in them that I go and watch them train – they're incredible athletes and immensely talented. We watch the handballers and swimmers. We do laps in the Olympic-sized pool as training. For two weeks we train hard. We eat well.

I enjoy the company of Bree and the other girls but especially of Bree. We get along fine. We spend our spare time hanging out and visiting the vending machines. The other girls have plenty of pocket money and buy lollies, chips and soft drinks but the ten dollars sits in my pocket the whole time. I don't spend a cent of it and when I walk back home through the door I proudly hand the note back to Dad. He puts it in his wallet, then asks me all about what I've learnt at the AIS.

It's hard being home because I am back in my hell on earth, a home filled with pain, pressure and tension. I wonder, *Am I a bad person for not wanting to return to my father?*

⊖

Big names in tennis start to hear about me. Craig Miller calls up Wally Masur and tells him he has to come down to White City to watch me play. When I meet Wally he's just retired from the professional tour, having been world No. 15 two years earlier.

Masur practises with my squad and, Craig tells me later, is astounded by my talent. Apparently he thinks I play beyond my years and also have a mentality beyond my years. Of course Wally is aware of my father's presence; as ever he is prowling around, doing laps of the court. At the end of the practice Wally waits for him to come and say hello. Instead my father lurks, scowling.

Outside of the squad I start to do some sessions with Masur. He's a lovely guy with a calm manner. I'm well aware of his talent and career. During one session he puts the net up to encourage me to get more top spin on my shots as I naturally hit the ball hard and flat. Almost two weeks into our practice partnership, my father fires him for this very reason – encouraging top spin.

'Go and tell Wally you are done with him,' he tells me straight after I finish a session with Masur.

Shocked, I almost refuse. But of course I have to comply. After delivering the news I feel awful. Masur takes it fine but I can see he is surprised. I am disappointed – I really liked him.

Next, Tennis New South Wales chief Barry Masters calls up an IMG sports agent, Brian Cooney, and tells Brian he should come and see this kid with incredible tennis talent, 'destined for amazing things', as he likes to say to me. Not that it matters what other people think of me, it only matters what my dad thinks.

Brian turns up and watches me hit. After practice Dad and I meet with him in the White City club, in Barry's office. Brian, a big guy with a soft voice and a warm personality, makes a strong pitch to manage me. He tells us that IMG is a huge, worldwide sports management company that represents some of the best players in the world. 'Jennifer Capriati is on our books,' he proudly points out. 'There's a reason why all the top players are with us and they stay with us. We've represented Chris Evert, Martina Navratilova and Billie Jean King throughout their tennis careers.'

He makes a strong point that the welfare of their players is paramount. 'We pride ourselves on our level of care, getting the best coaching for our players, as well as looking into strategy and careful scheduling when it comes to a rising junior player's career.'

Dad sits impassively as Brian finishes his pitch. The pop of tennis balls is all we hear outside – we sit in silence for almost a minute. Brian looks at my father, looking for a sign, waiting for some response from him.

But my father has worded me up before this meeting that I need to be the one to ask for money; that we will only do a deal if there is an immediate financial element to it as we need cash flow more than ever. So I speak up. I make it clear I will be the one coordinating business, and I translate everything for my dad. As he wishes, I am blunt and I get straight to the money.

'How good is your financial guarantee?' I ask Brian. 'Surely you're going to pay me to join you?'

Brian is taken aback. 'Well, we don't offer guarantees,' he says. 'We just don't do that. We're the leading sports marketing company in the world – we will go out and do the best deals for our clients but I can't guarantee you anything now. I am confident, though, that we'll bring in more money for you in the long run than any other management company.'

And with that I tell him my father's response: 'We won't be joining you without a financial guarantee.'

The meeting is over. Dad and I get to our feet and walk out quickly. I'm disappointed we can't go with IMG. I really liked Brian and I think he is somebody who'd look after us well. But as usual I have no say in the decision.

⊘

The tennis hierarchy at the New South Wales Institute of Sport has a board meeting to work out what to do about me and my father. He is making me unreliable. He forces me to suddenly pull out of a team trip to Darwin, so I don't turn up to the airport. Some days he decides on a whim I am not to go to other state events. Other days he decides I don't need to do physical testing – so I simply don't show up. I miss the Women's State League competition; I even start missing training sessions with Craig. All on my father's orders.

Later I find out that in these White City board meetings I am branded difficult, uncooperative. I know those people are rattled, too, by my dad's behaviour. In these meetings there are claims we are smashing up the etiquette of the sport. They discuss my questionable line calls in practice, his rattling of the fence to distract the other kids on serve. His boozing at tournaments, the distraction and chaos he causes.

The women's selectors, the coaches involved in player

development, the state tennis hierarchy in general are concerned. I am a tennis prodigy, but my father is trouble.

Do we ban her? Ban him? What do we do?

Nothing happens. I am just about the best hope they've had in women's tennis in years, so nothing will happen.

⊖

At the start of 1997, aged thirteen I'm offered a wildcard to the Australian Open juniors in Melbourne. I've learnt not to show emotion because it gets me into trouble with my father, so I dull all the happy and excited feelings I should have at this news. Not only is he beating me physically and emotionally, he's also beating the life out of me. I am emotionally exhausted having to deal with him and his outbursts every day. So getting this wildcard just feels like another step in the right direction, something I am supposed to be doing, a box to tick. Whenever I win, or achieve something pretty impressive like this, he says, 'It's no big deal. We need to keep moving forward.'

I lose in the second round to a seeded girl. My father is displeased with the result so he gets hopelessly drunk. He keeps drinking as we pack up our hotel room. We get to the bus station at Spencer Street and he's calling out and shouting. He looks like a madman. At one stage I physically start to move away from him – I shift to a seat as far away as possible and pretend I'm not with him. His drunken antics are ridiculous. This is the most embarrassing thing he has done to date. I am so ashamed.

I don't cry. I want to and am barely able to hold in the tears but still I make sure I don't cry because if I did he would lose it at me. He would think I was 'betraying' him by crying. He would say I was weak and call me a pussy. So I remain stoic as his voice rises and everyone around us watches, concerned about the crazy person yelling and staggering about. It doesn't take long for the personnel at the terminal to arrive and decide that Damir Dokic will not be boarding the bus back to Sydney.

Now we are in a jam. My father is fuming, pacing around, on the phone to my mother. Ranting, furious he hasn't been allowed on the bus. He's trying to arrange two plane tickets back to Sydney. We have no money but after three phone calls he has somehow managed to borrow enough to pay for these tickets home. God knows how. We certainly can't afford them.

There's not so much as a cent for another night in a hotel. We used it all to buy the plane tickets home. We have scarcely any money for food. Eventually the place is almost empty, deathly quiet save for a few late-night trains pulling into the station. The cleaners sweep and clean up. Dad and I are hungry and tired. He doesn't stop the verbal abuse. He's still very drunk and constantly talking at me. He is blaming me for everything even though he has made the scene and got us kicked off the bus. 'This is all your fault,' he spits and slurs at me. 'You are not working hard enough to get us all out of trouble.' After talking for a few hours he stops. Both of us fall asleep on the floor next to our luggage and my racquet bag. We doze for just a few hours until the first SkyBus leaves for the airport. On the flight to Sydney I go straight back to sleep – exhausted by the madness.

$\odot$

By March '97 my talent is acknowledged by the Tennis Australia hierarchy with my first overseas trip – to Japan. The night before I leave for Tokyo I lay out my green and gold Australian team tracksuit on the small bed I share with my brother. Slowly we have been buying furniture as we have settled here – deposit-free long-term credit from the local furniture store. Representing my country is a total thrill and I am travelling alone – that is, without my dad. Parents aren't allowed on this trip but he lets me go because of the value of international competition to test my skill. I can't wait for the time away from him.

I arrive at Sydney Airport eager for our Qantas flight but nervous. I look around at the other junior tennis players lining up to check in. They are all a good three years older than me and seem to walk tall, with confidence. They also seem to already have a firm bond, this group. A tight tennis clique – one that does not seem to welcome outsiders like me. I know the faces, I recognise them from state tournaments – all the cool kids of Australian tennis.

None of them say hello to me as I take my place in the queue. In fact, they barely acknowledge my presence.

By the time we arrive in Tokyo I am acutely conscious that I am an outsider. It's unmistakable I am different when we gather in the foyer to go out for team dinners. The others put on their best gear, jeans, nice t-shirts, fashionable shoes. I don't even own jeans or stuff like they have. We can't afford them, and anyway Dad thinks I don't need anything other than tennis clothes. So while the others are dressed in their trendy gear I have to wear my tracksuit. My teammates look at me weirdly. It's embarrassing. I make up stories for my odd dressing style. 'I didn't know we were going in jeans,' I say.

'It's okay. You can go upstairs and change,' someone says.

So then I have to lie, cover up why I can't.

The others all hang out together in each other's rooms, playing cards, being silly, whatever teenagers do, but I am not invited. One night I summon all the courage I've got. My father isn't here on this trip, dictating my every move, so with the possibility of this extra freedom I really want to join in. I want a shot at fitting in. I psych myself up: *I'm going to ask if I can play cards with them*, I think to myself.

I arrive at the door of the hotel room they've all gathered in. Nerves rush through me. I knock. They open it. Their faces are blank. I can see I am unwelcome. 'Go back to where you came from,' one player says to me, then slams the door in my face. The cackles of the players' laughter don't stop. It's like that person has told the funniest joke in the world to my teammates.

The words smash me to my core: I slink back to my room, sit on my bed and weep. I wish so much for acceptance. There's no longer any illusion that I might be welcome or accepted. Where does this racist attitude come from? For another teenager to be telling me to go back to where I came from … Is this what their parents are teaching them?

They are just as vicious the next day, telling me not to bother attempting to ask if I can hang out with them. 'Don't come,' they say. 'We don't want to hang out with you.' It is simple as that.

So I give up trying to make friends with any of them. For the rest of this trip I spend my down time either sitting alone in my tiny hotel room or hanging out with players from other countries, and the Australian coaches who have accompanied us to take care of us.

And even though I am far from the physical and emotional abuse, I still feel the pressure to do well, to win. My father might be thousands of kilometres away, but he's registering my every result and performance from home. If I don't win, if I don't do well, if I come home and my technique is somehow screwed up, I am never again going to go on another trip alone or with a coach, he tells me on the phone.

I win all my singles matches. We win the whole team's event.

The trip is a success. The tennis hierarchy are happy with my performance in Japan so in May 1997 they send me, along with several other players, on a six-week tour of Europe to play in the top under-16 tournaments. Once again my dad will stay at home for this trip.

Alicia Molik and I travel together. We get along, but I make better friends with girls from other countries. I find it easier to be myself with them – girls like Ansley Cargill, a rising US junior star who's the one to beat, we get on really well. With these girls, I feel like they don't care about my background. I am starting to think maybe there's nothing wrong with me; that I *am* perfectly likeable. Then I start to wonder, is it an Australian thing – something to do with a conservative culture within the sport that is suspicious of outsiders? Sure, my father wreaks havoc at the local courts in Australia but I believe their dislike of me runs deeper. There seems to be resentment that a refugee like me has benefited from an Australian government sports scholarship, even though I am by far the best in three age groups.

I come back from the trip and within a few weeks am picked to go on another one, this time to North America, through August and September. I take my school books on the road and put in plenty of time studying hard.

Lesley Bowrey is the head coach again, just like she was in Japan, on this trip. Lesley played in the 1960s and '70s. She was No. 2 in the world in 1964 and won at least one title at all four grand slams, including the singles title at the French Open twice. From the moment I meet Lesley, I take a shine to her. She's a whippet-thin woman who doesn't say much, but what she does say is meaningful and direct. She's a blunt, smart and strong coach who seems to bring out the best in me. In fact, she has a great knack of making us all feel really good, being gentle yet firm. Very quickly I feel comfortable with her, like we have a true connection. And I feel as though she cares.

Alicia goes on this trip too, and so does Rochelle Rosenfield, another talented Australian junior who's around the same age as me. Alicia and Rochelle always room together so again I am the third wheel, but I just get on with playing tennis and winning. In Philadelphia I defeat my friend Ansley Cargill in a tough match, 7–5, 4–6, 6–4, and then win against Alicia in the final. It's a tight match and I beat her in three sets. I feel relieved and satisfied – this is a big junior world title to take at the age of fourteen.

We go to Washington, where I make the quarters, and on to New York, where we stay at the Grand Hyatt, which is sandwiched between the iconic Grand Central Station and Chrysler Building. I fall in love with the buzz and excitement of this city. From my small beginnings in Osijek, to becoming a refugee not once but twice, now hitting New York City in such style is a huge moment for me. This is something I have worked my heart out for, and I am not surprised I have made it this far – there's no other choice. This time Alicia, Rochelle and I room together and we all get on fine. At the US Open juniors I lose in the first round to a Slovenian player.

After the States we go straight to Vancouver for the NEC World Youth Cup finals. Despite the loneliness and the exclusion I have experienced from my own teammates on parts of this tour and the previous one to Japan, I love representing my country and playing in teams. I love playing for Australia, and always feel proud to wear the colours. I treasure every team tracksuit I am given.

⊖

By the end of 1997, Mum has found a job working on the production line at the Tip Top bread factory in Sydney's west to help fund my tennis career and feed us. Savo now goes to school and is basically being raised by my grandmother as we are all away from home so much. My mum works long hours – we barely see her. She no longer attends my tennis tournaments as she works a maze of night shifts and double shifts. But even with her working so hard we still have hardly any money because tennis is expensive. My NSWIS scholarship only covers squad coaching and private sessions with a coach – we are not given financial support, and travelling around the country, which I need to do to improve, is very costly. Tennis gear, stringing, other equipment also come with a high price for us to bear as a family with little money.

Coming up in January 1998, we are to travel to Traralgon, a country town a few hours out of Melbourne, for the Victorian Junior Open. My dad considers buying a tent because we have so little money. To fund the trip my mum ups her shifts at Tip Top, for a while putting in sixteen-hour days. I'm very aware of how much my mum works and I feel so bad she has to.

Thanks to her extra shifts we can afford a hotel, albeit the cheapest place in town, the Motel Traralgon.

Traralgon's a sleepy place that wakes up for this grade-one tournament – the highest-level tournament before a junior grand slam event. Everything clicks and I'm in stunning form as my father barks orders from the sideline and I whip through my opponents. On my way to the final I drop only two sets.

In the final I take on Rewa Hudson, a talented Kiwi girl three years older than me. Once again fear is my motivator, but not of Rewa.

While most of the spectators sit in court nine's grandstand, my father stands off to the side, leaning against an old brick wall, almost in the shadows again. But everyone notices him because they hear him booming orders at me. He's speaking Serbian, but of course everyone can sense he's yelling out directions, and they must sound abusive in parts. But whatever they think he is saying, it's assumed to be coaching, and that is against the rules. A local racquet stringer and coach, Graham Charlton, calls my father out on it midway through the match. 'Pull your head in and stop cheating, mate,' Graham says. 'It's not fair.'

My father scowls at him and moves back into the shadow of the stands. I just get on with the job and win the final easily. My 6–3, 6–3 victory over Rewa pushes my dad into a state of momentary happiness. At fourteen, I'm one of the youngest winners of the title. There is no beating for me tonight, even though my father has been openly chastised for his behaviour. Lately, I have started to realise his behaviour escalates around finals times. Even though I am winning he gets extremely nervous and with that comes the drinking and screaming.

The next tournament we head to before the Australian Open juniors is the Australian Hardcourt Championships at the Notting Hill tennis club, between Melbourne and Dandenong. Savo has come on this trip too – it is school holidays and Dad wants him with us. We check into the Hotel Bruce County in Mount Waverley, near the club, and it is here that things start to fall apart badly.

The night before the championships – an international junior event – the organisers announce the draw during a barbecue at the courts. It's dusk, it's warm and the smell of sizzling sausages fills the air. Players from here and overseas and their parents and coaches all gather for a feed and some fun.

But there's trouble building up in a corner of this party. My father has been drinking. He reeks of wine.

All is calm until my draw is announced: I am to play Rewa Hudson. This stirs Dad's anger. He decides that there is some kind of conspiracy against me; he believes it's a set-up that I have to play Rewa, who I just played in a final last week, and so he starts to clap loudly in protest. His booming accented voice rings out in the balmy air: 'Rigged, it is rigged,' he yells.

Kids stop playing and chattering. Everyone falls silent. I am cowering now, eyes directed at the ground, wishing I could disappear. Savo looks alarmed, too. I am so embarrassed.

My father calls the tournament director a lesbian. He is puffing out his big chest as he shouts at her. Lumbering around and reiterating that the tournament is rigged. No one is eating their sausages. The tennis party's fun vibe has been killed. Everything is feeling out of control. In vain, I ask him to be quiet. Other parents try to calm him, too, but no one can talk him out of this state and he's intimidating people now. Finally other parents are able to placate him.

It's just a taste of what is to come.

In the first round the next day I defeat Rewa, 6–2, 1–6, 6–2. Despite the good result, my dropping the second set triggers a terrible mood in my father and he is seething as I walk off the court.

On the courtesy bus that delivers us back to the Bruce County Hotel, I am subjected to a quiet torrent of expletives and abuse – there are no other passengers. Apparently I am terrible. I am pathetic. I am hopeless. I will come to nothing. By the time we're dropped in the car park of the hotel, he can no longer contain his temper. Whack. He hits me. It's like he doesn't care anymore if anyone sees him. I flinch and cower. Try to avoid his big palm striking my face, leaving it red. But it comes at me again and again. *I actually* won – *why is he doing this?*

Finally he stops and storms off, thundering through the foyer, with me and Savo following him. Back in the hotel room he continues to berate me, and strike me with the belt, all – most unforgivably – in front of Savo. My poor little brother sits sadly in the corner witnessing our father's rage being unleashed on me. He only stops when there is a knock at the door. It is Maureen with Tyra. 'Does your little one want to play with Tyra?' she asks my father gently.

'Savo isn't allowed out,' he snaps and slams the door in her face.

Over the next few hours the beating intensifies. I am in severe pain and can feel the bruises starting to form on my back and arms. He has punched me in the stomach, which is agony. I am sobbing. *When will he stop?*

The beating stops when there is another knock at the door. My father opens it and in front of us are some men in pale blue and navy uniforms. Victoria Police. We are shocked. Someone has called the police because they have heard the yelling and screaming in our hotel room. People have heard him beating me. Yet the arrival of the police is not a relief for me – I know it will cause more problems and that I am going to have to deny everything anyway.

The officers tell my father he needs to go to the station for questioning. Chaos ensues – he refuses to go, denying anything is wrong. A well-dressed, calm woman from social services has accompanied the policemen. She tries to put Savo and me at ease but the sight of the uniformed men has us both scared.

As the police take my father away, my little brother starts screaming and crying, 'Papa, Papa,' his tiny voice rings out through the hotel corridors. It turns into a wail as he loses sight of our dad. I have never seen my brother so frightened. How I hate my father for putting us through this stress. Other tennis parents emerge from their hotel rooms and witness the traumatic scene unfold in the corridor: me sobbing, Savo distraught and the police trying to contain our father, who is wild with anger.

We're all taken to Mount Waverley police station, where we are questioned late into the night.

'Did he hit you, Jelena?'

No.

'Has he ever beaten you?'

No.

I won't budge. I don't even cry now. I am emotionless. I treat the Victoria Police like an opponent on the tennis court; I don't give them a thing. I am cold. They can't break me. They don't break my brother either.

My dad is kept in custody overnight; Savo and I wait all night on plastic chairs. We have to stay until he sobers up. There is no other parent for us – a fourteen-year-old and six-year-old – to go back to.

The next morning we are taken straight to the practice courts at Monash University, back to work. As I hit balls, out of the corner of my eye I notice some parents have congregated. I imagine they are all gossiping about the previous hellish night. Craig turns up at the court and comes over to see me. He's concerned, but I find myself being dismissive. 'I'm fine,' I say. He accepts my flat statement. But really my torso hurts. My arms hurt. Everything hurts. Beyond the physical pain, my mind and my heart hurt.

Still, I operate on autopilot and train like nothing has happened. I play Ansley Cargill and I am tough in the way I play and unemotionally beat her. The final score is 6–4, 5–7, 6–4. Considering what happened the day before it is a huge win. Craig is gobsmacked by this performance. In his mind he doesn't see this as winning – it's a tennis killing. He tells me it's an unbelievable performance considering the physical and mental conditions I must be playing under. Fear, yet again, makes me good on the tennis court.

After the match Maureen takes me aside. It's impossible not to notice the bruises, the lumps, the welts on my arms. She can tell I am in physical pain. 'Are you okay?' she asks me softly. Maureen is able to reach me in a way that the police didn't. Really, I want to tell her everything, I want to cry, I want to tell her about the hell I've just lived through. But he would kill me. Instead I say yet again, 'I am fine.'

A few days later I have to relive the ordeal when we appear in court. For days my father has been schooling me in what to say, and on the bus ride there he is still preparing me so I don't crack in front of the magistrate. 'You are to say I was just screaming at you. We were just talking, Jelena,' he coaches.

We are first up. I maintain my stony-faced demeanour.

Before the magistrate I lie. I say nothing happened. He didn't hit me. The magistrate tries to push but I am like a rock. I am not intimidated.

I protect my dad because I fear him, and he has made me, us, believe that we can't exist without him. That we would fail in life without him, that if we ever were to say a thing against him, we would be traitors. It would be the ultimate betrayal, in his eyes. It is 'us' versus 'them'.

The charges are dropped.

A day later I am at Melbourne Park for the 1998 Australian Open Juniors. It's another baking hot January in Victoria, and you could cook an egg on the green Rebound Ace. Again, despite everything, I'm on form. It is my third junior grand slam tournament and I outplay my opponents, dropping only a few games and making it to the semi-final. My father isn't happy I don't get through to the final, but this time he doesn't beat me. He is actually contrite after the Hotel Bruce County incident.

In the semi-final, people from the sports management company Advantage International are watching me. One of their agents, Ivan Brixi, comes to speak with me, and my father and I agree to meet with some Advantage people in Sydney. A few days later two of their agents, Rob Aivatoglou and Lisa Chaffey, travel out to Fairfield. In our tiny living room they make a detailed bid to represent me. They have a stack of documents detailing the opportunities if I sign with them – a breakdown of racquet and clothing deals. I do the translating again for my father as we negotiate this deal.

Advantage International offer something that IMG didn't: money upfront. They also have an agent who can speak our native language: Ivan Brixi is originally from Czechoslovakia – even though it is not the same language it is very similar and they understand each other. This appeals to Dad but mostly it is the money that gets him over the line. He feels we're at a critical point, and we can't keep scraping five cent coins together for train and bus fares to White City.

Advantage International offers me a three-year contract and a guaranteed income of nearly six-figures a year, excluding sponsorship deals. I sign with them and Ivan Brixi becomes my manager. At fourteen I have a racquet deal with Prince and a clothing sponsor in Nike. Finally we have hit pay day but we don't celebrate. My father doesn't do celebrations; in fact, he barely reacts to this big injection of cash. Still, I sense he is a little relieved because we were struggling with our small social security payment and my mum's long shifts at the bread factory. But there's no outward excitement from him.

I throw away my old and faded tennis-racquet bag. Into the bin go my shoddy threads. Out go all my shoes with holes in them. Much to our joy, we have enough money to buy a car – there will be no more hours spent on public transport. This really cuts our travel time and gives me longer on court. Mum doesn't have to work at Tip Top any more, and we can invest in more tennis trips and tournaments. But we stay in our modest apartment in Fairfield.

⊖

A few weeks later, on a muggy February morning, my father makes an announcement that takes us all by surprise. Like all big life decisions, he makes it quickly and apparently on a whim. He tells me I'll be quitting school so that I can fully focus on my tennis. He still wants me to finish my education, but I will now do it via correspondence with Dover Heights; Tennis NSW links me up with the school. This arrangement means I will get away from the bullying, which hasn't abated – I will not miss the crap I endure at school, being picked on, but I will miss the classes.

So I begin distance education and find that actually I like it. School work has never been a struggle for me. I love it, in fact. Whenever tennis gets in the way, I am able to catch up without much trouble.

But there were two parts to my dad's announcement. As well as no longer physically attending school he has decided I am to sack Craig Miller. He doesn't give me a reason; he just says my time with Craig 'is up'. And apparently it needs to happen right now. He has already lined up Lesley Bowrey, the Fed Cup captain, to start formally coaching me. He's seen her working around White City and she has a fantastic reputation as a player and coach. He thinks it would be excellent for me to work with an ex-player as good as her. He knows I've been on team trips with Lesley and that I like her. But first I must sever ties with Craig; yes, it is me who must fire him.

There follows an incredibly awkward few days during which Craig is trying to pin me down to attend an NSWIS annual induction night and physical testing session, as well as my usual training, and I'm trying everything to stall his requests.

It's so difficult to do my father's bidding. It doesn't feel right, but I'm fourteen: I don't know how to tell Craig straight and neither do I have it in me to stand up for myself against my dad. I find myself tossing up lies and half-truths on the phone to Craig to try to wriggle out of his plans. When I keep dodging whether or not I will be at the induction night, he says he'll be forced to refer the matter to the Tennis NSW CEO, Barry Masters, and NSWIS. On the inside, I am panicking. I don't want to let anyone down. 'I might be able to come to training tomorrow,' I tell him.

Under my dad's instructions I never turn up to training, and that spells the end: my time with Craig is over.

Whatever I may think or feel about this situation, it's too bad. I live by my father's rules. I never go against his word because now, more than ever, I know the hell he can unleash. Does any other fourteen-year-old girl on the courts of White City, or even in Australia, have this problem? Play with the fear that I have?

4

Lesley, 1998

Summer 1998. I am pounding the footpath beside the highway, sucking in lungfuls of carbon dioxide from the cars screaming by me. Semis rumble past on the Hume Highway. The thick western Sydney heat is suffocating. Sweat slicks my tanned skin. I am running as fast as I can; my arms ache, my legs are filled with pain, so I start talking to myself again.

'Things are all right. It will be fine.'

I mumble these words over and over as I run ten kilometres home, through smog and fumes.

This run from Bankstown station along jammed western Sydney roads has become one of my father's favourite forms of punishment if my performance at tennis training has not met his expectations. Which is often.

He trails me in our new car; I'm under constant surveillance. Sometimes he pulls over on the side of the busy road, winds down the window and barks at me to keep going, even though I feel like my sore legs won't be able to carry me home to our apartment. But the alternative to stopping is a catastrophic beating, so I do not stop.

The gruelling punishment comes after three hours on court on a boiling hot day with Lesley Bowrey. After the awkward cutting of ties with Craig, I have stopped participating in the state squad, and she is now my full-time coach, paid for by my NSWIS scholarship. At least training with her is a break of sorts, despite the fierce regimen she's instigated for me. Exactly as I sensed when I first met her in the States, Lesley gets me. I feel like we are similar people and athletes. Lesley is supremely organised and incredibly tough. She has a great intensity – and I think she can see that in me. I idolise her and I feel she's on my side.

We hit for at least three hours a day, six days a week. Then she doubles the sessions – three hours in the morning, lunch, and another two to three hours in the afternoon. Lesley is big on discipline. There is not a lot of stopping. She is not big on talking either. What she is big on is doing. 'Keep on top of your school work,' she also urges me.

From the shady spots of White City, my father is still in the habit of watching. Sometimes he goes for a walk, but most of the time he's watching. Making sure I am doing things on court correctly. If he considers I'm not, on our water breaks he'll call me over and whisper, 'You're going to get it when you get home. I'm going to beat the shit out of you.'

When he does that to me in training with Lesley, I feel sick with anxiety. The warning typically comes with an hour or 45 minutes of the session still to go. Once he's shown he's angry, it will be a miracle to get out of a beating, so usually panic sets in. My throat and chest tighten in anticipation of what is to come. I can't show Lesley I'm a mess, I have to just act normal, continue the rigmarole of training and not show any emotion. But my mind's already preoccupied with my trip back home and the hell that is to come. My thoughts go to the violent blows that will start the moment I get in the car with him. It's very hard to finish the session off well with these thoughts.

Sometimes Lesley gets Catherine Barclay to practise with me. Catherine is a decade older than me and she is currently in the top 200 in the world in singles and top 50 in doubles. She truly tests my limits, but if I'm losing to her I know it could send Dad ballistic, so I find myself breaking the rules of sportsmanship again. I call balls out when they're in. Catherine complains to Lesley; she says it's tough to play like this. But I know Lesley tells her to let it go. She says to Catherine one day, 'You know why? Because it's the pressure her father is putting her under to win this.'

Lesley has my back.

In training she starts changing my game one small adjustment at a time. I've always been solid from the baseline, but she raises that part of my game to another level. Lesley encourages me to start using my shots to their full potential; she introduces new things to my game, gives it more variety and also takes advantage of my good baseline game by telling me to come forward and finish off points. Under her tutelage I improve my net game. She works on my serve, getting better placement and more variety on it. My father approves. He begins to trust Lesley implicitly, so eventually I start to feel something else in these training sessions: freedom. Because Dad lets up on the pressure. Just a little. The huge number of hours spent on court see me dramatically improve, and the months of epic, punishing runs home from Bankstown have also made me fitter than ever. I can punch out six kilometres after a six-hour day and it barely hurts. Everything is starting to feel perfect. I have never been stronger. Lesley says I'm like a trained 'tennis assassin'. It's exactly what my father wants me to be and, unbelievably, even he now thinks I train enough. His basket of tennis balls goes into storage and we stop our extra sessions at the Fairfield courts. There have been a lot of tears on those courts.

It seems as though, in terms of tennis, I'm ready for just about anything. Here I am at fifteen years of age, in the top 10 in the junior world rankings and, we hope, on the verge of winning a junior grand slam. In the autumn Lesley says we need to go and play tournaments overseas; she thinks I should be taking on the young guns of the world again, this time at junior events around the world, including the grand slams. She floats the idea with my father, who naturally thinks it is a great plan. He's happy for me to go with her alone – he's always been reluctant to fly and now it's become a full-blown fear. So it will be just Lesley and me for the next few months. What a relief.

⊖

Being on the road is something all top tennis players need to manage well if they wish to have a long career. In Lesley Bowrey, I have a brilliant mentor. She teaches me how to hand wash my laundry in a hotel bathroom sink; she shows me a neat trick of wrapping the freshly washed clothes in a towel to squeeze them out thoroughly so they are dry by the morning. She tells me when to go to bed and when to get up. 'It's discipline that gets you through,' she often says. *If anyone knows about discipline, it's me*, I reflect, but Lesley's form of discipline is worlds away from my dad's – she's kind, and she really takes care of me. She feels like a mum when mine is thousands of miles away.

With Lesley I feel like I can be myself. She helps me slide into my new routine on the road, and I thrive in it. Life at home is temporarily forgotten, but while I put to one side all the bad stuff, I fight and play as hard as if my father were there. Although I speak to him as little as possible, I know that as usual he's keeping up with the results from afar. When we do speak he seems satisfied with my rise.

He should be because I'm winning everything. Since leaving Australia I have won three big tournaments – twenty matches straight – including the Belgian International Junior Championships at Astrid Bowl Charleroi, where I put an end to the campaign of their local hero, Kim Clijsters, 7–6, 6–2. Kim and I are on friendly terms as we have got to know each other in the course of a few international junior tournaments. She's a great player with tons of natural talent and tenacity, so I'm proud to have beaten her in a good match.

Going into the French Open, I'm ranked in the top five world juniors. I pummel my way to the final in Paris by downing Russian Elena Dementieva in the semi-final, but I lose 6–3, 6–3 to another smart-playing Russian girl, Nadia Petrova, in the final. Kim and I, having become friends in the last couple of weeks, decide we will play doubles together at the French Open. We're a winning combination – we defeat our opponents easily all the way through to the final. We play a great match in the final, beating Elena Dementieva and Nadia Petrova. Kim and I embrace upon victory. Our photo appears on the big screen at Roland Garros gardens. It feels like the highlight of my career so far. A true moment of happiness for Kim and me.

The singles final has been my best performance this year so far, and on the back of my semi-final appearance at the Junior Australian Open, my ranking rockets up to world No. 1. Ivan Brixi takes Lesley and me to a fancy Parisian restaurant to celebrate. Before we go I call my father, who knows about my new singles ranking already and is pretty happy, but says I need to *win* a junior grand slam. Right now, nothing can dim my elation, and I can express this in a small way because he is not around.

My shots have become more clinical and accurate than ever; my footwork is swift and agile. I win back-to-back titles on grass going into Junior Wimbledon, where I make the semi-finals. I grew up playing on grass quite a bit in Australia, so this surface is familiar to me. It complements my game because I am aggressive. I can take the ball early. So while I prefer the hard court, I am comfortable enough on grass.

It's midway through my Wimbledon run that Lesley pulls me aside after a match and gives me some exciting news. 'You're in the Fed Cup,' she says simply. 'I have you picked as the fifth player.'

The Fed Cup is the biggest international team competition in women's tennis, and Australia has done well in the contest in the past. Lesley's captained our team for four years now. It turns out that she knows she's going to cause all kinds of uproar by choosing me – at fifteen years and three months, I am the youngest player ever named into the Fed Cup – but she's unconcerned about that. This is not about her playing favourites; she simply knows I am on form.

Because I'm so thrilled, uncharacteristically I don't contain my emotion around the news, and at breakfast one morning in our Wimbledon accommodation I blurt it out to a fellow junior Australian player. She is three years older than me and a rival but we have been getting along okay on this trip. However, I'm mistaken when I think she will be excited for me.

'I am in Fed Cup,' I tell her as we eat the hotel breakfast.

'What, you?' she says. 'But you're not *playing*, right?'

'No, I'm a reserve,' I say, cowering slightly. Wishing I hadn't said anything.

She asks how I'll play against those girls.

'Yeah, probably not, it is fine, I am not going to play … I will just practise with them for the week.'

But I decide to ignore her response – it doesn't matter to me: I am officially on the team and that's enough. Nicole Pratt, Rachel McQuillan, Rennae Stubbs and Kerry-Anne Guse are the others Lesley's picked. When I get back after Wimbledon I have a few days before taking off to Canberra to prepare for the tie, which is against Argentina. For six days I practise with the girls and help them to prepare. This is a Fed Cup team under pressure, one that hasn't done well in recent years. Last year a core of disaffected players attempted to unseat Lesley, pointing to her as part of their problems. Since then she has vowed to introduce fresh talent, and here I am. They also have a problem that Lesley is my personal coach. They quietly think it's a conflict of interest having 'fresh talent', her charge, on this team.

Although I try to brush off the scepticism I face from the other women in the team, I'm self-conscious in their company. All of the Australians in this Fed Cup team are at least a decade older than me and in the top 150 in the world. They are a fiercely competitive bunch.

A few days before the tie Lesley brings the group together and in her matter-of-fact way says there will be a play-off for the singles spots. We are to play a set against each other to decide who will take the court against Argentina. The senior players go into meltdown – they hate the decision. Some of them confront Lesley but she doesn't flinch.

At the play-off I beat all of these girls. I play my way out of the reserves and into the team.

The president of Tennis Australia, Geoff Pollard, is watching this and tells Lesley afterwards he's amazed by my ability. Lesley's decision is vindicated for the moment: there is no question that I deserve my place on the team. She sits us down in a conference room at our Canberra hotel and tells us that Pratty – who has also been playing great – and I are playing the singles tie against Argentina. I am determined to play my best tennis and prove Lesley right – that rolling the dice with a fifteen-year-old has been a smart move. I don't want to let her down; I must win for her. I also want to win for the team and for Australia.

My first opponent is seven years older than me. Mariana Diaz Oliva is a top 100 baseline player with a powerful forehand. The local Canberra crowd roars; they are with me on every point. With their support I play with bolstered confidence and I emerge victorious. I defeat her in straight sets and become the youngest player to ever win a singles match in the Fed Cup. Lesley embraces me at the end of the match – her trust in me is being rewarded. I also beat my next opponent in two sets. Pratty plays well and wins too.

Lesley is overjoyed. I have played the best two matches of my life so far and I'm so happy we won for Australia as this was a play-off to get into the world group – only sixteen countries qualify. But most of all I am delighted I have won for Lesley as I privately vowed to. There has been a lot of pressure on us both, especially on her. It is one of the best weeks of my career, and the media can't get enough of me. The press coverage is glowing: they say I am the female star Australia has been waiting for, and I'm subsequently hailed as the finest Australian talent to emerge since dual Wimbledon champion Evonne Goolagong in 1970.

When I arrive home to Fairfield my Fed Cup performance is good enough to spare me being beaten by my dad. He is mildly happy. Not that there is any celebration for the performance. I had such a great time in Canberra – a joyful week. It dawns on me that all the great weeks of my life have been when my father hasn't been around.

The second half of 1998 is a sporadically positive time. I am winning and winning, though the joy it brings is always fleeting, pushed quickly aside by my constant fear of Dad – of when he might hit me next for mistakes on or off the court.

In August Lesley and I fly to Montreal, where I reach the final of the major junior tournament there, and then I hit New York. There, I steamroll my way into the Junior US Open final, and outplay Katarina Srebotnik to achieve a 6–4, 6–2 victory. It's my first junior grand slam title and I regain my No. 1 ranking, which is a wonderful moment. All the hard work with Lesley has paid off and I am playing the best tennis of my life.

Lesley takes me to a public phone in the Arthur Ashe Stadium and pulls out her calling card so I can ring my parents. When I get through and tell them I have won, they're both extremely pleased – especially Dad.

Afterwards Lesley surprises me and Evie Dominikovic, who is also on this trip, with tickets to the US Open men's final. It's an incredible year here for Australian men's tennis – No. 3 seed Pat Rafter and Mark Philippoussis, who's unseeded in this tournament, have both made it through to the final. Pat plays a magnificent match, overcoming Mark in four sets, 6–3, 3–6, 6–2, 6–0. But there's more: Lesley has managed to arrange for us to meet both finalists afterwards. It's the icing on the cake after my junior win. Pat is lovely – a huge star but so humble. He congratulates me on winning my junior title. Mark is a bit shyer than Pat, but I like him a lot too. The night feels like a dream.

◯

The next big move of this year is the decision for me to go professional. It's my father's call – naturally. Despite us having a considerably better income since signing with Advantage International – gone are my days of playing in old, holey shoes – he's still obsessed with money and how much I'm bringing in from each tournament. But to go pro is exciting, and exactly the path I want to take. Being only fifteen,

I have a tiny bit of worry about taking on the older women, but I don't express the slightest doubt to Dad as he would beat the shit out of me. Anyway, I am a fighter.

My ascent doesn't stop and in September I beat Daniela Hantuchova in straight sets to win the World Junior Championships in Osaka. But after that we decide not to play the remaining junior tournaments in the year – we give the famed junior tournament the Orange Bowl a miss because no one will be able to surpass my No. 1 ranking. We decide to go pro.

In October I enter an International Tennis Federation (ITF) 25,000 tournament in Saga, on the southern Japanese island of Kyushu. This entails four rounds of qualifying, which I win and I get through to the main draw. I make it to the final and beat the No. 1 seed on the way. It's a promising step forward.

Next up is the Thailand Open, a Women's Tennis Association (WTA) tournament, where I'm ranked 362 in the world. Again I make it through to the main draw by winning three tough qualifying rounds. I get a difficult draw and go down in the first round 6–7, (9–11), 6–4, 4–6 to the world No. 23, no less, Frenchwoman Julie Halard-Decugis. People are impressed by my fight in the match against her, especially when Julie goes on to win the tournament. I play an impressive match – particularly considering I've just turned fifteen. I'm very happy with my performance.

My dad calls me on my mobile when we're at Bangkok Airport on the way home. 'How much money have you made?'

'I don't know,' I say.

He demands I count it. So in the middle of the thronging airport lounge I place all the American dollars on the floor and start counting.

Shocked, Lesley asks me what I'm doing.

'My father needs to know how much money I have made,' I tell her, in a panic.

'Stop counting it here,' she says. 'You need to put it away.'

Disobey Dad? I have to finish and let him know how much I have as soon as possible; it turns out to be US$700 exactly.

Back in Sydney, I hand over all the money to my father. I never put a cent from my winnings in my own pocket. That's not how it works. Not at all.

⊘

As 1998 draws to a close there is some more exciting news: I've been picked to play in the Hopman Cup for Australia and my partner will be Mark Philippoussis. It's a mixed event in Perth every January, where countries from all over the world compete.

Lesley's excited about my selection; my father reacts in his typical low-key way. It's hard to read him sometimes because he rarely says much when big moments like this come up in my career. In his constant quest for me to get better, and improve our life here in Australia, his ambitions keep growing and he still doesn't seem satisfied by anything I achieve. He certainly doesn't back off with the pressure and expectations.

I fly into Perth with Lesley, both excited and overwhelmed by the prospect of playing three top ten players in the world in our group. South African Amanda Coetzer is to be my first-round opponent – she's in amazing form, and I know she'll be tough to beat.

All the players and coaches are staying at the hotel at the Burswood Casino. It's gorgeous, and I have my own room overlooking the pool and golf course, the nicest accommodation I've ever stayed in. The hotel is incredible. Here in Perth I'm confident in myself, and in practice I hit the ball well. Still, I'm slightly tentative about facing this tough competition.

My nerves are pumping when I take my place at the baseline. Coetzer turns out to be as tough as I imagined she would be and wins all the right points, practically smashing me off the court, 6–1, 6–0. But the score doesn't tell the whole story: like how hard I fought, a fact that earns me a lot of praise; that I was a rookie up against a seasoned high-calibre player; and everything about the experience was new and incredibly intense. The intensity of that crowd was something. And I loved it.

My next singles matches go my way: I take down the highly rated Frenchwoman Sandrine Testud and the incredibly tenacious Arantxa Sanchez Vicario, who's just helped Spain win the Fed Cup. I am also uplifted by the fact they are both top ten players.

Mark Philippoussis and I then combine and win the mixed doubles. It's the first time I've ever played mixed doubles and we're good partners. Mark has a huge serve and I watch in awe as his bombs fly past my head. He's also won all his singles matches and together we steamroll into the finals. Everyone is going nuts about the possibility of us winning the Hopman Cup for Australia. It's a big deal – the media has gone crazy. But from living under my father's brutal ways I've learnt to deal with these emotions by stuffing them down and hiding them away; still, I feel excited going into the biggest match of my life so far. It's a huge deal as Australia has never won the Hopman Cup before.

After comfortably taking the first set against Sweden's Asa Carlson a flurry of nerves takes over in the second: the crowd is electrifying and I'm so stunned by the support that I get ahead of myself, make the mistake of seeing myself winning. Not a moment too soon, I force myself to steady and win the tie breaker. There's a surge of confidence inside me – is it from having beaten some top ten players or the support of the Perth crowd? Suddenly I win match point and the crowd is going wild.

Following my victory I take my place in the stands to watch Mark overpower Jonas Bjorkman in what is also a nail-biting second set that goes to a tie breaker. And with his win we take the Hopman Cup for Australia! I receive a diamond-encrusted tennis ball and a cheque for $100,000; not bad for a fifteen-year-old. It's an extraordinary moment – partly because earning that amount of money in one tournament is hard to get my head around.

After this huge win, Lesley gives an interview to *The Age* in which she talks up my drive. 'Jelena wants it very badly,' she says. 'She'll work hard, she's very determined and she enjoys the competition. You have to really love competing out there to become a top player and a lot of players have fallen by the wayside in the past because they really don't enjoy competing. But she does. She is different. She's single-minded. She knows where she wants to go.'

Back in Fairfield, Dad is delighted – we have a peaceful time, no recriminations, everything calm. As always I am happy to see my little brother again; Mum, too. Yet I find myself wishing I was still with Lesley and miss her badly. After the high in Perth it is a challenge to return to reality.

⊘

My Hopman Cup performance opens more doors. Paul McNamee, director of the Australian Open tournament, gives me a wildcard into my home grand slam. Lesley and her lovely, friendly husband, Bill, borrow a friend's apartment in South Yarra and we base ourselves there to prepare. It's a beautiful place, and I reconnect with that high from the Hopman Cup. Every morning Lesley and I run along the Yarra River. We cook together. It's what I imagine a happy home to be so I pretend this is my real life, spent with even-tempered, balanced people. No dinner thrown against a wall. No beatings with a belt. No hours of verbal abuse. Just a calm, contented life.

After five days in this cocoon with the Bowreys, my family arrives in Melbourne and this little dream world is shattered. I move from the apartment into a hotel with them.

In an exhibition match at Melbourne Park, to my great pleasure I'm put up to play against Monica Seles, the very player who inspired my father back when I was six and who still inspires me. Monica is No. 4 in the world so it's no surprise when I go down 6–3. Still, I take some heart from this as it was a solid set. Monica has rebuilt her career and confidence after being stabbed by a crazed fan during a tournament six years ago. While I am shy, so is she. She doesn't speak much to anyone in the locker room, but I get a photo with her. It's a picture I will treasure. My dad meets her too and is delighted to talk to her briefly.

On the eve of the tournament, Lesley and I give a joint interview to *The Age*. I proceed to parrot my father's theories. One of the issues I'm facing as a fifteen-year-old on the women's circuit is that I'm limited by the WTA Tour to playing ten tournaments and four grand slams a year. I say that the WTA age eligibility rules are ridiculous and I might appeal them, and that I would prefer to lose in pros rather than win in juniors because it will help me to improve to play against better players.

Lesley sees it differently and tells the interviewer she believes I should play the junior slams until I win them all. After all, although I won through to at least the semis in all four junior slams last year, I only have New York to my name. Her view is the complete opposite of my dad's. I agree with her thinking, but publicly I put forward my father's proposed agenda when the journalist starts asking questions about plans for 1999.

Lesley: I think it's important Jelena does play grand slam juniors until she can get her [pro] ranking up there, until ...

Me: But then again –

Lesley: Wait a minute ... until she can play more tournaments because with the age eligibility rule, they can't play enough tournaments – ten is nowhere near enough for her – and I think being at the grand slams is very important.

Me: I don't agree with playing junior grand slams, because if I play Coetzer and Sanchez Vicario and whoever else in seniors, even if I don't win those matches, it's still good practice for me and then I'm moving back to play juniors, not going forward.

Lesley: The computer will tell us where she can play. I think that's something for us to work out when we see where she's at.

My words in this interview are my father's. He always briefs me before interviews, tells me what to say. If he were to read in the newspaper that I said something that contradicted his way of thinking, I would be in trouble; naturally I stick to his script. And my public face is completely different from my private one. I might seem confident but inside I'm a frightened girl who can't let on to anybody, especially the media, what is really going on behind closed doors. So I do what I am told.

Outside of the press conference Lesley lobbies my father, saying I should be pacing myself and stay playing juniors. He gruffly brushes her off, saying, 'Jelena should be going forward.' He has a conspiracy theory that everyone wants to hold me back.

Monica practises with me early most mornings during the Australian Open – a total honour. She's fierce, intense, keeps to herself. My father is in awe of her.

As I go into the first round I'm incredibly nervous. The stands are packed. When I come on there are yells and cheers. Like the home crowd in Perth, these are people who love tennis and are vocal about it. In this first match I'm taking on world No. 123, Russia's Elena Makarova, and somehow I manage to bring her undone, 6–3, 5–7, 6–4. In the second round, with my confidence boosted, my nerves settle and I take down 67th-ranked Kristina Brandi of Puerto Rico, 6–4, 7–5. I played a great match and the crowd is incredible on Margaret Court Arena. It is an unbelievable feeling to be a part of this.

Things are changing off the court: I am starting to be recognised around Melbourne Park. Fans come up to me in the street and request my autograph. Startled, I realise I am becoming famous – at fifteen. It's a lot, but I don't mind it. This new attention doesn't bother me.

What is more difficult is dealing with my father's presence at Melbourne Park. These past months I've been able to forget how he makes me feel. I've become used to it just being Lesley and me, and everything working smoothly and without pressure and abuse. It's really tense with him around. I wish he wasn't here, and it could be like it was in Perth and on our trips in 1998.

My next opponent is on the cusp of becoming the best women's tennis player in the world: Martina Hingis. She's ranked No. 2 in the world. I walk out onto Rod Laver Arena to play against her and I feel nervous. The last seven, eight months everything has happened so quickly and now I am here.

She is too experienced for me: she brushes me aside, 6–1, 6–2. There were a lot of close games and it's not a really bad match for me. Of course, my father isn't pleased. He doesn't hit me or scream at me, but as usual he thinks I could have gone further and played better, never mind that I've reached the third round at a grand slam, aged fifteen.

After the match Dad, Lesley and I meet underneath the main stadium near the locker rooms to discuss the next step. Lesley suggests I play the Australian Open juniors, and this sets my father off. He remains adamant I won't play juniors; he sees it as 'going backwards'.

Lesley thinks it's simply taking a measured approach to my development: 'It doesn't matter, it is another week of tennis,' she says. It's more matches and I agree with her.

My father refuses to budge. It's a firm no.

After the Australian Open Lesley decides it's time to go on the road again. I play WTA tournaments in Colombia, the US and Dubai – Dad doesn't come, it's way too much flying for him.

I don't do badly but I don't do great either and the results don't sit well with him. When we get back from the trip he tells me he *is* going to start travelling with us – my heart sinks. He thinks he needs to be court-side for me to really succeed. He is also still annoyed by Lesley wanting to have me play junior tournaments.

As usual he insists that I act as conduit: I'm to go and tell Lesley he will be back on tour with us. She's tactful about my announcement, but I sense she doesn't want him there. Who can blame her? She knows he drinks. He often reeks of alcohol. That it works far better with just the two of us. But if Lesley's thinking of dissuading my dad somehow, she doesn't get the chance to say her piece because he now decides to fire her. He has decided I have 'outgrown' her.

Once again, I am to tell her this. He, of course, won't do it. I am kind of numb with shock with this order to cut her. We have spent so much time together and I truly feel she is the only person who really understands me and the pressure I am under. She sees it. I am mortified by the idea that I have to get rid of her.

At my next practice session at White City Dad reminds me that I must inform Lesley she is no longer coaching me. I don't know why he's doing this: she and I have done a great job together. I am miserable, utterly deflated. The refuge I had when I travelled with her is about to disappear.

With Lesley gone, I am alone. Confused and afraid.

5

Birmingham, 1999

Martina Hingis invites me and my mother to stay at her palatial home on the outskirts of Zurich. I have seen her on tour over the last few months and have exchanged hellos but it's our shared management company, Advantage International, that brings us together. Martina needs a strong practice partner before the clay court season starts, so I am there to train with her. Generously, she insists we stay at her house rather than bother with a hotel.

My father remains home with my brother. I don't fear leaving Savo in his care – my dad never harms Savo; he behaves completely differently with him. Thank God.

In Zurich, Martina and I practise hard together and talk a lot. Quickly we become friends – well, as friendly as you can be on this tennis tour. I might struggle to find a friend in the Australian tennis community but the best player in the world doesn't mind my company.

We talk a lot. We have a lot in common.

Like me, Martina has been raised to exclusively play tennis. Her mother, Melanie, has been coaching her since Martina was a toddler.

Nadia Petrova, another up-and-coming junior, joins us to serve as one of Martina's hitting partners. Melanie takes us through the sessions and I admire everything she and Martina say and do. I think Martina is very smart. Brilliant, even. She is composed on the court. She plays using her head. At sixteen, in 1997 she was the youngest in the world to become No. 1 and to win Wimbledon. In 1998, she won the Australian Open singles and was the third woman ever to be No. 1 in both singles and doubles simultaneously. She might have won grand slams, is also No. 1 in the world, but she's completely unaffected, impressive off the court as well as on it. She is nothing but kind to my mum and me.

Although I am in awe of Martina and her achievements, I am not overawed. That is partly because I have my dad's words echoing in my ears: 'Don't look at who you are playing,' he has told me countless times. 'Don't look at who is on the other side of the court, what ranking they have. You should never respect anyone in your way; don't respect them so much that you become afraid of them.' While I am not to respect them or be afraid of them, my father also doesn't want me to underestimate anyone.

Also, there is a feeling of ease in spending time with Martina. By the end of my stay in Zurich it seems as though she and I have become good friends. But I know what will happen when I leave Zurich and get back on tour: my father's rules will apply again and I won't be able to maintain a friendship. Still, in this moment I enjoy Martina's company.

In our downtime she drives us around Zurich and shows us the sights of the city. She takes us to a macaroon store. 'You have to try these,' she says. 'They are the best.' When I taste the sweet meringue biscuit

I see what she means. We also go walking, bike riding, to movies and restaurants. Often we just hang out together. For breakfast, lunch and dinner all six of us eat together: Martina, Mum, Melanie, Martina's stepfather, Nadia and me. We sit around talking about tennis and life. Martina's mother and stepfather are lovely and very hospitable. My mother is surprisingly comfortable in this environment. She, like me, is more relaxed without my father around. When my mum and I are alone we have a great time.

All the practice with Martina and Nadia has been incredibly helpful, but getting back on tour – back to business – proves challenging. My mum and I are flying blind – staying in tiny hotels, navigating WTA tour events. Being without a coach proves especially hard. Mum doesn't have a deep understanding of tennis. She was always at work or looking after Savo and has barely watched me play in Australia. On my father's orders, at times she pushes me, trying to tell me how much I should train, what I should do. And I still manage to make a few quarter-final appearances in WTA tournaments, which is pretty good for a sixteen-year-old. My father manages to convince me this is nothing special though. It doesn't take long for me to start to feel alone again.

Next it's on to the Fed Cup 1999, where I play singles and win one of my two matches, beating Austria's Barbara Schett. The air in the Australian Fed Cup camp this time is not too frosty – I get on with my Australian teammates. And I get to see Lesley – still the Fed Cup captain. To my relief, we get along great. There is no weirdness, even though we are not working together any more.

My father is calling constantly – like, all the time – the pressure is there from him. He's giving direction, advice, instructions, yet I feel so alone on the court. I look to the stands, the crowd, and there is not a face to help me out. My mother can't help. So, I do what I know on the court, and it's fine but it's not great.

I get a wildcard into my second grand slam – the French Open. The first round sees me playing Frenchwoman Emmanuelle Curutchet. Naturally, the French crowd screams wildly for her; when I hit a winner, there is nothing but a smattering of polite claps. My opponent takes the first set in a tie breaker but in the second set I pull it together and win it, 6–3.

The third set is a total grind. We play on into the evening, neither of us willing to give an inch. It goes to 11–9 in the third set – her way. I look up at the scoreboard and everything feels dark. *I am shit*, I say to myself. *I am hopeless.*

The match has gone for more than three hours and apparently is one of the top five longest women's matches ever played at this slam. I am uncharacteristically emotional, heartbroken by the loss, beating myself up. All of a sudden, it hits me – I have lost my confidence. All the confidence I gathered from my big year in 1998 as well as my performance at the Hopman Cup through to the 1999 Australian Open has disappeared. I feel lost on court, as though I don't know what I'm doing anymore. It feels like my tennis is going in the wrong direction and I don't know how to fix it.

Perched against the tan wooden locker, I sob as all my negative thoughts stream out. I'm full of disappointment I haven't played to my best. My mother arrives and sits down next to me, trying to console me, but I just sob harder. 'I don't want to play tennis,' I say to her. 'I don't want to play tennis.'

I thought we were alone in the locker room and no one could hear me. But there is movement off to the side. Someone must have been getting a massage in one of the curtained-off cubicles. The player who emerges is Monica Seles. My childhood idol is standing before me as the tears still stream down my face. I am shocked to see her. 'It will get better,' she says to me softly. 'You feel like you want to stop now but it will get better. You won't feel like this tomorrow. You are only sixteen and you are already so good.'

'Thank you,' I say, grateful for her words.

Momentarily I am boosted by her unexpected support. Next thing my mother's phone rings and it's him. She passes me the mobile and I let it all out. A jumble of words and thoughts. 'I don't feel good, I don't feel confident. I have no one with me.'

Then I say it. I say the words I never imagined I would even want to say. 'Please come over, Dad.'

At that moment, I feel as though he's the only card I have left in my hand, tennis-wise. I am totally torn. I know it's going to be hell with him, but at the same time I need his help. I know he is going to come over to Europe sooner or later anyway, so I think it's better he comes now than when things get worse with my tennis.

⊘

Within 48 hours, my father's plane touches down in Paris and as soon as I set eyes on him I bitterly regret my cries for help. He is hungover because he's been drinking to help him cope with the hated plane trip. At least he has brought my beloved Savo, whom I scoop up into a big hug, while my father mutters a subdued hello – he is not big on pleasantries.

With my dad's arrival, my mother and I are back to walking on eggshells. Tension fills the air. I know I need him here to help my tennis but I immediately fall back into a state of fear and anxiety. *Why can't he be normal?* I think.

The next day we head to Birmingham in the United Kingdom for a WTA tournament – this one is the warm-up tournament to Wimbledon, held here every June. We cram into a tiny, cheap hotel – yes, we have money now, but for all of us, and especially my dad, splashing out on a hotel room still feels frivolous. It's time to get back to work.

The rain won't let up in Birmingham so I train indoors on lightning-fast courts. My father returns to his practice of loitering in the background, calling out instructions. And despite my misgivings, I do find that his presence gives me more confidence on court. I walk taller, stand straighter. Yes, I'm scared of him, yet I always feel he knows best. He only has to say a few instructions to me and I know I'll be okay tennis-wise. 'That's the way you should hit that shot.' So, I am torn. Constantly torn. Put aside his antics and the abuse, my father knows what he's talking about when it comes to tennis. He has absorbed the technical and tactical elements of the game from my coaches, especially Craig and Lesley. From the first moment I stepped on to the tennis court he has been listening to and watching the experts. He has memorised all the drills he thinks work and employs them when he coaches me.

It's because I know he knows what he is talking about, because he has steered me to this rise, that I get confidence from him – but that doesn't change the fact I am afraid of him. And him coming over now 'to my rescue', even though he hates flying, would be to make sure I am successful. That my rise continues. He doesn't care if I am happy or sad. He hasn't said to me once in my life that he loves me. I so wish he could be normal because he really understands tennis.

For seven days I practise well and then win through two tough rounds of qualifiers, beating South Africa's Liezel Huber and the Bulgarian player Lubomira Bacheva, who is ranked world No. 97, to make it into the main draw for Birmingham.

My father seems okay with what I am doing. Everything is back on track. Or is it? I never know.

The tournament begins and out on the back courts I'm playing an Italian woman, Rita Grande. I've steamrolled her in the first set but am losing the second when I notice a mild commotion in the crowd. Later I discover that whenever I make a mistake my father thinks he can hear two British women in the crowds laughing. It incenses him so eventually he turns to them and calls them 'old British cows'. There's a lot of yelling after that – the people around the women thoroughly disapprove of him and his words. I try to ignore it. Although I'm used to his disruptions during a match, they still fill me with trepidation.

As I forge on, trying not to be distracted, I see him leave the stands all of a sudden. Whatever's happened, there's nothing I can do so I try to focus even though it is really hard as I know something is going on with him.

What I hear later is that he has gone to the players' lounge, where the television is showing news footage of the NATO bombing of the Belgrade hospital Dragiša Mišović. My father was once operated on in this hospital – it's a place that means a good deal to him and now NATO is blasting it to pieces. Not only that, but hearing the explosions brings back awful memories for him. So of course he starts drinking. He drinks to get rid of the pain, the pressure, the annoying crowd, anything that angers him.

He orders a wine in the players' lounge. And another. Soon he has drunk two bottles and it's then he decides to return to the court to watch me play. He is drunk and he is now very angry. Near my court he starts shouting at officials and spectators all over again. This time he is louder. It's getting more and more difficult to focus on the match. Now my focus is completely on him, and we are in the third set.

Anyway, Brenda Perry, a WTA tour director, takes my dad aside and asks him to leave the area. She has already cautioned him for yelling during my qualifying match the day before. But he pushes Perry away and refuses to leave. The shove seals his fate: security personnel step in to end the sideshow my father is putting on. It takes six security guards to lift him. Struggling with his burly frame, they eventually get him past spectators to the exit at the rear of the grounds of the Edgbaston Priory Club.

Once they're outside the complex they set him free, but his rant doesn't fizzle out. He continues yelling, shouting how good Australia is and how terrible England is. He shouts that the Edgbaston Priory Club members are 'Nazis who supported the bombing of Yugoslavia'. Then he jumps on the hood of a car, rolls off again, sprints zig-zagging down the street and throws himself into the middle of the road in front of another car. It's being driven by a woman with a child in the back, and she narrowly avoids running him over.

Security detains him for an hour until the police arrive. His bizarre behaviour continues – several times he falls on his knees in prayer in front of the guards. When the police turn up they arrest him for being drunk and disorderly and detain him.

Meanwhile, on I play, completely unaware of the chaos that has unfolded as I have tried to win this first-round match. It's late in the evening and the light's too dim. Play is suspended when I'm leading in the third set, 2–1.

It is at this point an official comes over and informs me that my father has been arrested.

I'm not surprised when they tell me this news, but I am furious. I ask someone to drive me to the police station to see him.

There, the police tell me he has been arrested 'for his own safety'. They release him without charge three hours later, after he has sobered up a bit. He returns to our hotel. When he arrives back to our room it's like the incident didn't happen. None of us mentions it. We don't dare. I go to sleep very late, worried. I know it will be extremely hard to continue the match tomorrow.

⊖

Dad's outburst is all over the papers the next day. There are blow-by-blow accounts of how the father of one of the 'most highly regarded junior players' behaved like a lunatic, of how he 'flipped his lid'. The tabloids have started to call him 'the tennis father from hell'.

I read that Bart McGuire, the chief executive of the WTA tour, has barred my father from Edgbaston for the rest of the week. Another man involved in the club, member Roy Dixon, tells the media, 'I've not seen anything like this before. I know of the Mary Pierce incident [Pierce's father was banned from the women's tour after 'continual verbal interference' during her matches and two misdemeanours at the French Open – one of these involved him punching a fan] and others that have happened in tennis. I've played forty-five years of tennis and nine years at Wimbledon, and, no, I have not seen anything like this.'

I turn up for a warm-up before my match against Rita continues. Because of the chaos the day before I haven't been able to line up someone to warm up with. I find a brick wall and hit against that, feeling miserable. I want to slam that neon ball through the brick. When I finally take the court against Rita I'm completely distracted, almost panicked. It's hard to put aside what happened the day before. Rita isn't relenting and the match just – only just, mind you – slips away from me: she wins the final set, 9–7.

After the loss I front a press conference. Feeling like a sitting duck I sit in my seat and wait for the questions to come. But even before I say a word I know I have no choice but to back my father. This makes me feel sick because I certainly don't think or act the way he does.

I am the total opposite to him. The whole episode has embarrassed me so much – this is no longer the juniors, it's an international tournament. The questions start. Of course everyone wants to ask about my dad and the commotion he caused. I force myself to say he was just 'cheering'. 'I don't think anything bad has been done,' I say. 'It was just a person cheering. I don't think there's anything wrong with that.' When they persist with asking about the chaos caused, I come up with this: 'Nothing bad has been done. It was nothing different from what you see all over the world … Probably my father will not be as loud next time.' Privately, I am so sad I have to defend him and the bullshit that he does.

If I don't defend him, guess what: I might actually end up in hospital. There are players on the tour rolling their eyes about my defence of his behaviour. Yes, I can imagine it's hard for people to understand it. But what choice do I have? And I don't understand why he can't handle the pressure of these tournaments. There was more pressure when I was in the juniors in Australia because I hadn't yet made any mark on the tennis tour. But now I have proved to him I can deliver on the court at the professional level: this year I have already beaten three top-20 players, and I've only just turned sixteen.

Surely, the pressure should be off him now – am I not showing him that I am on my way to achieving what he has always wanted me to achieve? Is it a financial thing? That doesn't make sense either, because I'm earning hundreds of thousands of dollars from sponsorships, endorsements and prize money. This is the money he told me I had to earn to get us out of this 'hell', and I've done it! Our situation is so much better than it was three years ago that he has rented a bigger, though still modest, three-bedroom townhouse in Fairfield. We have a new car.

So, yes, I am utterly confused as to why my father isn't a happier person. If anything, the Birmingham outburst signals to me that he is actually worse.

That night I look at him watching television in our small hotel room and I ask myself – for what must be the thousandth time in my life – *What do I have to do to make you happy? Why are you doing all this? Aren't you embarrassed? You are embarrassing me and our whole family? Why?*

⊘

I compartmentalise – just bury my feelings and get on with taking on the tennis world. I've been programmed to be unaffected by the chaos and low moments I go through. But the public embarrassment is slowly starting to affect me. We are in hiding following his drunken performance and the subsequent wave of bad press, so Ivan Brixi has arranged for us to practise at a private club before Wimbledon.

For eight days we lie low and I train my heart out. We're staying in another budget hotel; this time it's a place in Putney Bridge. I'm on the court three hours in the morning and two hours in the afternoon preparing to qualify for Wimbledon. My life has again become a cycle of sleeping, eating and relentless training, and I remain confident because I have my father telling me what I am doing right on the court, and what I'm not doing well. The six months I've endured since parting company with Lesley have shown I just can't do it alone. I am only sixteen, after all.

We head to the tennis battleground of Roehampton, a leafy suburb a few kilometres from the prestigious All England club, where the Wimbledon 'qualies' are held. Here, a bunch of juniors like me and long-time players trying to crack their first Wimbledon, are on a mission to secure a spot in the main draw. Everyone is hungry for the chance. But I doubt anyone is hungrier or has worked harder than me.

I cast aside Belgian player Patty Van Acker, who's ranked 146 to my 129. Austrian Evelyn Fauth doesn't stand a chance – she only wins one game off me. Then I play fellow Australian Rennae Stubbs: I take her down in two sets.

I am sixteen years old and I have powered my way through three qualifying rounds to gain a spot in the main draw of Wimbledon. Qualifying for this prestigious tournament is met with no praise from my dad: he doesn't consider praise helpful. He thinks I need to be pushed to work hard to succeed. He has me on diet of fear and punishment.

But I can handle it for now, I think.

6

Wimbledon, 1999

I'm careful not to let my father observe my reaction when they tell me I'm to play Martina Hingis in the first round of Wimbledon.

'That's okay,' he says flatly. 'You can beat her.'

Yes, I nod, trying to smile. On the inside I am kind of freaking out. The world No. 1? I just got here.

Sure, I could have got a better draw, but I remind myself I have slayed three other players trying to qualify and immediately start thinking of ways to beat her.

'At least you'll be on one of the two biggest courts,' says the official.

I smile and nod again. Where this match will be played doesn't matter; all that matters is beating Martina. I'm nervous but I can't let my father know this when he's told me over and over I must never decide someone is better than me; he doesn't want me to even think about losing. If I give him any indication or hint that I'm scared of losing, that I could somehow feel weak – he will punish me. That could be a beating with the brown belt I dread so much.

After the announcement that I am to play Martina, Dad adds, 'You have to think you can beat anyone.' He's right, I know in my heart he's right. And that's the last conversation we have about the match.

One morning my father spots Steffi Graf around the practice courts. He goes up to her and asks if she would mind hitting with me and she says she will. I'm shocked she has agreed, but delighted and very nervous. So one rainy day before I am to play Martina, Steffi and I hit for two hours on Wimbledon's indoor courts. It's incredible just meeting her let alone being on the court with her – I'm in awe. She is tough, serious and professional. To have practised with Monica earlier this year and now Steffi are dreams come true. They are my idols.

By this stage I've managed to shove aside the shock of the draw, and in the days leading up to the match I'm feeling good. As my father told me, I can take anyone down.

He has been warned he will be under surveillance at Wimbledon. From my management group to the very top echelons of the tour, everyone is on full Damir Dokic alert. He himself dismisses the warnings. He thinks none of it is his fault.

My mother is not allowed to say much to me about tennis. Or anything really. In keeping with Dad's wishes, she stays quiet and doesn't even wish me good luck. She never wishes me good luck anyway. My little brother is oblivious to what a big occasion this is but I love that he is here.

On the morning of the match I warm up at a back court and I don't experience any nerves. No one watches me – I am still a relative tennis nobody here, just a junior with a couple of good wins behind her. So despite the magnitude of this clash I don't feel any pressure, just fresh and strong. I know Martina's game inside out thanks to the stint

I spent at her house in Zurich before the French Open. Our match at the Australian Open earlier this year has also given me a good insight into her game. As I warm up I mentally park the friendship and I focus on the game plan in trying to win this match.

I walk onto Wimbledon's Court Number 1 as though it's a grass court at White City. I feel confident. I don't play with a lot of top spin, so with an aggressive type of game style being my strength, the ball on grass really skids and goes away from the opponents and stays low, making it very difficult for them. I also take the ball early. I switch myself to automatic. I feel no sense of occasion; in fact, I feel nothing. As the thousands of spectators cheer and clap, I'm not nervous – I don't take much notice of the noise – I am focused; I make myself believe this is just another tennis match.

Up in the players' box my father sits alongside Mum and Savo. My dad's quiet and anxious – I can see it from where I stand. I sense that he expects me to beat her – the world No. 1. I think and feel nothing.

Oddly, in Martina's box her mother is absent.

From the get-go I force Martina to stay back; I don't allow her to dictate and play her game. I don't allow her to move the ball around, to take the ball early and come forward, which is what she likes to do. I hit a lot of great two-handed backhands, cross-courts and down the lines. As well as a lot of great drop shots. Here on Wimbledon's Court Number 1 I hit some brilliant winners, and when I do I barely react. I don't engage with the emotion of the occasion. After some astonishing play I simply lower my gaze to the ground or adjust my racquet strings. Barely smile. Occasionally, after a winner I glance up to my father and permit myself a small fist pump. But I remain as impassive as possible as I dismantle the world No. 1. I play without feeling just as my father has instructed. I am not allowed to talk. I am not allowed to pass comment on my opponent or the match. I'm not allowed to show negative body language or throw my racquet. If I do any of these things, as I learnt in my early junior days, my father beats the hell out of me.

I take the first set 6–2.

By now the crowd is loud and they are cheering for me, the underdog, as they watch 'the Swiss Miss' lose her composure. I can hear and feel that the crowd are in shock.

By the second set Martina is truly floundering – she can barely win a point; the momentum's with me – I'm unstoppable. The crowd gasps at my tennis and the cheers become louder with every winner I hit, the Australian qualifier coming from obscurity to crush the top women's player in the world.

It's a clinical victory. After I take eleven straight games in one stretch and get up 4–0 in the second set, I can see that Martina is more and more dispirited where I'm full of energy. Adrenalin pumps through my body. I am bursting with nerves and excitement on the inside but I have to temper it as usual.

In the end Martina doesn't win a game in the second set. On match point her backhand return pops out of bounds. I throw my hands into the air, in shock, and look at my dad. But I don't see his face, only the back of him – he is walking out of the stadium already. My heart sinks as fast as it rose. In fact, all my happiness disappears instantly. His walk-out makes me feel that this victory somehow doesn't matter to him. I have won, 6–2, 6–0, in just 55 minutes, pulling off the biggest grand slam upset of the Open era, but my father can't even wait to applaud me. Am I asking for too much? Am I being too sensitive? This makes me so sad.

I find him in the players' lounge, but there is no hug, no congratulatory words. He doesn't even say 'Well done.' While he appears satisfied, it's as if I've just beaten someone on a court at the Fairfield tennis club. All he says is, 'I told you that you could beat her.'

In her press conference Martina is really gracious. 'It happens to everybody sometimes,' she says, and adds that her loss is due to my great play.

My conference is packed with Fleet Street journalists and international media. I am the new girl on the block, the steely-faced blonde ponytailed giant-killer. I too heap praise on Martina. 'She's got all the shots in the book and she can do anything – I mean, she's number one in the world. But once I got going, I played very well. Everything worked today: I knew I had to keep it deep, put pressure on her forehand, be aggressive, take the ball early and not let her dictate. I don't think there was any pressure at all, because she's the one who was supposed to win.

'I'm going to try and do my best to go as far as I can, but there are no easy matches, everyone's tough to play. There was no pressure on me today. No one expected me to beat the world No. 1. Even if I lost the match it would have been good to get close.'

Then I say, 'It's still hard to believe I've beaten Martina, but I have to keep my feet on the ground because anything can happen in the next match.'

Though I say in public that I'm finding it hard to believe I have beaten Martina, to be frank that's a lie. I am not shocked that I have beaten her. My father made me believe I could do it.

'I owe him a lot; he knows what I have to work on and what I have to fix,' I tell the press.

They bring up Birmingham and ask what my father said to me after the match. I lie. 'He was out of words,' I say. 'But just because I've beaten Martina doesn't mean I'll win the tournament.'

Back in the players' lounge I notice other players giving me side-ways glances: 'Who is this?' kinds of looks. This is how they react when a new gun is on the scene. Yes, I have arrived. And in the days after the victory my popularity soars. It's impossible for me to walk out of the lounge without getting mobbed. People are clamouring for my autograph. The Wimbledon organisers have to give me security. Journalists keep on writing about me; they can't get enough of our story. They write about the 'blonde and beaming Dokic, who arrived in Sydney [five] years ago by way of Serbia ... and is coached by her father, Damir, a truck driver turned tennis sage.'

None of them knows our dark truths. Our secrets.

The media writes that we have a celebratory dinner with bread, cheese and pizza. In reality, while there is bread, cheese and pizza, there are no celebrations. The four of us simply go back to the Travel Inn in Putney Bridge and eat in silence at the hotel. It's like beating Martina never happened.

In the days that follow it becomes clear that my 'dad from hell' and I have become the new fixation of the British press. They dub my father 'controversial' and endlessly bring up him harassing English fans over the NATO bombing campaign in Serbia and subsequent arrest in Birmingham. They love that my family is living in the budget hotel, sitting on a bed watching television while eating cut-price bread-and-cheese dinners. 'Bread and cheese in a cheap hotel for new golden girl,' reads a *Daily Mail* headline. A British news-paper compares the 'Dokic Hotel Hovel' to the weekly rent of £4500 (AU$7200) for the three-storey residences in leafy Wimbledon village preferred by millionaires such as Martina and Russian star Anna Kournikova.

A British television commentator likens the hotel we're staying in to a brothel. 'She's staying in a cheap bordello down the road,'

Julian Tutt says while commentating one of my matches. The £59.99-a-night room I share with my parents and Savo is modest but it is certainly not a brothel. Tutt is later forced to apologise for fear of a lawsuit from the hotel chain and us. A tabloid photographer paps me emerging early in the morning from the hotel. In fact, every member of my family is papped, including Savo.

I try to ignore my newfound fame and concentrate on my second-round match, in which I take on Slovakia's Katarina Studenikova on Court 13, one of Wimbledon's outer show courts. The large crowd is dotted with green-and-gold-painted faces shouting, 'Aussie, Aussie, Aussie, oi, oi, oi'. Although not everyone in the Australian tennis community has accepted me, the fans have always been unfailingly positive towards me. And loudly so. Today their cheering boosts me. As the match opens, I'm still on my Martina-slaying high and come out firing to claim the first set 6–0 in 23 minutes. But I fade in the second; my second serve is inconsistent and I lose, 4–6.

In the third set there are five consecutive breaks of serve and my nerve is stretched. At one stage a line call goes against me when I'm certain my ball was in. My lips tremble and I catch my father's eye. He grimaces back. He, too, knows my ball was in. As usual, whether I am winning or losing he has an expression on his face that frightens me – and especially when I am losing.

Here in the third set I can see he is very angry and nervous. He is sitting in the fifth row from the front and I hear him throwing out advice quite loudly. Yet his shouting is muffled by the crowd noise. I can't quite make out what he is saying. He is not allowed to coach me, but he ignores the rules. As always.

I cling on to the match. I take the third, 8–6.

The press chase Dad down after the match as he tries to make his way back to the players' lounge. He is grumpy. Later I read that he's described the match as 'Very bad today … a different match from the last one.'

The WTA official instructs the press room to ask only 'tennis questions'. I tell the media: 'It was a bit scary today. I dropped my game a little, and also concentration, and it was hard to get back. I didn't play as well as against Martina. But she didn't play as well as Martina did. Martina forced me to play well.

'Now I've got to keep my feet on the ground, and it's hard to do that with all the attention and the press and everything. It's a bit different now, definitely. More people talk to me and everyone knows me. And there's a little more respect. And I've had lots of faxes from Australia.'

They want to know more about me. 'Is your name pronounced Dok-ik or Dok-ich?' someone asks.

I shrug and smile. 'Whatever,' I reply. When pushed I tell them 'Dok-ich'.

A British reporter asks me about the mark on my face. Yes, I confirm, it is a birthmark. They ask about how my relationships in the locker room have changed since my rise in the tournament. Of course, I don't tell them that Dad doesn't allow me to spend much time in the locker room. It's one of his rules: I'm to go in and out of there as quickly as possible; chatting to other players is strongly discouraged.

I'm asked about how far I could go on the Wimbledon grass but, as I explain, I haven't looked at the draw. I don't even know who I'll be playing in the next round. What I am really feeling – that was notably absent before my match against Martina – is pressure. I'm beginning to feel burdened by the fact I have brought her down and there are now new, high expectations of me. Coupled with this, thanks to my growing popularity tennis fans are following me everywhere.

The Wimbledon organisers capitalise on my sudden rise in popularity and award me a match on Centre Court in the third round, where I'm to play Anne Kremer, who's ranked 31, from Luxembourg. I beat her 6–7 (9–7), 6–3, 6–4 but again it becomes a terribly scrappy match – I keep on double-faulting, and making unforced errors. Still, I fight and pull through.

'After losing the first set you have to think positive,' I tell reporters afterwards. 'I definitely didn't play as good as I did against Hingis, but I have come from nowhere in this tournament so there will be no pressure against [my next opponent, Mary] Pierce. Hopefully I'll play well again.'

The night before I play Mary, Dad invites my sports agents, John McCurdy and Ivan Brixi, over for dinner at our hotel, the Travel Inn. The six of us sit in the hotel's modest restaurant, where my father has pre-arranged for the hotel chef to cook up all different types of fish. Fish dish upon fish dish arrive. He's an enthusiastic host – charming even. I'm relieved John and Ivan are able to see a better side of my father. He is boisterous but not out of control. I hope that to them he seems like a solid father, albeit a slightly erratic one, who only wants the best for his daughter.

Mary Pierce is another player I have a deep respect for. Tall and confident, and seeded ninth, she'll be a fierce opponent. Sure enough, in the opening games she crushes me and all of a sudden she's up 3–0. I'm floored by her power and five games in I have only managed to win one. Still, I don't lose hope. I gather my thoughts. This isn't a match I should be expected to win but I continue to believe I can do so.

Serving at 1-4 I feel confident even though I'm down. I hold my serve and focus hard on trying to break hers. I am starting to feel the ball better and better. My shots begin to hit the lines. I manage to break her serve and I am back in it. Pierce can hit the ball hard, but I try to move her around the court. I come back and take the first set 6–4 in 35 minutes. When I look up to Dad, his face is blank.

As the second set opens I spot Lesley watching from the players' area. It's a tremendous surprise to see her and there's a real boost from her presence, as well as a pang of sadness she is no longer on my team. Still, my momentum rolls on: I take the second set 6–3. I honestly can't believe that I have beaten another top ten player in the fourth round of Wimbledon.

Again my father leaves his seat without acknowledging my win. He rushes off from the stands and afterwards, when I find him, he acts as though nothing special has happened. Just another win.

Privately, I am ecstatic but I try to remain modest at the press conference. 'Today I played better than in my previous two matches, though not as well as I did against Hingis. I've got great confidence right now, and it's anybody's tournament. Beating Mary today proved to me that I can beat top players.'

Mary is left shaking her head. 'She's a good fighter. She just never gave up. She moved around the court well and hit some great shots when she was in trouble. She's a baseliner. She plays aggressive and comes forward, taking the ball early.'

To me this win is on par with my victory over Martina. This is another win, in two sets, over a player in the top ten. People will now realise that my victory over Martina wasn't a fluke.

After my press conference I hurry back out to see my parents and we return to our hotel.

I am in the quarter-final of a grand slam but there are no celebrations.

In my next match I come up against another junior on the rise: Alexandra Stevenson. She is a tall, powerful eighteen-year-old. I know not to underestimate her; she's a strong player with a big serve and a good grass court game.

They put us on show court 2. We play a few games and then there's a rain delay, which means the rest of the match must be played the following day. They move us to show court 1. I go back to the hotel, my father gives me a pep talk; he's on my back, he's constantly on my back. I go to bed and sleep well. But I play terribly the next day, from the first ball. I feel wrung out – not physically but emotionally. I am really, really emotionally drained from the hectic tennis schedule. Emotionally drained from beating Hingis and Pierce. It's been a huge few weeks.

Stevenson is all power with her thundering 190 km an hour serves. She is running me around and I'm now the one floundering all over the court, hurtling from side to side, struggling to get her shots back, to read and return her big serve.

The turning point comes at 3–3 in the third set. I'm serving and she breaks me and from then on I have nothing left. I don't win another game and she ends up beating me, 6–3, 1–6, 6–3.

I am done, my Wimbledon is done. After the press conference, in a quiet corner, my dad goes mental. As usual he chooses a spot where nobody is around – between Wimbledon and Aorangi Park, where the practice courts are. His face is just centimetres away from mine when he unloads a torrent of abuse.

'You are hopeless.'

'You are a cow.'

'You are pathetic.'

'You are worth nothing.'

Over and over. He is furious that I have lost in the quarter-finals of Wimbledon by, in his eyes, playing badly. To him I have thrown it away. I have thrown his, and my, Wimbledon dream away.

As I stand there copping his spray, his words sear my soul. He makes me feel like I am worthless.

My usually stoic exterior drops – I can't hold the tears back any longer and I start to heave with sobs. Suddenly this and the emotion of the last three weeks – the high of winning against Martina and Mary, and now the low of this moment – it's all too much. Here I am with my father telling me I am a piece of shit, when at sixteen years of age I have made the quarter-finals of Wimbledon from 'qualies'. To hear that I am a hopeless, worthless human being in my father's eyes after this achievement leaves me devastated, sad and scared.

When we get back to our hotel in Putney he doesn't strike me – instead he inflicts another punishment from his catalogue of abuse: standing. For three hours he makes me stand while he delivers a torrent of insults. My little brother and mother have to listen to this shit. It's not the first time I have endured the standing punishment and this outburst is not even close to his worst tirade. Sometimes he takes breaks from bellowing at me and watches television while I have to continue standing. My legs ache from a gruelling period of competition but the emotional pain is worse.

He keeps me awake with this until two in the morning. I just think, *Hit me and get it over with.* Sometimes I'd rather put up with an hour or two of physical pain than hour after hour of psychological torment. This yelling frightens me to my core. It's more exhausting than physical pain. It's almost worse than when he punches me in the stomach.

And I figure that people are bound to have noticed the bruises from his physical abuse. As much as I might try to cover them up by playing in long-sleeved tops in practice, it's impossible to hide them when they're all over my legs, my arms.

When people have asked what is going on, I have offered up plenty of excuses. All the ones you'd expect. 'Oh, I ran into a table,' I used to tell a coach. 'I fell down the stairs,' I once told someone. I never tell the truth about what is happening to me because I don't want it to come out. Certainly not to the whole world. Rather than risk my family falling apart, I will take the hits and keep us together. Of course, I don't want to be physically abused but I am trapped – I am sixteen years old, and I can't fathom telling anyone what is really going on. I worry if people find out from me that he abuses me – and he finds out that I told someone our horrific secret – he will literally kill me. And I don't want people to feel sorry for me, so I keep making up excuses about my injuries.

By now many have glimpsed the worst sides of my father and how frightening he can be – I've seen people looking scared by his behaviour. Generally they turn a blind eye to it all. He's too much to handle.

For the time being, I will continue to lie on his behalf. Already I have stood up in a courtroom and lied for him. I will always defend him, no matter how awful the abuse, how vile his words are, how fragile he makes me feel. I will always defend him because I'm afraid of him, and I hold out hope that if I hang in long enough, this abuse will stop one day. I defend him to keep my family together.

The media is all over him and us but it's his own fault. Not that I would ever dare to tell him that. I need to keep my focus on my tennis, despite all the new distractions around me – because he is constantly asking for more from me.

7

Canada, 1999–2000

August. Trouble starts to brew on a plane trip to Toronto as we head to the Canadian Open. Mum and Dad are with me and as usual my father slams back a heap of white wine and scotch to help calm his nerves. Pretending he is nothing to do with me, I look off into the distance.

Since Wimbledon, my life has changed. Now that people know my name, there is strong interest in me.

In Toronto I draw a wildcard in the first round – Croatia's Iva Majoli, a former French Open champion coming back from injury. I give our match my all, play solidly, and get through 6–3, 6–4. Next I face Conchita Martinez, who is ranked 18 in the world. She's eleven years older than me and the kind of opponent who can expose every weakness in your game: terribly efficient, with a great top spin forehand and an excellent slice backhand. She is very difficult to play against. Makes few errors and is extremely patient but at the same time aggressive. I know it will be a difficult match.

I take the first set 7–5, but it's total grind against the Spaniard. It feels like every ball is coming back. The rallies are relentless and in the second set Conchita starts winning them all. She is signing the cross and looking to the sky after taking the big points. It's intensely hot and the match is a marathon. Despite fighting so hard, in the third set I feel it slipping away. After a three-hour match I lose the last two sets, 6–1, 6–4.

Thoroughly spent from the match, I have few reserves with which to confront Dad's pent-up fury. The moment we are in the privacy of our hotel room, the beating starts. My mum is made to sit there and witness it. Today he chooses the bathroom – in a small space, I have nowhere to run. He removes the brown belt from his trousers and instructs me to take off my top. When he is hitting me, he talks non-stop, berating me. First he goes through the specifics of what he thinks I did wrong in that match, each flaw punctuated with a lash. Then he starts on my character: 'You're a whore [whack]. A hopeless cow [whack]. A dirty bitch …'

Dropping the belt, he resorts to bare hands. A few hits to my face to begin. Next we're out of the bathroom; he makes me stand in the centre of the hotel room while he pelts me with verbal abuse. He pulls my hair. He yanks my ears. He spits in my face. I hate it so much when he spits at me.

This beating is more intense than any that have gone before. Soon I am physically in agony, emotionally pulverised. Without let-up he's told me how terrible I am, hit me, whipped me, pulled my hair, tugged my ears – over and over and over. There are bruises all over my body. My ears sting. My scalp hurts from where he has pulled my hair and my head is throbbing.

Evening gives way to night. My mother, totally voiceless, is also watching this live horror show. I am denied all food and drink, even though I spent three hours hurtling around the court in that heat. This punishment is familiar. One he has been inflicting regularly since I started playing juniors. My mouth feels dry. I am desperate for water and feel faint. My last meal was breakfast. But I refuse to break. Somehow I always reach a stage where I feel like I can push through the pain. I make myself feel nothing.

Morning breaks in our Toronto hotel room and finally my father calms and sits me down. 'I went overboard,' he says to me. 'I am not going to do this again. You fought and you lost.'

That's all he says. It's not an apology but it is an acknowledgement that this has gone too far. If he says this beating was bad then I know it was really bad.

I nod, profoundly grief-stricken, sick to my stomach, on the verge of passing out and weeping. All I want to do is curl up in a corner and hide so I can cry my eyes out. Not only because of the hitting and the emotional abuse, but out of sadness that this is the state of my family life. That this is my life. I am seventeen, earning all this money, playing well, yet in his eyes this is not enough. *What's wrong with him?*

The three of us fly to New York for the US Open. The Toronto hotel incident isn't mentioned; it isn't reflected upon. None of the abusive episodes ever are. For the moment my dad's attitude towards me has mildly softened, but I'm still reeling. Even though that was the first time he expressed regret to me about physically and emotionally harming me, his words about going 'overboard' certainly can't take away the pain he has caused me. I've lost all focus. Questions swirl in my mind. *Why does he punish me when he's supposed to protect me? Why does he seem to hate me when he's supposed to love me? Do I deserve what he does to me? Why am I not enough?*

My emotions are a mess and the draw at the US Open doesn't help. In the first round I'm to take on Aranxta Sanchez Vicario, who's seeded No. 10. Her 'never say die' attitude on court is something I just can't deal with right now. Sure, I'm a fighter too, but not at the moment. I am broken after Canada. Still, I win four of the first five games in the first set, breaking her serve twice. And then my thoughts go elsewhere and my shots go everywhere. He gives me no encouragement from the stands. After only a few errors I can feel my headspace clouding with negative thoughts. *I am worthless; I am nothing. What am I even doing here at the US Open? I am hopeless.*

I lose. His words have really got to me: it's the first time in my career that I feel I can't focus and perform because of him. It's because of that extreme beating in Toronto: the fear of him has got to me rather than driven me. And I am hurting on the inside more than ever before.

After I lose to Arantxa there are a handful of questions in my press conference at Flushing Meadows before journalists hit me with my dad's behaviour in Birmingham. *Here we go*, I think. *Time to start lying.* It's exhausting and demoralising having to cover for him, again. Especially when I think he is wrong and way out of line.

'How were you able to focus so clearly after what happened a couple of weeks earlier? Was that difficult to block out?'

'No, I don't think it was. What came out of [Birmingham] was pretty much blown up. A lot happened there, but it didn't bother me because I knew half of those things weren't true anyway. I think it was just a story that people had something to write about at Wimbledon.'

It's the last thing I want to talk about after being beaten by Arantxa. The questions finally turn to the match. I know there were too many unforced errors, I say. I think I just gave the match away. As my father likes me to, I throw in for good measure my distaste of the age limits at WTA tournaments. 'You've got to pick your tournaments. Even after this now, I've hardly got anything to play. I'm struggling to find tournaments where I can go to, [when] I'm going to play them. I can't just go to any tournament.'

We head to Tokyo. I lose in the first round of the Japan Open. I play doubles with Amanda Coetzer and make the final. We lose and Dad is mad. He has been drinking all day. On the plane he continues to drink spirits and whatever else he can get his hands on. He gets louder. He needs to go to the bathroom. All the cubicles are taken so he starts going around and banging on the bathroom doors. I look at the window and pretend I am not with him, that I am travelling alone, that I have nothing to do with him. His drunken antics go on for a couple of hours. He is yelling at the hostess for more alcohol. I am actually stunned they are still serving him. He cruises around the place like he owns it. Eventually after hours of embarrassment he gets back to his seat and passes out.

⊖

Tony Roche's Turramurra home is beautiful. It sits in lush green bush on the outskirts of Sydney's north. It's quiet, peaceful; a haven of garden that boasts a perfectly maintained hard court, which you can see from his comfortable living room.

In my dad's eyes Tony is a coaching genius. He has guided Pat Rafter to great heights – this past July Pat reached world No. 1. Unfortunately, he lost in the first round of the US Open and is struggling with an injured shoulder, which isn't getting better quickly. But as a consequence Tony has some time on his hands and Tennis Australia have connected me with him and asked him if he'll work with me on a part-time basis. Tony's agreed, so now every day we travel from Fairfield to Turramurra.

Tony's mild-mannered but tough. He's kind-hearted, like Lesley, and he has the same ethic as her: work hard, do a lot of hours on the court with not too much of a break. He focuses on improving my net game and helps me with my serve, which needs some work. Pat sometimes joins us on the court and hits with me. Like Tony, he is kind and nice – their characters are completely opposite to my father's. And despite Tony's gentle but firm methods, my father likes him; he has deep respect for him and his history with the game. He often engages Tony in conversation about tennis. Not in English – I stand there and do a lot of translating. I wish my dad wasn't here, but like he did with coaches before Tony he's absorbing everything that Tony's teaching me.

One downside to being coached by Tony is that it causes the resumption of the beatings. It happens after sessions my dad deems 'bad' or 'pathetic'. There's no way he'd hit me on Tony's property; he waits until we're in the car at the front of the house. The ensuing car trips home are always excruciating, too – especially since he is trying to teach me how to drive now too. I'm beaten for being a bad tennis player and a bad driver, and he strikes me while I'm driving if I make a mistake so it's a petrifying experience. He keeps his arm on the back of my headrest ready to hit me in the head at any time if I make an error. In heavy traffic he strikes a blow to my head sending my focus off course. Imagine if I crashed? I *have* almost crashed more than once. My excitement about learning to drive has quickly turned into fear of a hellish experience.

Some days when we get home from Tony's, my father makes me stand for hours on end as he hurls abuse, my muscles aching while I endure the standing torture. He'll then send me on another long run around Fairfield. These days almost break me. While I am pounding the pavement I sometimes dream about running away.

As the millennium draws to a close, I'm clinging on, but only just; life is getting worse. I can feel more trouble around the corner.

⊝

I have just lost to a little-known Hungarian, Rita Kuti Kis, in the opening round of the 2000 Australian Open. Although I briefly pulled myself together in the second set, generally my game was error-ridden: 1–6, 6–2, 3–6. At my father's insistence I skip the mandatory post-match press conference and we return to our hotel – as the press writes, I go 'missing for four hours'. With my no-show I've risked being fined $10,000.

Then he decides on a whim that, after all, I will address the press. I never know what he is thinking or why he makes decisions. What I am supposed to say is that Rita is a hopeless player who will never cut it at the top of the sport. For once I am defiant: the thought of doing that to another player sickens me. 'I don't want to say that,' I tell him.

'You have to,' he replies. 'Don't you dare not say it.' And the way he looks at me, I know if I disobey him he will unleash the full force of his brutality on me. I think back to that hotel bathroom in Toronto and I start shaking. He instructs me to write down a statement, including the sentence 'She has never been a player and never will be.' These are horrible, ungracious words and not my thoughts at all. I feel sick having to say them.

Preparing the statement takes a while, and I arrive late to the rescheduled press conference. Hesitantly, I take my seat in the theatre-style room in front of the assembled journalists in rows, their eyes on me. First, I quip that I'm late because I went to church to pray for better results. It's what he has told me to say – mad bullshit. I take a breath and read out my father's words, feeling like I'm feeding myself to the lions. 'Basically, I lost to a player today that has never been a player and I guess probably never will be,' I say, dying inside.

> She played well against me today, but people have never known her and she beat me … If anyone saw my practice, there is probably not even three or four players at the moment who can beat me if I play like that in the match. It's just that I've been having trouble putting it into my matches. It will probably take time to do it, a couple of months, six months maybe, but once it gets going it will always be like I did at Wimbledon.
>
> It will be tough to beat me – like in the juniors in [five] months I got to be number one in the world in juniors. Like I said, I've just got to get it together in my matches and once I do that I think I'll get up there pretty quick.

At the conclusion of the press conference I can see journalists whipping out their mobile phones to call their editors because of my brattish words. The headlines the next day shout statements like: 'BE A GOOD LOSER – Dokic told after outburst'.

That's just fuel to my father's crazy fires. I am thinking on the inside about my father, *It's all your fault. What did you think was going to happen?* He instructs me the next day that we're to do an interview with a journalist from the *Herald Sun*, John Ferguson, in which I'm to say that the WTA tournament draws are rigged. It makes me feel sick, numb and dumbfounded I have to make this statement.

We meet John in the foyer and I do as I'm told – I tell him WTA matches are being deliberately changed to stall my career, that a run of bad draws since Wimbledon last year has left me convinced something is going wrong. It's an outrageous claim; blatantly untrue.

Dad sits by my side as I say exactly what he has instructed me to. 'For all this trouble, it's a bit hard to believe getting draws like that,' I tell Ferguson. 'They say they pull them out [of a hat] but I don't think so.'

And I don't back down from my attack on Rita. John asks if I regret my comments. 'No, I don't think so,' I say with uncertainty, then I add, 'I just basically said if you look at where she is and her age, you will see you have never heard of her and probably never will.'

If I go against his word I know he will punch me in the head behind closed doors but I acknowledge to myself how fed up I am with spouting this nonsense. My father then starts giving his thoughts in the interview; again, I have to translate for him. He claims that our family has no friends on tour except for Tony, and he prompts me to say again that much of our motivation has come from the fact that we were refugees from Serbia before coming to Australia in 1994.

'He [my father] says I have a lot of pressure on me because of where we come from,' I tell the journalist. 'I came to be number one junior in the world and ranked number thirty-seven in the world when we had nothing – only social security.'

My dad then accuses the WTA of acting out of order in Birmingham and tells me to pass this on to John. Obediently I do so.

John Ferguson's story hits the front page of the *Herald Sun* and is all over the front pages of other News Limited tabloids across Australia. 'WORLD AGAINST ME – Dokic's conspiracy theory' reads the headline.

Chaos erupts.

The media knows that Damir Dokic is a livewire, that he is likely to come out with who-knows-what if he's pushed. Media crews camp outside our hotel and appear at my practice, and a Channel 7 TV crew tracks us down in a Melbourne car park as we try to go back to our hotel. My father is angry and can't control his emotions – he lunges at the cameraman as we walk up to the lobby and snatches the camera. He offers cameraman Adrian Bray $500 for the return of the camera, minus the film.

As the day unfolds, some people speak in support of me – those who know me, who know that what I've said surely hasn't come from me. My doubles partner Jennifer Capriati defends me. We are friendly; she has an inkling of the pressure I am under and she speaks her mind. 'Who really knows what the influences around her are,' she says. 'You don't know if it's coming directly from her.'

Still, my reputation is slowly falling apart here. Every television station in town has camera crews at the ready around us. At my next match, a doubles with Capriati, the media attention is immense. It's a slow news day and I've become the story of the tournament even though I'm not even in the main draw now. I would never give up my tennis, I don't wish for a normal sixteen-year-old's life, I love tennis, but I just wish I could play without the hell he puts me through. Without him. I hate all this public embarrassment.

Jennifer and I defeat our opponents 6–2, 6–0 and afterwards I front a packed press conference and again trot out every word my father has asked me to say: 'So, you know, that it's clear what I said ... What [John] wrote ... we had a totally different conversation. He wrote a totally different story the next day. I asked for the tape because I didn't say what he wrote.'

I also deny saying that WTA officials set up my matches. Then I offer $50,000 for the interview tapes to be released so that people can find out the 'truth'. In response the editor of the *Herald Sun*, Peter Blunden, comes out and states that the paper stands by its story and will not release a copy of the tape recording: 'We don't release transcripts of tapes. We don't feel obligated to release anything,' he says.

It's occurred to me that my dad's lost his mind and that the problem's getting worse and worse. This 'draw-fixing' allegation, then my retraction, are, I am well aware, big mistakes in the public eye and they tarnish my image. Until now there hasn't been a bad sentence written about me – the stories have all been about my meteoric rise after coming over here with nothing. Now the attention is almost purely focused on my apparently petulant and unreasonable behaviour, and on my crazy father.

The next thing he does is to lash out at Tennis Australia – for, of all things, not being able to control the media. I have been named an official ambassador for the Olympics to help promote the Games, which are being hosted by Sydney this year amid huge excitement nationwide. It's a great honour and I am truly moved. But now Dad informs Tennis Australia I might not take part in the Olympics. For the first time ever, he threatens Tennis Australia president Geoff Pollard and Open tournament director Paul McNamee that our family will go back to Yugoslavia. It's a genuine threat – he's actually serious. My mother, as always, plays no part in this decision and doesn't even express her feelings about the threat. She is not allowed to say anything. For my part, I am worried and scared as I absolutely do not want this to happen. I have come to think of Australia as home. It's where I belong and this is the country I want to represent and play for.

But my dad thinks he can do whatever he wants with my life. He thinks he has made me.

One day in our Fairfield apartment I gently try to encourage him to change his mind about snubbing the Sydney Olympics. 'Please don't rush with the decision,' I say. 'Please think about what is the right thing to do. I really want to play at the Olympics.'

'I don't care,' he says. 'Everyone is against us. You are not playing.'

He comes up with a plan to pay back officials and media who have 'ruined' my reputation: a paid interview with the women's magazine *New Idea*. Of course he briefs me prior to the interview – I am to say I will almost certainly boycott the Sydney Olympics because I was 'betrayed' during the recent Australian Open.

'I'm ninety-five per cent certain I'm not going to play in the Olympics, because of everything that happened to me over the summer … It's my revenge.

'I didn't feel like I was supported, no one got behind me, and that really hurt me. I feel betrayed, ruined. It's left a sour taste in my mouth and I don't really feel I have to give anything back.'

I add that the boycott is a desperate measure to clear my name over the draw-fixing comments.

'I want to prove my innocence,' I declare. 'To make the decision not to play is very hard. It was something I discussed with my family. We will probably go to Europe for holidays instead.'

None of it is true. I *really* want to play at the Olympics.

By now there are whispers on the tennis scene that my father physically abuses me. The stories from my junior days – the incident at the Hotel Bruce County – have filtered back to the press. But in this interview I deny he has ever hurt me. I think, *What would the consequences be if I told the truth? Would I be responsible for breaking up my family?* At this point of my life I can't bear that burden. So, I praise my family and emphasise that my father is my greatest supporter, say he'd never harm me. I feel sick to my stomach about this. I am tired of lying. 'Everything has been blown out of proportion about my dad. There have been all sorts of stories about him. I've heard rumours that he was beating me, but it's all lies.

'I have a very close relationship with my dad because he's always been there for me.

'I trust my dad more than anyone and there's no one I can rely on more than him.'

As I say these words I realise how trapped and stuck I feel. *I wish I could be free of this*, I think. *I just want to be happy. I just want to play tennis.*

The *New Idea* article and the subsequent publicity about me wanting to pull out of the Olympics cause a huge headache for Tennis Australia as the country is preparing to host the Games. They go into damage control. Paul McNamee makes a mercy dash to our Fairfield home from Melbourne. My father actually likes Paul a lot – he's the only person at Tennis Australia whom he trusts. Paul walks into our small home and my dad offers him a drink. They talk amicably. But Dad is standing firm: 'Jelena is not playing Olympics,' he reiterates to Paul.

So, I'm an official ambassador for the Olympics but I'm refusing to take part – Paul knows this is ridiculous, that being upset by a newspaper article is not going to cut it with the Australian public. There has to be a much better excuse for my stance and Paul suggests one as he stands near the barbecue while my father cooks. 'If she doesn't defend her quarter-final at Wimbledon, she can say she's down on confidence and needs to focus on her form and her ranking. That would work, I reckon. For the record, Tennis Australia obviously cannot endorse her declining to play in the Olympics, but we will be sympathetic and supportive. And if we all stick together, at least the PR damage will be minimised.'

My dad agrees to go along with this plan. He's cooked up a feast for Paul's visit, and Paul compliments him so Dad is chuffed. As the evening is ending and Paul is talking about ordering a taxi, my father offers up a new deal. 'You have one glass whisky with me, she play Olympics.'

And, just like that, the deal is sealed. A glass of whisky secures my participation as a player at the Sydney Olympics.

I cannot believe how ridiculous this is. So much drama for nothing.

The next day, eight days after the *New Idea* article, I confirm in a statement released by Tennis Australia that I will take part in the Games after all. The gist of it is that my annoyance over the article which appeared during the Australian Open was not worth denying myself the opportunity to play in my home town's Olympics.

'I'm obviously upset with the Melbourne *Herald Sun*, but I shouldn't have directed this frustration at the Olympic Games,' the statement reads. 'It's got nothing to do with the Olympics, nor Australia.'

The spot fires of bad publicity have been put out – for now.

$\odot$

During March on the US hard courts I manage wins at Indian Wells and Miami plus a couple in Florida. At the Hilton Head tournament in South Carolina I amp up my form and make the quarters, beating Nicole Pratt on the way. There's a ruckus caused by my father in Hilton Head. He loses it when there are no courtesy cars available. In front of players and coaches he starts yelling. 'You have not delivered a car on time on purpose,' he shouts at the tournament transport officials – I translate, mortified. He ignores their apologies. In protest he turns to me as says, 'We will walk home to the hotel.' On the walk home I feel heavy with embarrassment.

Still, somehow, despite his chaotic conduct, my good form continues on court. I capitalise on this form to beat a host of top players – Kim Clijsters, Anna Kournikova and Sandrine Testud – at the Fed Cup world group play-off. I win all my matches in tough three-setters. Lesley is the Fed Cup captain again and I love the week in Moscow. We have a strong team environment. It's great without my father around, but then it's time to go back to Saddlebrook for a couple of training weeks with him. It's back to reality.

After the training block my next tournament is the Rome Masters. I play an excellent tournament. At the Rome Masters I take down Venus Williams, world No. 4, to make it into the quarter-finals, where I play Monica Seles. Monica wins in three sets but I've played respectably, even though fatigue is setting in a little. My dad is mad that I have lost to Monica, one of his tennis idols. He doesn't beat me up but he is pissed off. As an unseeded competitor, I get to the second round of the French Open.

A few weeks out from Wimbledon I lose terribly in 's-Hertogenbosch in the Netherlands. Tony is here for this tournament, in keeping with our part-time coaching deal. It's not a good day. I fall to world No. 48 Kristina Brandi, and it's a dismal loss: 6–0, 6–1. My father is livid with my performance. As usual he calls me a host of awful names and declares that I'm hopeless. Rochey, who doesn't observe any of this, of course, sees that it's just a bad day for me; not the end of the world. After the match he comes up to me to say bad luck, knowing that now isn't the time for analysis.

My father is incensed that Tony can simply tell me 'Bad luck', and loses his mind. Out of nowhere he instructs me to translate to Tony: 'We are finished. You can go home.'

I am appalled when I hear this. The words are utterly disrespectful. To the pit of my stomach I feel awful. And I don't want to finish with Tony – he's a wonderful person whose coaching has helped me out immensely. I am so mad my father has done this, and so embarrassed. How can I face Tony ever again?

Tony is such a nice man and he doesn't seem too shocked by this sudden sacking. He probably knows that my father is mad. Still, in years to come, whenever we cross paths I feel uncomfortable and ashamed. Years later I apologise to Tony, but even now I'm mortified at what unfolded that day.

8

Wimbledon, 2000

I can see that my father is unravelling from the moment we hit the tarmac at Heathrow and check in to the Travel Inn in Putney once again. The staff here love us and welcomes us back warmly. This time we splash out by hiring two bigger rooms instead of the single 'family room' we all shared last year.

My star continues to rise. This year I'm expected to haul in two to three million dollars. My management company tells the press I'll be promoting, on top of my FILA clothing and Head racquet deals, everything from mobile telephones to computer games across Europe and Japan.

Somehow I will have to fit this in on top of my schooling. At night, after long days on the tennis court, I cram in study. Although no longer a straight-A student, my marks are good despite the time constraints and fatigue.

My father has got what he always wanted: I have become the breadwinner. Our saviour. While we still live in working-class Fairfield, we own a car and rent a roomy townhouse. I have delivered on the court, put more money in the bank than we could have imagined. But still Dad is tormented. He wakes in the morning and often the first thing he does is pour himself a glass of white wine. He usually stocks up on cheap white wine from a local bottle shop near our tournament hotel. Now that he is constantly drinking throughout the day I worry he's becoming an alcoholic.

The next morning we're sitting in a room at the All England Club and Dad is loudly interrupting me as I try to give an interview to an international news agency about my straight-sets victory over Hungarian qualifier Greta Arn. Every ten seconds he's stopping me to tell me what to say; he's already stressed that this is to be my only interview. So I sit in there with one international journalist as my father speaks in Serbian to me and I translate his comments as mine.

'It feels good to get past the first match,' I say. 'Considering the pressure I've been under … I've done well.' I explain I am under pressure because of 'the actions of officials'.

The interview is calamitous: it's obvious it is not me doing the talking. The WTA officials put a stop to the charade. People on the tour are wising up to the fact that my father is unhinged. The media, the players, the WTA – the whole tennis world is aware. But none of this helps me much because I still have to deal with his physical and mental abuse on a daily basis, and it is inflamed by his increasingly serious drinking habit.

⊖

As I try to win my second-round match against Spaniard Gala Leon Garcia, I can hear Dad in the crowd. He's sitting near Australian fans with their green-and gold-painted faces, bellowing, warbling and loud. He's the loudest man at Wimbledon and I know he's smashed. From the sound of his voice, I'd say he's had about two bottles of wine. I ignore him so as to focus, and win in straight sets, 7–6, 6–1. I scribble a few autographs and hastily head back to the locker room, praying we can get out of Wimbledon and home with as little fuss as possible. But by the time I get to the locker room an official tells me my father is really losing it – he points outside.

I creep out and spy my dad on the footpath outside Wimbledon's new Millennium Building courting his own crowd. He's wearing the St George flag like a cape, behaving like some kind of deranged clown capturing the attention of the Wimbledon crowd. Soon the small huddle of tennis fans swells to almost 50 people and he starts posing for photographs like a celebrity. Then he begins shouting, 'The Queen is for democracy; everything else in this country is fascist.'

I run back inside and hide. Why is he doing this? I'm winning at the most prestigious tennis tournament in the world, but he's still falling apart? I still can't quite fathom how it has come to this: that the better I get on the court the more he seems to lose it.

Later I find out that he continues to hold his audience outside the media centre before declaring that the WTA is 'fascist and political'. Two police officers try to calm him down. He introduces one of them to a passerby as 'Mr Bobby'.

My mother is witness to all this as she stands nearby, her face grim. She doesn't try to stop him. She can't – she's too frightened of him. At her side is my little brother, who stands by watching helplessly as well.

With the flag now draped over his shoulder Dad starts chanting, 'England is a free country, England is a free country.' He yells out that President Bill Clinton is a 'dickhead' and makes obscene sexual gestures at a female American sports reporter, which prompts Sky News sports correspondent Mark Saggers to intervene. 'I am not having you speak to people like this,' Mark apparently tells my father. 'You can't speak to women like this.'

Dad, now angry, complains that no one will listen to him. 'No one wants to listen to my message about me and my daughter. Our real thoughts,' he adds.

'Well, if you want to walk across the road to the golf course where we have our camera crew set up, I can interview you, but I want to talk to Jelena as well,' Mark says.

'How do I know you're going to tell the real story?'

Mark replies, 'I'm not – *you* are going to tell *me*, in your own words.'

'I want to speak to my daughter,' says my dad. 'Give me your mobile.'

Mark hands it over, and Dad smashes it into the balcony. Part of the phone bounces onto Court 14, where two men are playing. My father then raises his arm threateningly, as if to hit Mark, but seconds later offers to pay for the phone, though he doesn't apologise – he never apologises.

He calls for my mother, and shouts at her to hand him our credit card. She pulls the Amex out of her purse and he waves it Mark's way, offering him £750 for the damaged phone.

Finally, four police officers come and remove him. They take him to their temporary headquarters under Centre Court, where, briefly, he holds the flag in front of him like a shield, chanting, 'I don't want to fight with England police.'

While all this is happening I'm hiding in the locker room. I should be delighted at making the third round of Wimbledon; instead I'm shaking and near tears. I am seventeen years old, one of the top 30 women's tennis players in the world and dealing with this rubbish. I cancel my post-match interview. Both the police and the All England Club ask me to reason with my father. I go to see him at the cell underneath Centre Court, sad and angry at the same time. *Am I the parent here coming to get you?* I think. *Who else deals with this?*

Eventually the police say he can go. Wimbledon organisers say that he will be free to return as he hasn't been charged with any offence. The All England Club issues a statement to the press: 'We will be monitoring the conduct of Mr Dokic closely. Should this again fall below acceptable standards, it would lead to Mr Dokic being banned from the grounds.' The WTA says it will investigate the situation.

My managers, John and Ivan, don't get involved. They don't say anything. Clearly no one wants to get involved in this chaos. No one can blame them. I certainly don't.

How I wish I could fall into a hole somewhere and disappear.

The next day I walk around the corridors and courts of Wimbledon and people look at me with sorry eyes. *I just wish it would all go away and I could play tennis without this drama.*

The physical abuse I can handle behind closed doors. But this, the public carry-on, is awful. It rocks me to my core. The embarrassment is worse than the physical abuse because the public meltdowns are out of my hands. I can control the pain around physical abuse. But his public meltdowns and their repercussions are out of my control.

We go home that night to the Travel Inn and Dad drinks more. I guess he drinks to push away the memories of the day. He drinks so much that he barely remembers a thing the next day. I don't dare to ask why he acts like he does – I fear the retribution for questioning his behaviour.

Dad wakes and has no idea that he has done anything wrong. He goes out and buys some cheap wine and soda water and starts the day off with a spritzer.

The headlines are hurtful to me but true: 'Tennis Dad from Hell'; 'Father from Hell Does It Again'. But I try to ignore them – and the front-page photographs of my father draped in the St George flag, flanked by police officers, waving his gold Amex; the fact that my dad has become the mad, embarrassing star of Wimbledon 2000.

He blames everyone else for this drama. In his eyes it is always everyone else's fault. This time my reaction to his 'tennis dad from hell' act is fury, and I channel it into my tennis. American Brie Rippner doesn't stand a chance when I take her on, on Court 13. I coldly demolish her. My father watches on quietly and soberly. She's gone, 6–2, 6–1. It takes me only 44 minutes. I still haven't dropped a set on my way to the fourth round. The sports journalists agree that there is every chance I could make the semi-finals. On the court I feel unstoppable even though off-court it's all come undone.

My father is on his best behaviour as I play Kristina Brandi. He's wearing his trademark scowl but he applauds quietly, barely speaking. A few weeks earlier, at 's-Hertogenbosch, Kristina brought me down – the match that triggered my father sacking Tony. Today I beat her, 6–1, 6–3.

During the match I can't help looking up at him and today the spotlight is on him more than ever so everyone notices it. In my press conference a reporter asks if I felt like I was playing for two people out there. My response is that whatever I do is for myself, but it's a grossly untrue statement. Because I don't play for myself, as much as I love tennis. I'm in a never-ending battle trying to please him.

Following my victory over Brandi I reveal that we have sacked Rochey. Basically the nicest and best coach on tour and the kindest person ever – we sacked him heartlessly. The way in which it was done continues to mortify me. Anyway, having told the press, I deflect all the questions about his axing. I tell them we've decided to rely on my father for coaching. 'He is the one I probably turn to most,' I say. Asked for Roche's reaction to the split, I say, 'I think he was disappointed,' adding, 'I think my dad and I thought it was something that we should try, have a go at – just try a few things that we thought might work, just sort of do our own thing without anybody else.'

The day before my quarter-final I practise at Bishop's Park, Fulham, for my quarter-final. The point of coming here is to get away from all the media attention, but today it doesn't take long for the paparazzi to arrive and start snapping away. I practise my serves with Dad and do some fitness training as parents play with their children and dogs run around the park. The cameras are distracting, but I make myself see in tunnel vision as I get ready for this big match – one of the most important of my career so far.

The next day there are 10,000 people watching my every move on Court No. 1 but I don't notice a single one of them. My mind is in overdrive thinking about the chaos my father has caused and could cause again today so I'm on autopilot and play the match as swiftly as I can. In straight sets I take down Magui Serna from Spain, 6–3, 6–2.

Fronting the press I talk about what an indescribable feeling it is to make it to the semi-final, to be in the final four at Wimbledon. As far as I am aware it is a terrific result to be a seventeen-year-old in the semi-finals of Wimbledon. It's a pity I am so unhappy on the inside. Shouldn't I be excited?

Lindsay Davenport, the world No. 2, is my next opponent. She's tall, imposing and a magnificent player. While I have stormed into this semi-final, I know it's going to be extremely difficult to overcome her. But I am not thinking much about tennis anymore. The media furore, my dad's rantings about conspiracy theories on the tennis tour, his paranoia – they have overshadowed my playing. Minimal energy is spent thinking about my game plan. Going into this match I'm not nervous. I am merely surviving, barely keeping it all together. Constantly on my mind is what I'm likely to face if I lose a match. My focus is less on my opponent than the ramifications of a loss.

Ominously, on the morning of the semi-final, in the plush players' lounge at Wimbledon my father orders a white wine. We're there with my agent John, my mum and Savo. Dad orders another and another. Nobody can stop him. We watch him throw back a bottle of white wine in 40 minutes. Next thing he is loudly muttering about the WTA, how everyone is against us. His angry voice makes everyone in the lounge look over our way.

I leave to warm up and try to put out of my mind everything except the task in hand. It's hard to focus. Him being drunk is a bad sign. Against Lindsay I need to play the match of my life. Although she arrived at Wimbledon with a bad back and little match play, a question mark over her form, she's looked nothing but strong at the All England Club. Will my vicious double-handed backhand be enough to bring her down? Her serve is massive, the best serve on tour, and she also has some of the most powerful accurate ground-strokes. As I walk onto the court my mind is still scrambled, my focus not where it should be. The wine my father has drunk in front of me signal that trouble is not far away.

Even as I glance towards the stands, all I can see is Dad, inebriated. As the match slips away from me I can tell he is not just drunk but furious. Catching sight of my father's darkening facial expressions distracts me even more.

She beats me, 6–4, 6–2.

My comment to the press is that she was an intimidating figure. 'But, you know, that's probably not an excuse for, you know, how you play. You should just go out there and play your game. I say the nerves of the occasion got to me a little bit. I was thinking about the occasion and about who I'm playing. It sort of takes over a little bit.' The truth is that everything off the court has taken me over.

Then the question comes. A journalist gently asks how I survived the chaos of these two weeks and made it to a semi-final. 'Overall, does it give you any extra inner strength knowing that you achieved what you did under not really normal circumstances? You had the drama with your father last week; you got rid of Tony Roche before this tournament. It wasn't exactly an easy road for you off the court. Does it give you any extra pride, considering those factors?'

Like a seasoned politician my reply ignores all the angles regarding my dramatic father and Tony's sacking. For press conferences I have perfected an ability to be emotionless and to deflect. 'Well, overall, again, getting to the semis in this tournament, overall result is quite good. I've got a lot of confidence coming from this tournament. Hopefully I'll use it in the next tournaments. I think, like I said, my level of tennis is probably raised over the last couple of months. You know, hopefully I'll do, you know, well in the coming tournaments. But, like I said, overall this tournament, result-wise, it's been fine, it's been good.'

Lindsay does her press conference next and she doesn't hold back about my father's behaviour.

'It's totally a shame,' she observes. 'Whether she plays tennis or not, it's hard to have a parent who distracts from the overall good of what the child is achieving. I know it took Mary [Pierce] a long time to get out of the shadow of her father. Jelena is a very young, very good player and it is just sad when you get negative publicity for something that could be really good.'

She is so right.

After the match I can't find my father. When finally I get him on his mobile phone he tells me I have brought shame on our family. That I am a disgrace.

I just made it to the semi-finals of Wimbledon at seventeen and in my father's eyes I am the worst person in the world, an awful embarrassment to the Dokic family name, and am not allowed to come back home tonight. So me and my racquets, as well as the medal I've got for reaching the semis – we don't come home.

◎

All the top players are going to Saddlebrook these days. We too head to the impressive tennis resort in Florida for the hot weather and some anonymity; and flying to Florida is easier than making the long commute back to Australia. Following the Wimbledon ruckus, I sense my dad doesn't want to go back to Sydney: he knows the media will be all over us there. I train solidly at Saddlebrook as I prepare for the du Maurier Open in Montreal.

We are in a strong financial position and this confuses me – isn't this what my tennis journey has been about for years: getting us out of poverty. So why is Dad drinking so heavily, not satisfied by all this money I am earning? And I don't see a cent of it. Not that I care as I would rather have a normal, peaceful family unit. I would give anything for that.

Meanwhile, my father has picked another fight with the Australian Olympic Committee (AOC). Though I am an ambassador, promoting the Games, and have been given the privilege of holding the Olympic torch, my father is making me go to war against them. What he wants is to send a firm message to the AOC – he likes to threaten people to show he is in control. But rather than talking directly to them, he instructs me to do an exclusive interview with the Sydney *Daily Telegraph*. My job is to tell the newspaper that I will not sign the Committee's compulsory athletes' letter of agreement, a contract that contains the rules of being a member of the Australian Olympic team. He gives me a list of demands that the AOC must meet before I'll agree to play at the Games in August.

The first is that I'm not to stay at the Olympic Village. A place of fun, partying, socialising, it's the last place my father wants me. We live ten minutes from the Village, and he wants me there at home. The AOC are okay with this but security and transport arrangements – getting me in and out of the Olympic compound every day – are going to be a problem for them.

He's also demanding special accreditation as my personal coach. The third demand he makes is to do with sponsorship. The AOC has rules in the team agreement about what brands we can and can't wear, to fit in with the Olympic team's main sponsors. According to the athletes' agreement, while I can use my Head racquet, which is part of a multi-million-dollar racquet and clothing contract I have, I must also wear the official Australian team uniform on court, which is sponsored by Nike. But Dad is adamant I am to wear my sponsored Fila clothing. His worry is that my wearing the Nike uniform might cause chaos with my Fila sponsorship, which it won't. The bottom line is that he doesn't think we should sign the agreement. As usual he simply wants to generate a fuss. I am so tired of this.

Delicate negotiations take place between the AOC, my management and my father. Gradually they gently talk him around. It's hard to reason with my dad but the AOC and my management finally succeed in changing his mind. He backs down on me wearing Fila at the Games and the issue of transport is sorted out; he's also given special accreditation. Because he can be difficult and aggressive, persuading him to change his mind on this is a big victory for everyone involved – including me. I don't expect anyone to stand up to my father – it would be very different if this was a coach/player relationship, but this is a family situation. In the end I sign an indemnity statement to the effect that the AOC is not responsible for my security outside the venue, transport to and from the tennis stadium or for my accommodation.

The resolution of the complications my dad's caused is an enormous relief: I will be an Olympian. I just love that I will be able to represent my country, Australia, at the Olympics.

Mum and Savo leave Florida to return to Australia for my little brother's schooling. Just as my father is deteriorating day by day, so too is my relationship with my mum. Nowadays we are frequently in different countries and have drifted further and further apart.

In Montreal at the du Maurier Open I play Belgium's Sabine Appelmans in round 1. The first set is a dog fight, which I win in a tight tie breaker. As we change ends I spot my father move from the players' box to the lounge that overlooks Centre Court. Aware of the precarious situation unfolding, I become distracted and lose the second set, 6–4. In the third I am unable to hang on and Appelmans wins the match. Barely, 7–6 in the third. By the time we finish the match I can clearly see my father is hammered.

From the moment we hop into our courtesy car back to the hotel I know there is hell to pay. That hell comes at full force the moment we step into our hotel room and are alone. There's the usual hits to my face, familiar lines of abuse about being a hopeless cow. The blows start getting harder, and then he clenches his hand into a fist and strikes me. The blow to the head fells me and as I lie on the floor he starts kicking me. He kicks me near my ear and my vision blurs. I feel dizzy. I stagger up; he hits me again in the head. I pass out, but when I come to, he makes me stand again. My head is aching.

This is not the usual standing punishment. For the next round of torture he makes me stand still, then kicks me in the shin with the sharp-toed dress shoes he is wearing. When I cry out in pain he gets me back in my position, lines up and boots me in the shin again.

Again and again he kicks me in my shins. This is a first and it hurts like hell – they start swelling instantly. This assault will leave permanent bumps on them.

Sometime during the beating my father announces I will not be playing doubles with Rennae Stubbs the next day. We are supposed to play doubles here in preparation for the Olympics.

Soon after this I hear a knock at the door and it's Rennae herself. He drops into the background as I go and speak with her. When I set eyes on Rennae, I force out the words 'I can't play tomorrow.' I know I look awful. I feel awful. I know I am wearing an expression of fear and horror. I can't hide how frightened I am. My father emerges and orders me in Serbian to tell Rennae I am injured, that I've hurt myself in my match against Sabine and we are going back to Florida. Reluctantly I translate this. Rennae is nobody's fool; I'm pretty sure she can tell it's all a fabrication, that she won't swallow it.

She confronts my father. 'Why are you pulling her out of the doubles?'

I try to put an end to that conversation. She turns to leave, saying, 'I've come here to play doubles with you, Jelena, and you and I are going to play doubles tomorrow.'

The punishment continues well into the night. The intensity is vicious. He doesn't allow me to shower. He doesn't allow me to eat, although I am ravenously hungry. Eventually he heads downstairs to the hotel restaurant for food for himself. He instructs me to sit on the edge of the bed but not to fall asleep or watch television. I am to sit in silence.

The room is dark. Terrified, I tell myself over and over, *Don't fall asleep*. But the exhaustion hits me and in the end I collapse on the bed. My father walks in at two in the morning, which wakes me up. I'm petrified the punishment will start again because I have fallen asleep, but he lets me rest.

The next morning my shins are swollen, blue and purple. My head hurts. My heart hurts. Emotionally I am a wreck. My father orders me to get ready to go to the hotel gym. Off we troop downstairs and he demands I run. Despite being in considerable pain I clock up 3 kilometres. At the end of the gym session he makes an announcement.

'You can play doubles,' he says. It's both a gift and a punishment. Above all I'm relieved because I really didn't want to let Rennae down.

It's impossible to hide the marks of my father's rage – the purple welts on my legs are there for all to see. I move around the practice court dissociating myself from those awful hours – my only way of enduring this. When Rennae sees the bruises she asks me if I'm okay. 'I am fine,' I say. It's hard to say those words, but of course he would kill me if I said anything else. Dad doesn't watch me play. And I do well considering the ordeal of the night before. My shins ache from him kicking me; still, I play through the pain. But we lose to Amanda Coetzer and Lori McNeil, 2–6, 7–6 (4), 7–6 (2).

His beatings are more ferocious than ever before, worse as I've got older. It's as though he saves up all his rage for a few days, then lets it pour out. It's hard for me to have any love for him and I feel guilty about this. But how does he feel, I wonder. You can't do this to someone you love. This is not love. This is torture. I can't fathom why a father would do this to his daughter.

⊖

We go to New Haven for the next tournament and he tells me once again, just like he did after Toronto last year, that he has gone 'overboard'. He says he won't do it again. I don't believe him. I struggle in New Haven emotionally. I lose in the first round and he doesn't take it out on me, but to be honest I feel like he is really using all his might not to beat me.

The next day I go to play doubles. He is nowhere to be seen during the match. Afterwards I find him drunk in the players' lounge.

My father has had a skinful of white wine. This time he is making a scene in the players' lounge. He's commanding a small audience and complaining about the food. He is throwing bagels across the room. He storms around whingeing about the standard of food.

Another coach sees it unfold. Instead of going and dealing with my dad, I hide in the locker room. I pretend it is not happening. I look at my racquets. Neatly fold up everything in my bag and hope that the storm he is causing eventually dies down.

But it never ends softly. I must eventually go and find him in the lounge. I manage to convince him to come with me to catch the bus back to our hotel. We have a ten-minute wait at the bus stop and he is still complaining and ranting.

To cope with this I stare into oblivion. I pretend, again, he is not there beside me.

The bus arrives. 'Come on, let's go,' I say to him.

As I look out the bus window I think to myself, this is not the way it is supposed to play out.

We arrive at the hotel. I suggest he goes and eats something because I hope it will sober him up.

We sit down at the hotel restaurant. Suddenly, he gets an idea. He decides I need to eat a whole bowl of brussel sprouts.

He insists on me ordering and eating them.

By trying to make the situation better I now must endure eating a whole bowl of these awful vegetables. I can't stand the taste of them. But I have no choice but to finish them.

I don't know why he has done this. He is so drunk.

Everything is getting worse. I am afraid he is going to do something publicly shocking again.

9

US Open and the Olympics, Winter 2000

When I walk into Flushing Meadows for the 2000 US Open my mind is scrambled. As I make my way around the grounds, I can't look people in the eye. The place is buzzing in the heat, but I can't indulge in the excitement of this slam, I am in my own private hell. Birmingham, Wimbledon, New Haven: they have scarred me. As the southern hemisphere winter gets under way, I know I must help my father through this meltdown. It's impossible to know why he behaves the way he does, but I still believe that my tennis can make it better. Unfortunately, this belief is about to challenged again.

For my first-round US Open match I am down – the physical and emotional scars of Canada remain. My shins are still swollen. I go into my match against world No. 41 Anna Smashnova with my mind a blank. On the court I have become an emotionless robot. Playing clinically, I end Smashnova's New York campaign in the first round,

6–1, 6–0. In the absence of all feeling when I play, victories like these give me relief not joy.

The next day after a doubles match he calls me on my mobile and tells me he wants to see me. I find him in the players' lounge, staggering around drunk, causing people to stare at him. *Food might sober him up*, I think. *He needs food.* I tell him we should get something to eat.

He orders the salmon at the players' lounge restaurant counter. The server gives him a small serving. 'How much is this piece?' he asks.

'Twelve dollars fifty,' she answers.

'Is this it?' he yells at the server, complaining about the size of the salmon portion.

'Yeah, that's it,' she says, moving on to another customer.

He starts yelling about the size of the salmon for the price tag. Quickly he progresses to throwing stuff around. Cutlery. Bread rolls. And then the piece of salmon goes flying through the air. 'It's too small. It's too expensive,' he yells.

He doesn't let up. 'Twelve dollars for a piece of fish – it's criminal,' he shouts as I stand by his side. Now he flicks the salmon straight at the lady. By now most of the diners in the cafe – players, parents, children, officials, coaches, well over a hundred people – are watching him throw food around. Everyone is open-mouthed with shock and I literally want to die.

His rage grows. He calls the food server a 'cow'. WTA official Brenda Perry, who is also in the food line, tries to calm him down. Security is called, which aggravates him further. He is now full swing into a stream of abuse. He calls Women's Tennis Association CEO Bart McGuire a 'gangster'. He lunges at me and violently rips my competitor accreditation from my neck. 'Fucking US Open,' he shouts. He throws his accreditation at Jim Fuhse, the tour publicity director.

The director of security, Pete Pistone, arrives and grips my father tightly on his shoulders, steering him out of the lounge and to the parking lot. They want to get us out of here, for the commotion to be over. The crowd is building – there are hundreds of people, players, coaches, parents watching this hell break loose. I feel as we make our way out of the players' lounge and restaurant down to the car park that this is the most humiliating moment I have ever had to endure. Everyone is staring.

My father swears at Pistone in particular and at the United States in general. He says Pistone is fighting him and calls him a 'fascist'. He yells that New York is 'dirty and bad-smelling'; that America's heart is made of 'cold concrete'. More security officers take him into a parking lot and I follow him in tears, my usual stoic demeanour cast aside.

It's not until we're standing in the service street in front of the stadium, waiting for a car to take us back to our hotel, that my father notices I'm crying. For a moment he softens. He hugs me, wipes away my tears. But even then he won't drop his volume. Now he's bellowing at a group of onlookers: 'He fight me. He grabbed me.' He wags a finger in the face of Fuhse, who's standing with us, and shouts, 'This is the fucking biggest crime in the world.'

Finally a mini-van pulls up. It takes two attempts to get him into it, as I sit in the back crying, willing him through tears to get in.

As we drive off, my dad winds down the window and waves to the crowd, who has just witnessed my 'tennis dad from hell' at his worst.

That night the phone in our hotel room rings. It's a News Limited journalist, Michael Cameron. My father, still drunk, and still drinking – whisky now – agrees to speak with him. He starts another rant – in Serbian this time – about how he has been unfairly treated by tournament organisers and makes me translate for him.

'He says he's having a fight with some Jewish people from New

York and that was what the problem was about. When he asked for the food they didn't give him the fish.'

Michael asks me to get my dad to explain these comments, and he obliges, saying, 'Before the election of Gore and Clinton this was a democratic country, but not now. It is a question of politics.'

I continue translating. His thoughts become more outrageous. 'We have to fight the Jewish in New York … We are not scared to fight … We don't care if they put a bomb in a plane.' *What on earth*, I wonder in despair, *is he talking about?* He has lost his mind.

He then takes a call from Melbourne radio station 3AW. I curl up small as he continues to rant.

'She's very upset,' he says, looking at me sitting hunched in the corner of the room. He's waving his hands. Swigging some more whisky. 'USA Open is crime organisation. USA Open, this moment, this moment … all organisation for New York … USA, USA is big crime organisation.

'Other coaches, when she loses, say, "Take your time. There is always next year." I say, "No, you don't have time. You must go faster, harder. If you stop, it's over."

'I don't make problems. Others make problems. If you make something bad to me, I react. But it has to stop. It must stop. It's no good for Jelena,' he says. 'She can be one of the best players, easy. She can be like the Williams sisters. She can be like Graf.' On he goes, admitting something that makes me cringe for my mother: 'I love women, wine, food and kids. And by women, I mean women. Not wife.' I feel disgusted as I hear his words.

'She will never need another coach,' he says. I am thinking, *Are you mad?*

Mercifully he hangs up. The phone rings again; it's the *New York Times*. My father is such easy prey for the press. Never says no to them; grips that media spotlight with his big hands and points it directly on himself. Undoubtedly he gets a kick out of attention. I've seen him get on some kind of high from the drama. Pretty much any journalist can call him on his mobile – they all have his number now. And depending how drunk he is, they can always get a sensational line for their story.

Next he tells me to call up the FBI and a local synagogue. 'Call them both and tell them they are conspiring against us,' he says.

I think, *I am seventeen years old. I just want to play tennis. I do not want to be part of this craziness.* But, as always, I do what he tells me. I pick up the phone and pretend to dial the FBI. Then I fake a conversation with an FBI chief. Either I am a very good actress or he is so drunk he literally can't make any judgements, because he's buying the illusion that I'm actually talking to the FBI, telling them that we, the Dokics, are sure they are conspiring against him. There is no need to fake a call to the synagogue for long because minutes later he passes out.

I imagine he won't be allowed back at Arthur Ashe any time soon.

$\ominus$

Morning breaks. My father wakes dusty and mellow. Figuring he needs to know what he did, I recount it all to him: the swearing, the rage, the ejection, the salmon-throwing. How he called Bart McGuire a gangster, got on the phone and spewed to the Australian and American media. He doesn't remember a single thing.

'No, I did none of that,' he says. 'No.'

Incredulous, I explain to him he was like a drunken tornado ripping through Flushing Meadows.

'Are you serious?' He can't believe it. It's as though I have told him they are going to make him the prime minister of Australia.

Then I give him the very bad news. He's been banned – USTA

officials confiscated his credentials. He cannot enter the grounds and he will not be allowed to buy a ticket. I tell him that the USTA has circulated his photograph to all security personnel and ticket officers on the grounds. For the rest of the US Open he's not allowed back, and the WTA have backed the ban. He has become tennis's most unwanted man.

'Are you serious?' he asks again, shocked. He thinks again he has done nothing wrong. That everyone is conspiring against him by banning him. He thinks it's come out of thin air.

It's time to go and play my second-round match. When the courtesy car arrives my father has a few words for me as I get into the car. 'Just play tennis, don't worry about me,' he tells me. 'The officials, they are very bad, they want to take me away from you.'

Later I find out, and from press reports, that after I leave he heads straight for the InterContinental Hotel bar. He's knocking back a glass of white wine, dressed in a tracksuit and smoking a Cuban cigar, when Michael Cameron finds him.

Michael asks if he can take a seat. My father welcomes him and offers him a wine. The journalist starts interviewing my father, who remains unapologetic, unabashed by the shenanigans of the previous day. He blames 'communist' tennis officials who wanted him off the circuit. Remarkably open, he concedes that alcohol had something to do with it. 'If you touch me … any time … I will not touch you,' I read later in the article. 'If I drink one or two wines and you touch, who knows.'

Regarding his future, he's philosophical, saying he now expects a total ban from all tournaments by the WTA, but that he could live with it. 'Lots of people think Mr Dokic is bad,' he says to Michael. 'I am not bad. When somebody makes something against me, I am very angry. But the WTA is always provoking me.'

When the photographer is summoned Dad happily poses.

The formal repercussions from his explosion over the price of fish continue when the WTA release a statement: 'Based on Mr Dokic's past history of such incidents, a formal review is being conducted to determine what action will be taken by the Tour. The Tour will announce its decision shortly after the US Open.'

The chances of my father touring again look remote.

For my part I put my head down and get to work. The next time I walk out onto the court the support in the crowd is rapturous. They've had another glimpse into the hell I have to live with. Media seats are packed and my every move is under scrutiny. *Am I going to cope under this pressure, especially considering the terror and embarrassment I endured yesterday?*

This is my paradox: without him, I feel good but alone. I have no one to turn to or look up to, which is worse when I know I'm being scrutinised like this. However, as I've done before and no doubt will have to do in the future, I shut it all out. When I step onto the court, the chaos of the day before dims. I demolish my second-round opponent, a Dutch player called Miriam Oremans, 6–1, 6–4. I find it very hard to focus but somehow I do.

I take my seat in the press conference room after the win and psych myself up for the questions. Here at Arthur Ashe, the media don't go softly.

'How were you so able to focus on your tennis today, given what's happened in the past couple of days?'

'How was it possible that you can just switch on and focus so well, given the last couple days?'

'Is it going to be difficult now, not having a coach on the premises for the rest of the tournament?'

'Will you think about perhaps having someone else accompany you at tournaments, if you have to?'

'Do you worry that you might face more of this in the future?'

Not that I let on to them, but I'm not coping well in this pressure-cooker environment anymore. Here I am, ranked world No. 43 at seventeen, something I should be proud of, something others should take note of, but it doesn't mean a thing. Overshadowing my story is my 'controversial' father. I am thinking about leaving him but I am not sure how I would escape.

My third-round match is against the Italian player Francesca Schiavone, and it's one I should win – she's ranked 108. But I'm struggling with those feelings of isolation. Out of habit I keep looking up to the players' box in the Louis Armstrong Stadium for approval, but of course Dad's not there. Between this disorientation and the stinking heat I fail to get into my stride and Francesca surges through the first set. It's as though I blink and suddenly I am 4–1 down. What a terrible start – I can't let myself slip further. *If I can just get to 4–3, I'll be back into the set.* I've been here before – I can reel her in. And I do. We go to a tie-breaker in the first set and I win it.

But I start floundering again in the second set. My concentration is such that I continue to look for my father, in vain. Yet I manage to come back from a 5–4 deficit to win the match in two sets. I've just scraped through to the fourth round with hardly any focus.

Ever watchful, some of the press pick up that I was searching for my dad during the match and question me about it.

'I think whether you're up or down you always look for support,' I say, matter-of-fact. 'If you're down, you start believing that maybe you can come back or that you can win matches. I mean, you feel like you're lonely out there, you've got to try to get that from yourself, inside. It's hard to do that sometimes when you've got to really believe in yourself, and not a lot of people can do that. Like I said, I believed that I could come back in both sets, and I played well when I needed to.'

A journalist finishes off the press conference with a confronting question: 'And if you could change one thing in your life, what would you change?'

'At the moment, I'm happy with the way things are going. I've done what I wanted to this year, considering the circumstances, the number of tournaments I can play, which has been really tough to pick them out. You know, I've just enjoyed the game, win or lose. That's what I'm really proud of. I've just kept on going. I have no regrets about the tour.'

Heaven knows, if I answered the question honestly there would be plenty I would change. For starters I would have my father love and accept me for doing my best. He wouldn't embarrass me publicly. He wouldn't sack my coaches. He'd be gentle and look after our family rather than ripping it apart. How I would love to start telling the truth in press conferences. Pretty well everything I say in them is bullshit; these are his thoughts and ideas, not mine. I wish I could stop being controlled by him. But I can't. I am a scared seventeen-year-old girl living under his violent rule.

⊖

In the fourth round I play Serena Williams, who is all muscle and fight. At eighteen, she is the reigning US Open champion. We have never met off the court – but what I do know about Serena is that she is a great player and it will be hard to beat her. Sure enough, it's a tight tussle, a teen thriller in the first set – she's the strongest player on the tour, and in the blistering sun I know I've got to give this match everything. I take a lead in the first-set tie breaker and then hit a backhand which I know is a winner to take the set. But it's called out. The television replays later show the ball might have caught the outside of the line. When I question the decision, it isn't reversed and that rattles me. I have one more set point, at 7–6, which Williams fights off as well. She wins the tie breaker, 9–7.

In the second set she is thundering down aces my way. She hits three aces to open the set. While I have put up a fight in the first set, I can't manage to do it in this one. It's disheartening, and I imagine I look disheartened too. I can't win a game: I'm out of the US Open, 7–6, 6–0. I am mentally, emotionally tired but although I'm disappointed it's over, in a way I'm also glad. A fourth round at the US Open is a solid result, especially considering the chaos of the last seven days.

The press point out that the WTA could elect next week to ban my dad from the tour as my coach.

'Whatever the decision is, I'm just going to have to deal with it when it comes to that,' I say. Then I pause. 'You've got to block things out.'

But blocking out the chaos is becoming harder and harder. I don't see a light at the end of the tunnel.

⊘

It turns out that when I return to Sydney in September, the city is buzzing with Olympic vibes; the place has turned into a big party. Tourists jam-pack the streets. There are sparkling new sporting venues and the country's focus is on the joy of the Games.

Not that my family get the chance to experience it. My dad doesn't attend the Olympic venue despite his accreditation. I am annoyed that he made a huge fuss demanding accreditation and now he's not even bothering to turn up to the greatest sporting event on earth. I am, on the other hand, happy he is not coming. Nor will he allow Mum and Savo to go to Sydney Olympic Park. They are to stay at home in Fairfield. The country, the city might be pulsing with excitement but my dad's mood is flat, cold and dark. To him the Olympics have no meaning. *Unbelievable*, I think to myself.

Lesley is the coach of the women's team, and it's brilliant being back by her side – I've missed her. There is no talk about the hell that unfolded in New York and Wimbledon.

Anyway, I am distracted by the electric atmosphere of the Games. I love the vibe at the Olympic venue.

I am competing in the singles and the doubles – Rennae is again my doubles partner. One day, after our practice, she confronts me about the physical abuse she suspects my father is dishing out. She suggests that I stay at the village, assuming I need to get away from him. 'Stay here. He can't get in here; he can't get to the courts,' she says.

Even if I do stay at the village, what do I do after the Olympics? Of course, my father has forbidden me to stay in the village during the games, and made sure I don't have to. Taking care not to confirm to Rennae that I am being abused, and without really opening up to her, I try to explain that it's almost impossible for me to get away from my dad.

Not staying at the village complicates each day's training and will affect my matches, but, as she has in the past, Lesley comes to the rescue. She offers to pick me up and drop me back to Fairfield when I'm competing, and even after the opening ceremony. My father has negotiated with the AOC that I'm not required to attend the opening and closing ceremonies and as the opening of the games draws nearer this starts to upset me – I'm desperate to be part of what's anticipated to be a huge, thrilling show that will make us all proud to be Australian. One day as Lesley drives me to training I tell her how much I want to stay in the village on the night of the opening ceremony, and how much I want to take part in it with all my compatriots. As always she totally gets it, and doesn't want me to miss out. 'Let me see what I can do,' she says. She says she will try to talk my father around so I can go to at least the opening ceremony.

The evening before the Games begin, when Lesley drops me home she comes in to see my parents. My dad offers her a whisky, which she politely declines.

'She's going to have stay in the village tomorrow night, Damir,' she says. 'It will be too late to try to get her home.'

My father is quiet, his broad chest puffed out. He knows the transport situation that night will be difficult, and he trusts Lesley.

'Okay. That is the only night she can stay.'

The opening ceremony is one of the best experiences of my life. I walk into the stadium with 500 Australian athletes to the orchestra playing Men at Work's 'Down Under'. I swirl around the stadium waving and marching with fellow Olympians – giants of their sports such as Cathy Freeman, Kieren Perkins, my tennis teammate Pat Rafter. For a few hours all my problems are forgotten. There are more than 100,000 watching in the stadium and apparently more than 3 billion on TV. Everything feels magic and I'm on such a high, laughing, joking with my teammates. I haven't felt this carefree since I was a little girl back in Osijek. It's an experience of joy – unconditional joy – something I'd almost forgotten. I'm having fun. I could get used to this. Olivia Newton John's performance is another highlight. I watch Cathy Freeman light the cauldron. It's a beautiful moment. A special time. It's an experience that will stay with me for the rest of my life.

◯

Even the crowds at the Games are loud and loyal and help make it a fun and uplifting atmosphere to play in. It's such a pity Savo and my mother aren't here to witness it.

In the first week I play some terrific tennis and get through to the semi-finals, where I face Elena Dementieva. The first set is mine, 6–2, but she comes back at me in the second to take it, 6–4. In the third set

I manage to get up 4–1 and have two break points. But I can't close it out and to my dismay she claws back the third set. And that's the end of my chance to play for an Olympic gold medal. After the match I'm really dark on myself, feeling that I threw it away. It was tough and could have gone my way but didn't – what can I say. At least a win would have meant a shot at an Olympic gold medal. That night when I get home to Fairfield Dad heaps abuse on me for losing.

Any joy remaining after the opening ceremony, my effort getting to the semi-finals, completely evaporates; I'm horribly deflated by the latest outpouring. In my bronze medal match I lose to my childhood hero Monica Seles, 6–1, 6–4. She is just too strong for me. Her experience counters my youth. Rennae Stubbs and I had already bowed out in the second round of the doubles earlier in the week.

Although Dad doesn't bother attending, he manages to steal a headline with an outrageous interview. In it he says that he and I are sick of Australia. It's grossly untrue that I am 'sick' of my adopted home, I love it, but everything he says in the interview is off the charts.

'The people here think I am crazy and dangerous,' he says to the reporter. 'Sometimes I drink, but so do other people. So what. I am nothing when President Clinton likes his sex and Boris Yeltsin was drunk every day. I am not dangerous.'

And that's it for me as far as the Games are concerned. My father has forbidden me from attending the closing ceremony. There's no one to talk him around this time and I am not even allowed to watch it on television. Instead, while most other Olympians enjoy that one last party, my father is berating me for not winning gold.

10

A Return, Spring 2000

An October editorial in *Australian Tennis Magazine* suggests that Damir Dokic should 'seek psychological counselling' after his forcible ejection from the US Open and subsequent six-month ban from the WTA Tour. When he's alerted to this my father is affronted that the magazine has suggested he needs professional help to control his volatile temper. He goes ballistic and tells me we must do something. *The Age* calls and he lets it be known he's considering legal action against the magazine through the Human Rights and Equal Opportunity Commission. Either the magazine editor apologises or we're going back to Yugoslavia, he says.

Is he serious or not? It's such an extreme statement. Then again, over the past year, whenever Dad's been in a foul mood, which is often, he says stuff like, 'Everyone is against me and you; everyone in Australia is racist; they are always causing us problems.'

I don't talk about this with anyone. I barely discuss anything in depth with Mum these days. She doesn't have her own opinions; she seems to believe in his and trusts him; she goes along with all his decisions. The man who treats her so awfully he even refuses to marry her. She constantly submits to him. Despite the way he treats her, the beatings, the verbal abuse, she appears to be in love with him. She always takes his side; she will do whatever he says; I find her adoration of him both confusing and perplexing.

Over the course of my life so far I have seen that while my mother is regularly abused, it's not to the same degree I am. He treats me with a ferocious anger, and her a rage founded on annoyance. He slaps her, while he pummels me. She is also subjected to relentless mental tirades – I feel for her so much during them, but they are nothing like the torture I go through with him.

I don't want to go back to Serbia. I want to stay loyal to Australia. This is my home. Despite being born and spending some of my childhood in the Balkans, now I feel like I am Australian. I respect very much where I was born and where I come from, the culture I was raised in; that will always be a part of me. However, I really want to represent Australia.

Dad announces that he is going to the consulate in Sydney to organise passports for the family. He says it's too dangerous for him to live here anymore; that he feels Australia is turning its back on us. He declares that it's the media's fault, Tennis Australia's fault, everyone else's fault that he has an image problem. Throwing fish, calling tennis officials 'Nazis', labelling the WTA 'fascists' and Bart McGuire 'a gangster' – how could any of this have contributed to his bad name?

'They are making me out to be a monster,' he asserts.

I think to myself, *Are you aware of what Australia has given us? Even though it has been very hard at times, we haven't always been accepted, sure, but we did get a lot of help.*

But he just can't understand that everything, all the negative publicity, he has brought on himself.

He organises a photoshoot back in Serbia and makes it known to the national press that he's arranged for me to get a new passport. Then he books for my mum and me to fly from the last tournament of the year in Asia to Belgrade, while he and Savo stay in Saddlebrook.

On the plane trip back from Asia I wonder if he is going to go through with this move. It is likely that this is just a stunt, a chance to get a passport, a move to keep Tennis Australia on notice. I hope he won't make us move countries. I hope he won't make me switch to Yugoslavia.

When we touch down at Belgrade airport it feels weird. In Serbia I have become enormously famous. I can barely walk down the street without being mobbed by fans wanting my autograph. The attention doesn't come as a complete shock – I know there's been a lot of coverage from Serbia's press over the last few years. It turns out that the possibility of my homecoming has electrified their interest in me. Everyone is lovely. They treat me with respect. The passport presentation turns out to be a full-scale ceremony, with Interior Minister Zoran Živkovič doing the honours. I shake his hand, smile for the photographers. An interview with a bunch of journalists follows – of course the whole affair is a carefully orchestrated rebuke from my father to Australia.

'I came here for the Yugoslav passport,' I tell them. 'I'm grateful to Australia, it helped me a lot. But I always wanted to come back.' I add for good measure, 'I wanted to come even sooner, that was always my biggest wish. Now that wish finally came true. I'm a Serb and that's why I wanted this passport.' It is such bullshit.

On Dad's instructions, I announce that my family plans to buy a house in Belgrade so we can travel easily to tournaments in Europe.

'Australia is far away,' I say, by way of explanation, knowing as soon as it rolls off my tongue that it sounds like a weak excuse. This is not the ideal country to be based in to commute 'easily' to tournaments. There are better options.

When asked if we're leaving Australia, I deny I'd cease to represent our adopted country. But deep down I'm beginning to wonder if this is a way for us to leave, to retreat because my father can't handle the attention he has created for us here anymore. This is a big step – travelling to Serbia and being photographed with a passport. I'm finding it harder and harder to believe it's merely a threat. Perhaps this could happen – despite everything, we could actually move back and switch nationalities. It frightens me.

There will be no calling up of old school friends or coaches now we're back in Serbia. In the years since we arrived in Australia, Dad's refused to allow my mother any contact with old friends, not even with her sisters. It's always about control with my dad. Her sisters care for my mother deeply – they know my father is aggressive towards her – so it makes him even more determined that she will not have contact with them.

Pretty well straight after the press conference we leave Belgrade and join Savo and Dad in Florida. Savo goes to school here now and earlier this year Dad bought a fancy four-bedroom house in Saddlebrook. He didn't consult me on this but the place is an especially welcome sanctuary after the relentless attention of the past weeks. I enjoy some privacy and I tear into my off-season training. I finished last season as No. 26 in the world and am determined to continue my rise up the rankings. The beginning of 2001 starts in Asia and I play well: I beat Elena Dementieva in the semi-finals in Hong Kong and then Anna Kournikova in the final.

$\ominus$

Summer 2001: three days before the Australian Open, the draw comes out. I return to the Park Hyatt hotel to my family and let them know who I am playing in the first round: Lindsay Davenport. The No. 2 seed and No. 2 in the world. Dad goes crazy. He is wide-eyed and starts ranting. My mum, Savo and I sit quietly as he blazes around the room yelling and screaming.

'You are not going to play for Australia anymore,' he screams. 'You are done. We are leaving. The draw is rigged. The draw is rigged. It's a set-up.'

My heart sinks.

'Maybe we shouldn't do this,' I say, measuring my words. 'Maybe you should think about it ...'

He shoots me a glare that shuts me up immediately. He has made up his mind and I know if I challenge him further he's likely to attack.

Just as I suspected, it turns out that sending me to Belgrade was a calculated move. It's possible that this was his fallback plan all along – to 'defect back' to his home.

It weighs on me that I have no one to talk to about this decision. No friend to lean on. No confidants who know my story, people I could call up and cry to. With all hell about to break loose I feel more alone than ever before.

Now that I have drawn Lindsay, my father feels entitled to vent his gripes publicly – his conspiracy theory that the WTA 'fascists' are against him and me. He calls up Tennis Australia and tells them that from now on I will be playing under the Yugoslavian flag. On the Friday night before the grand slam, he gets me to call Sydney's *Sun-Herald* journalist Matthew Benns. My dad has decided to trust him and so he wants to give him the scoop. Matthew comes on the phone, my father talks loudly in the background and I translate.

'My dad wants to see you and we have a big announcement to make,' I say. 'You must come to Melbourne.'

Matthew turns up to my practice session at Melbourne Park on the Saturday morning, and with no other press around we give him the exclusive. Again, Dad talks and I translate.

'I am playing under the Yugoslavian flag, not for Australia,' I tell Matthew. 'It is a decision we have come up with and we have talked about it.'

In my father's words I describe to Matthew how the final straw came when I drew Lindsay, that our family sat up in our Melbourne hotel room until 5 am after the draw:

I think the draw is fixed just for her. If it is not, the country should protect its own player … Jelena was crying for the first time ever last night. I have never seen her cry about tennis in her life and she was saying that she could not believe that she got that kind of draw in Australia.

She feels betrayed. She feels that no one here likes her and when you feel like that it means you have no spaces here where you can just go.

This is not a lightly taken decision. We were forced to do this and now she will always play for Yugoslavia.

After this draw we don't have anything left here. We will move to Florida straightaway in one or two weeks. Now I must sell everything and leave this country. We are all very sad.

What a lie. He has put it all on me. I am thinking, *Are you fucking serious?* He is calling all the shots and making all the decisions for all of us, but now publicly he is putting it all on me? Like this is my idea and decision to leave? He says I am 'betrayed' but I have been betrayed by him. I can't believe he said he had never seen me cry about tennis until last night. I have been in tears for half my life because of him beating me after playing. How could he forget all the tears he caused as he viciously lashed out at me? Since he is making these decisions he should have the guts to own up to them.

I keep on translating his twisted logic. 'If anybody has been attacked the way I am in the media they would feel the same way.' I say the hostile media reports about myself and my father hurt because 'It is not something you do to a number one player in Australia. If they cared enough about me they wouldn't write stuff like that.'

My father tosses in the line that he is worried about how the Australian tennis crowds will react to me and how this will affect my safety. 'I am scared very much what Australians will do to her, I am afraid there will be an incident if she plays well,' he says.

The story of 'me' turning my back on this country, my home, is splashed over the Fairfax newspapers on the Sunday, and a media storm breaks loose. I am the story of the tournament and a tennis ball is yet to be hit. Once more I have become the headline act for all the wrong reasons.

I am mortified by the situation I am now in.

Dad has a few drinks and does other rambling interviews: 'I'm not surprised that in Melbourne boards are sabotaged,' he tells another journalist. 'Australians are racists and fascists: they killed the Aborigines as if they were rabbits. From sons of criminals and prostitutes cannot come out a healthy country.'

The tennis authorities know the situation can't be rescued. The decision happened so quickly that the WTA hasn't spoken to me. My agent John McCurdy has, but he knows things are too far gone to reverse. The WTA puts out a brief statement: 'Jelena Dokic has officially requested her listing on the Sanex WTA rankings, and subsequently the Australian Open 2001 draw, be updated with her country reading Yugoslavia.'

Geoff Pollard, president of Tennis Australia, confirms: 'We've received this advice from the WTA Tour. We will accept this and amend the Australian Open 2001 draw accordingly.'

My management goes into damage control and Tennis Australia tries to contain the fallout. Geoff and John take me aside to a small room to brief me before the usual pre-tournament press conference. They believe that the best thing would be for me to tell the Australian public that I don't believe the draw is rigged. There's nothing any of us can do about my defection to Yugoslavia but, they urge, I need to salvage a few pieces of my reputation. We huddle together in the room with a WTA official, and they ask me how I feel about the decision and my father's allegations of draw-rigging. I tell them I don't believe the draw is rigged. They are sympathetic and kind. They know it is all Dad's doing. John looks relieved and suggests again I go out there and tell the media exactly that.

'Can you do that, Jelena?' he asks.

I nod my head. 'Yes, yes, yes. I will do this.'

Even as I say it, I am aware I'm not being honest with him. To tell the truth out there will have devastating consequences for me. I'll be beaten, perhaps thrown out of the house. The Wimbledon banishing goes through my head again. Where will I go? What about Savo and my mum? My mind's racing – I'm in a bind. I agree wholeheartedly with them that I ought to tell the Australian public the draw isn't rigged. But I'm caught in this double life. I have a flashback to the beating in Toronto. Even the thought of publicly betraying my dad is something I cannot entertain.

I take my seat for the press conference. 'I'm number one in Australia and yet I have to play Lindsay Davenport ... That was one of the reasons for my decision,' I say. 'And also I've been unhappy with the media coverage.'

John McCurdy's face is full of disbelief. He also looks concerned and sad for me. Geoff Pollard and tournament director Paul McNamee have similar expressions. I feel sick.

⊘

Up and down the country my dad and I are leading news bulletins and taking up the front page of newspapers. There are cameras in our faces. *Today Tonight* is stalking me, *A Current Affair* as well. Once more the Dokics are a grand-slam sideshow.

My father is bemused. 'Why are they making such a big deal out of it?' he says. 'It's not that bad.'

It is. It is the worst thing we could have done to this country, which has supported my tennis dream and helped me so much. Tennis Australia has been supportive from the beginning, despite the behaviour of my father. And he knows he's hit them right where it hurts. He rubs in their faces that their finest hope since Evonne Goolagong will now play under a different flag at their home grand slam. He couldn't have made it any more difficult for me. He couldn't have made it any worse. It is torture.

I walk into Rod Laver Arena to take on Lindsay. 'Do it for Australia,' someone shouts, cheering. And I know very well that cheer is for Lindsay.

'Would you welcome, from Yugoslavia, Jelena Dokic,' booms the court announcer. The announcement of my name is met with a chorus of boos and a smattering of cheers. I find out later I'm the first player at the Australian Open to be jeered walking out onto Centre Court.

This is the worst moment not only of my career but my life. It's a terrible feeling to know that people who had once passionately willed me on are now sneering at me. I feel that I have let everyone down. Even though I can understand why they're booing me, this situation makes me crack. I stand on Centre Court and I can't think about tennis.

I lose 6–4, 4–6, 3–6 to Lindsay. Even though I play okay.

Afterwards, in the locker room, I crumble. Huge sobs roll through me. Lindsay comes and finds me. She hugs me. I can't talk, I feel so rotten and shit. I am incredibly sad and can hardly get any words out to say so, but I very much appreciate her coming over and seeing me. I want to thank her for comforting me. I want to thank her for graciously handling the situation on court – I could see out there she felt uncomfortable because of the hostile environment. I could see she felt sad for me. But I can't get the words 'thank you' out of my mouth because I'm sobbing. I never get the chance to tell her, but I am forever grateful for her compassion.

In the press conference she remarks that this is the worst thing she has ever been a part of.

With red-raw eyes I face the assembled journalists when my turn comes. Taking a deep breath I say I'm not surprised by the reception. 'It was okay. I expected worse. I feel good because I got close to the world number two and I'm more concerned with my tennis right now than anything else.' Total bullshit, of course. I feel awful.

Foolishly, I've assumed things can't get worse, but then a journo mentions my father's claim – news to me – that if I'd beaten Lindsay I would have walked out of the tournament. *That's enough*, I think: *I'm not upholding any more of his insane thinking.* So I scotch that.

'I probably would have gone on and played, but I didn't win and that's something I don't have to consider now,' I say.

It's a tough press conference. My role is to be the dutiful daughter protecting her father; few people know how well I play it. As usual I come out with things I don't mean, which don't come from my heart. When I'm asked what I say to my supporters, I take the chance to try to explain how grateful I am to them, and add, 'I think a lot of people don't sort of understand some of the things, but I think they will stand by me no matter what my decision is because I've played for Australia for quite a few years.'

Another journalist probes me about my dad's relationship with the media. Again I know I have to defend him. I say that we have been 'assaulted by the media', that my father has been 'attacked'.

'There was never positive things written about my dad or about me and my family, especially in the last couple of months. A lot of people telling us that, you know, they don't want me to play for Australia and that I don't belong here, which I don't think is right after everything I have done.'

Surely I have said enough on behalf of my father. I go home exhausted.

But my Australian Open isn't over. Next up is my mixed doubles with Yugoslavian Nenad Zimonjic. Although we've never played together before, we manage to get to the quarter-finals. Then shortly before that match Dad suddenly announces that I am not to play anymore. 'Call Nenad and tell him you are done; tell him you are injured,' he says. 'We need to go home and pack and leave Australia.'

I'm shocked enough to argue with him. This is a terrible thing to do to Nenad, especially at this stage of the tournament. I'm denying him the chance to go out and play in a quarter-final grand slam. 'But we're in the quarters. I'm not going to leave Australia. I'm not going to tell him I am injured.'

'Just tell him you can't play.'

'I can't call him. I can't let him down.'

But I do. I call Nenad. I lie and tell him I have a back injury. The disappointment in his voice is plain. It also sounds as though he doubts me.

Fantastic! I have become someone who lets people down. I have become a liar because of him – I feel as though I am always lying.

Nenad joins the ever-growing list in my head of people I will be ashamed to talk to in the future. There's Tony, Lesley ... All those my father has disposed of.

Then my dad hits the media again, this time in an interview with Perth radio station 6PR. 'For the second time in seventeen years she is a refugee,' he tells the presenter. 'She don't have one friend in the stadium last night, she don't have one person,' he says in broken English. 'Australia people is big racist. This is discrimination country.'

I listen to his deranged words as he gives this interview. *How much longer can you go on like this?* I think to myself. *Isn't he tired already?*

⊖

We're back in Sydney and my father orders me to throw all my trophies in the bin. They are not to come with us to our new home in Florida, he stipulates. Hundreds of junior mementos are to be tossed out.

I shove dozens and dozens of them into the big green wheelie bin that we keep down the side of the house. Each one represents a proud achievement, but in my father's eyes 'junior trophies' are worth nothing. 'You don't need these anymore, they are worthless, meaningless,' he says. As I squash in more of them I manage not to cry, but on the inside I am awash with unshed tears. Every trophy tells a story of hard work. I have also gone through a lot of beatings to win these trophies. It once again rams it home to me that he has neither respect nor care for me.

My dad and Savo depart for Saddlebrook, leaving Mum and me

to pack up our rented townhouse. Over the next two days we throw more stuff out and clean the walls and floors. On the third day we fill two suitcases each and take a cab to the airport. It's a beautiful Sydney morning and I am sad to my core. Tears slide down my face. 'This is not right,' I tell Mum. With my father so far away she dares to admit that she too thinks this the wrong move. Yet, while she is sad to leave Australia, I can see that she trusts him implicitly. She considers whatever he does is best.

Maybe I am not allowed to express an opinion but I am positive this is a terrible mistake for our family; in fact, I'm seething with anger as well as sadness. He has forced us to turn our backs on a country that has helped us, a government that has provided us with social security payments when we had nothing. A country that has become my cheerleader. A tennis federation and coaches who have basically funded my junior career, who poured in hundreds of thousands of dollars and helped make me a star; who covered my coaching and travel when I started delivering results. How can he say that this country, the tennis authorities here, haven't supported me?

And it's also not only about help. I actually feel Australian. Yes, there have been tough periods, when I had to prove myself, and more so than other kids. Periods when we were discriminated against because of our background. Parents and their kids who have told me to my face, 'Go back to where you came from.' Who have been mean-spirited. But now I feel as though I belong here. That people care about me and what I do.

And now he is causing me more pain, not to mention my mum and Savo, by ripping us away from all this.

As I sit on the plane I reflect that this is the worst decision of his I've ever had to accept. I will never forget this day. I don't agree with doing this. Deep inside I know that I will fix this one day.

11

The Circuit, 2001

The circus is well and truly getting to me and for the first time in my life I am starting to think about how I can escape it. The media merry-go-round my father has created feels as though it's slowly destroying me.

As angry as he can get, I can handle that. As violent as he can get, I can usually handle that as well. But this sick publicity circus is something else. He has forced me to comply with it and I don't want to be this person – it's not me.

In Saddlebrook I meet Mike – a tennis coach – and my dad organises him to be my hitting partner. My father remains my coach but Mike and I practise together and he hits the ball nicely. Our sessions are productive; as well, I focus on getting fitter in the gym and on the court.

After two months of training, in March I play in the Miami Open. It's one of my first tournaments as a Yugoslavian national and straightaway I realise that some of the Australian players won't talk to me. Many of them have seen my bruises and heard him screaming at me but it's hard to find any sympathy from them. I know some of them think I sponged off Tennis Australia and then left. None of them have come to me wanting to know the truth about why I was made to leave. They don't seem to care.

I defeat Amanda Coetzer to make the quarter-finals but can't get past Venus Williams, by now the world No. 3. It's not a bad loss. I had a great tournament to make the quarter-finals of a major event. I am still only seventeen so to make the quarter-finals of a Masters is a big achievement.

Two days before my eighteenth birthday Dad can make his comeback as his WTA tour ban is now at an end. His presence immediately makes me tense. He's like a silent and intimidating statue in the stands at the Bausch & Lomb Championships in Amelia Island, another Florida tournament. All eyes are on him, but he's not yelling. He's not drunk. He's on his best behaviour. For now.

And I am trying to do my best on the court. Swiss player Patty Schnyder is in my way in this second-round match. She's a hardy competitor but I shoot out from the blocks strongly. I get a 5–2 lead before I start to make a bunch of mistakes. Schnyder gets close then pulls even before finally I get myself together and manage to close out the first set.

In the second I steady. I serve for the match at 5–3, then face six break points before holding my nerve to win. It takes me 70 minutes to beat Patty, 7–5, 6–3. Afterwards there aren't many questions about the match. As usual the media want to know about my father. I have nothing but praise for his return, telling the press he's a good influence on me. That it was a tough adjustment not having him around but it made me a better player. Everything I trot out in this press conference about my father is garbage. It is all just something to say. The truth is I would prefer it if my dad was not around. If only he would stay off the tour and out of my life. Although I am two days away from turning eighteen, I know that momentous birthday will mean nothing: for as long as we are living under the same roof he will always be running things. So it's safer to talk the talk he'll approve of and tell the press how important he is to me. 'We're really close and there's no one except him that knows my game and knows me,' I tell the small gathering. 'It's your parents who always are the ones that want you to do the best you can.'

My father ignores my birthday. He doesn't even say 'Happy birthday'. There is no cake, no party, no presents. Perhaps this is all he thinks I deserve: nothing. Doing things his way means that my mother and brother don't celebrate my birthday either. They must do what he decrees.

And I may have just become an adult in the eyes of the law, but my dad is still controlling me. Not only does he do all he can to control my tennis, but financially he is completely in charge. While I have a credit card for travel costs, and I am privy to what my sponsorship deals are worth, like my FILA and Head contracts, not a single cent is mine – it's all in his name. For sure I can spend money and buy things. But I don't fritter money away. I'm not a materialistic person. Coming from nothing has taught me to be frugal. I buy clothes I need but mostly I live in the tennis gear from my sponsors.

On my birthday I play my third-round match against Amanda Coetzer. I lose the first set. Calmly my father lights a cigar during the second set when I rally to take it, 6–2. By the third Amanda is all over my game again and she beats me with two breaks of serve. After match point Dad bolts from his seat. This is a bad sign. But later he doesn't beat me – maybe that's my gift today. He does, however, give me a brainwash, hurling buckets of abuse at me into the early hours and making me stand all the while.

Next stop Charleston, and out I go in the first round. My father continues his bullying ways. The latest bizarre development is his unfounded fear that I could become a lesbian. Some days he launches into full-on lectures coupled with scathing attacks on gay tennis players. The message is that I *can't* be a lesbian. That I am not to hang out with any lesbian tennis players. That being gay is not acceptable. Then there are the lectures about how I am never to be 'a whore'. Sleeping around is immoral, I am to understand.

The way he plans and controls my life leaves time only for tennis and little bit of study to finish off my schooling. I certainly don't have a boyfriend. I have never had as much as the chance to hang out with a boy. Not that I want to right now: if I spoke to a boy I swear Dad would kill me.

Many times my father has told me I'm the priority and that he loves me the most out of anyone in our family. I don't like hearing this, especially because there shouldn't be any favouritism between me and my brother. Frankly I don't believe him anyway, because look at how badly he treats me.

Mum and Savo join my father and me on the road for one European leg of the WTA tour. At the Betty Barclay Cup, they are in the stands to see me win through to the semis, beating three-time Hamburg champion Arantxa Sanchez Vicario in a tight tussle, 3–6, 7–6 (5), 6–2 on the way. My game is more aggressive than hers. This win against the fourth seed here is a pleasing one. It's my second victory over her. In the semis I lose to Venus Williams, who's climbed to No. 2 in the world. She beats me 6–3, 6–1.

The women's game is booming at this time in history. It's a dogfight at the top, an incredibly tough competition and there are talented tennis guns everywhere. Lindsay Davenport is dominating the game. Also battling it out in the top tier are the likes of Jennifer Capriati, Serena and Venus Williams, Martina Hingis, Amelie Mauresmo and Monica Seles. Justine Henin and Kim Clijsters are also in the thick of it. And right now I am on the verge of breaking into the top 10.

Dad's in a state of simmering anger, as usual, and the tension of the Eurocard German Open in Berlin tips him over the edge. After I win the first round, in the second I take on third seed Jennifer Capriati. She's in the middle of her tennis renaissance and for me the match is nothing but difficult. For 101 minutes I doggedly try to stop her, and I show true fight in the final set. In the end I lose, though: 7–5, 3–6, 6–4. It was still a good performance from me, but from the moment the umpire calls 'game, set, match', I pick up on my dad's angry mood. When I glance in his direction I notice him mouthing words, berating me. Afterwards, rather than taking me back to our hotel, he instructs me to go out to the practice courts. There he makes me serve until the sun is going down, and during pauses he gets me to run. Finally he turns to me coldly and tells me to run back to the hotel.

The following week we fly to Rome for the Italian Open. For some mysterious reason, here he is a model of composure, sitting almost impassively in the Foro Italico stands during my matches. All four of us are here. My mum assumes her customary position beside my father, mirroring his emotionless demeanour. Savo, my quiet supporter, subtly makes it beautifully clear he wants me to win.

It is indisputable that my dad's composure helps me. Everything is so much easier when he is not behaving like a maniac. I skittle all my opponents including Rita Kuti-Kis, Patty Schnyder and Conchita Martinez. Playing Rita was very difficult after being forced to publicly berate her. I am glad I beat her this time but I still feel bad about everything I have said about her, especially because she is a lovely girl.

Conchita Martinez and I have started playing doubles together this year and I know her game well. It can be slightly weird to play against someone who is your doubles partner. Win or lose, doubles is where you have to come together and be a team.

In the final I face Amelie Mauresmo, a fierce competitor on the verge of breaking into the top five. I don't know her well but she's always nice and says hello to me. I have a lot of respect for her, not that I would ever disclose this to my dad. There's a light drizzle when we get underway and the Italian crowd is boisterous and loud. In this upbeat atmosphere I am focused. Amelie will be very hard to play against and tough to beat but I believe I have a chance.

I win the first in a tie break, a very tight first set. I think if I can win this first set I might have a chance to win the match. I continue to play well going into the second set and I manage to break her early on in the second. From there on I cruise to victory – 7–6, 6–1.

This is my first WTA title. It's a big one. Beaming with joy I hold the shiny silver trophy above my head, even kiss it. Thanks to this victory, when the WTA rankings are released the following week I will enter the top 20 for the first time. I am extremely happy to have won this tournament, it has given me a lot of confidence and belief. This is my biggest result to date.

'My goal for the year was top fifteen and I think I'll be seventeen next week,' I tell the press. 'There are points to defend but I think there are also points to gain. I always set goals as I go along, so you know, top ten's not very far away.'

Then I voice my dream because I now believe I could achieve it. I tell them I believe I have the ability to win a grand slam. 'Hopefully it is only a matter of time,' I say. 'I definitely have a chance. I have beaten a lot of the top players, which is something that goes towards winning a grand slam.'

My confidence is back. It's the best I've felt since I was playing with Lesley.

Dad is not jumping for joy or heaping praise on me, but, to my amazement, to celebrate he takes me to Rolex in Paris a few days later and we spend more than $30,000 on a watch for me – and one for him too. It's a shame material things cannot make up for his lack of love.

⊘

It turns out that Rome was an exception – at the French Open everything's back to how it's always been and my performance suffers. I lose in the third round and he screams at me afterwards. He's verbally abusing me, calling me a cow, pathetic, the usual, and then he orders me out of our hotel room. 'I don't want to look at you because you have lost,' he says. 'You've played like shit.'

Until now I have been sharing a suite with my brother. Dad banishes me from that luxury room and says I must sleep in the other hotel room with my mother.

There is still doubles to play here and it goes much better. Conchita Martinez and I reach the French Open doubles final. The excellent tennis that we have played in the tournament isn't enough in the final against a Spanish and Argentinian duo, however, and we end up losing 6–2, 6–1. Dad goes nuts. As soon as I come off the court he starts screaming at me and he keeps it up all through the Roland Garros players' lounge. I don't even get a chance to say goodbye and thank you to Conchita, I am just trying to deal with and contain my father's escalating anger. It's a joke and I feel ashamed that I can't even go to my doubles partner and say 'thank you'.

The abusive rant continues on our trip back to the hotel and up into our room as he calls me a whole host of awful names. Even though Conchita and I lost, getting to the final was a fantastic result, a continuation of a rewarding, successful partnership. But my father doesn't care about this. *I am eighteen years old, a grand slam doubles finalist, a player on the verge of entering top ten in singles; what is his problem?* I ask myself.

Our next stop is Birmingham, to play at the DFS Classic. I am the No. 2 seed at the tournament, but I'm not living up to that. When I face Alicia Molik, ranked 92, she plays better than me and manages to beat me in the third set. In the post-match press conference, Alicia takes the opportunity to condemn my switch to Yugoslavia and makes known her feelings about the support I received from Tennis Australia: 'Jelena had all the help she needed from our governing body, Tennis Australia, when we were both playing junior tennis. I'm baffled by her decision [to switch countries]. You'd have to sit down with her, preferably without her father, and ask her.'

Alicia is right, I did get a lot of help from Tennis Australia. She's baffled by me switching countries; I'm sick about it. I wish I'd had the chance to sit down with her and the other Australian players for them to get to know me, perhaps to understand more deeply the dreadful duress I've always been under. But I wasn't given that chance.

As we leave Birmingham, Dad's undesirable behaviour shows itself again. I become fixated on making sure he doesn't get drunk. It's not easy – there are liquor stores close to every hotel we stay at, which provide easy access to booze for him. I try to distract him, tell him I need him to help me with warming up before matches. But of course it's always possible for him to find something. There are bars everywhere at all these tournaments – usually sweet-looking places with white umbrellas and nice outdoor chairs – which provide petrol for his madness. So after my matches I run around flagging down courtesy cars to get him out of the public eye before he can cause another scene.

⊖

On my first day of competition at Wimbledon my 'tennis dad from hell' signs autographs in the stands on show court 3. It's a year since he was held in a police cell underneath Centre Court for behaving like a drunken lunatic and now he's chatting to his new legion of fans, being charming, scribbling his name on pieces of paper and tennis programs, as I play Paraguay's Rossana de los Rios. I'm seeded No. 14 as Wimbledon begins.

Sure enough, when I'm in trouble in the first set my father gets edgy and his charm disappears. I've lost a 3–0 lead and soon trail 4–5 on Rossana's serve. He is yelling: 'Fight, fight!' Another mistake, another point lost and once more I hear his booming voice: 'Fight, fight!'

He lights up his pipe court-side, puffing plumes of smoke over the people around him. The All England crowd, composed faces, sticklers for rules, thoroughly disapprove. Of course, you're not allowed to smoke a pipe at Wimbledon. But this is my father. He does what he wants. Soon a security guard reminds him he can't smoke here and, thank God, rather than take him on he puts out the pipe.

Despite my country switch some Australians in the crowd, draped in flags, their faces painted with green and gold, are cheering for me. I hear their 'Go, Jelena' sporadically throughout the match. This is unexpected and really heartening. It's uplifting. I rally in the second set to win, 7–5, 6–1.

The pipe-smoking incident makes the news – obviously we're not going to escape Wimbledon without incident. 'Babsi v The Beast' screams the *Mirror*'s front page. Dad reads it over breakfast at the Travel Inn in Putney and immediately combusts with rage. The Beast – that's him. There's a photo of him looking menacing. And Babsi? That turns out to be Barbara Schett – the Austrian player. She's seeded 21 here and, it turns out, and is being backed by the

Mirror and is even wearing their logo on her shirt. She also happens to be my next opponent.

Underneath, the story describes my dad as a 'bearded father from hell' who 'will try to psych Babsi out from the sidelines ... He has already been reprimanded by Wimbledon security staff this week for smoking a foul-smelling pipe during his eighteen-year-old daughter's first-round match.'

My dad is off his brain with fury. In the midst of his meltdown we have to get to the courts because I have a match to play. But our transport is late and we hang around the front of the Travel Inn waiting anxiously. The car is so late I start to worry I might miss my match. Finally former player turned TV commentator Sam Smith pulls up and asks if we need a lift. Before I can say a word Dad starts screaming at her. Telling her to 'piss off and go'. Sam quickly drives off in shock.

'What did she say?' he asks.

'She wanted to know if we needed a lift,' I explain.

'She's been sent here on purpose because our transport is late,' he says. 'Everybody is screwing us over.'

He then decides there's a connection between the newspaper headline and the car failing to turn up. 'This is on purpose,' he says. He believes the All England Club and the tabloid press are conspiring against me; that they don't want me to win against Barbara today. This would be funny if it weren't so ridiculous.

We make more calls. There is still no car. I have missed my warm-up. We order a taxi and get to Wimbledon that way. He is so sure the tennis and media hierarchies are systematically working against us that my father decides we will boycott the players' lounge. So we sit in the public area – me in my tennis clothes, head down, trying not to let anyone in the crowd see me, while my father starts throwing back white wines. I am preparing for my match on Court 1 at Wimbledon by sitting in a public cafe while my father tries to get drunk. Madness. Who else goes through this? No one.

I go to change into my match gear in the locker room five minutes before the match. As I'm rushing into the locker room, Barbara and I cross paths. She stops me. 'I'm sorry – I had nothing to do with the article,' she tells me.

'I am sure you didn't,' I say sarcastically. 'You will see on the court.'

As soon as the words come out I feel terrible. I've lashed out at Barbara because of my own anger at him, and my panic that I haven't had a chance to warm up for my match. Between the transport debacle and his drinking, I am under a ton of stress and pressure and my emotions are heightened. I didn't mean to take it out on her. I know it is not her fault.

Finally it is time to play. I can see him up there in the stands and he's on the way to causing his regular commotion. He's loud. Bellowing abuse and crap again. I just want the match to be over. Schett plays pretty well, but I'm still so mad that I'm aggressive and she's no match for my determination today. I win in straight sets and pump my fist on victory.

Afterwards I front the press and go off at the *Mirror* article. 'It was really a nasty article about my dad, and I think it's really not funny anymore. I think it was as bad as it could get. If they have nothing else to write, that's really sad … I think my dad doesn't deserve that. Especially, you know, since he's gotten back on the tour.'

Afterwards a sports journalist writes in a posh English newspaper that '[Jelena]…doesn't seem to be happy unless she is surrounded by turmoil. Fortunately for her, she has a father, Damir, who often creates it.' *Do I look happy to you?* I think. To write 'fortunately for her, she has a father, Damir, who often creates it' – what the fuck? If only they all knew the truth. How miserable I am.

I wish completely the opposite. I just want a calm life and to play tennis in peace. All this public embarrassment and turmoil is something that I dread.

$\ominus$

My opponent in the fourth round, on Centre Court, is Lindsay Davenport. It's a year on from my loss to her in the semi-finals here. She has been sidelined with a knee injury for three months of this year but she's not playing like it, she is living up to her No. 3 seeding. She hits the ball very hard and flat, with great depth, angles and placement. Today she's serving smoothly, sharply. She's cool and composed. Unlike me. When I have break points Lindsay nails really big serves – I have one in the first set but I don't manage to convert it.

Afterwards, I tell the press I know it was a missed opportunity. I agree the 'best Jelena' didn't play today, that I couldn't get it together in the moments that mattered. They ask me about the off-court pressure. Someone asks me about transportation. All stuff I don't want to talk about, though I reluctantly answer.

I go and find my father after the match. While last year he banished me from the family hotel and told me to sleep elsewhere, today he doesn't give me grief after my fourth-round exit. Such an unpredictable man.

But he has something to say and informs me he won't be travelling anymore. He says he can't stand it. It's obvious he can't handle the pressure. It's seems that the 'Babsi v the Beast' headline here at Wimbledon, and our drama with the transport that day, have been the final straws. Of course, he struggles with the flying too. Every time he boards a plane he thinks he's going to die so he keeps drinking himself senseless on almost every flight. He hates hotels, he tells me. He says he's had enough. He's not screaming. He is almost measured. 'I am staying in Saddlebrook. Your mother can go with you,' he says.

But there's always a little uppercut, a few words to keep me on notice. 'I got you to this ranking [I am almost in the top ten in the world] – let's see where you go to now,' he adds sarcastically.

As I listen, a sense of release washes over me. I almost feel joy. 'No problem,' I say nonchalantly, trying to conceal my delight.

⊘

My mum and I go on the road and this time round it feels right. I don't feel lost. I am that bit more experienced; I have faith now in my ability to work hard without my dad around. Although my mother doesn't have the tennis knowledge the travel gives us an opportunity to get closer again. We do everything together. We find a good balance that brings us both some happiness. There is no friction between us. We don't fight. My mother is pleased to be on the road with me and I am pleased to have her with me. Things are good. My little brother remains in Florida with my dad so he can attend school. And my father? Of course, he is present – over the phone, telling me to do this, do that, trying to control my game from thousands of kilometres away. But these phone calls are nothing in comparison to what I know would be unfolding if he were here.

Because of his decision I schedule the rest of my year to be away from Saddlebrook. I am able to convince him that I should be playing as many tournaments as possible – which he thinks I should be doing anyway because he is money-hungry. He is also obsessed by my ranking and results. I don't discriminate against surfaces, I just want lots of match play, far away from him.

I play a few tournaments in Europe then return to the States, where I achieve solid results in San Diego and LA. I travel to Toronto and lose in the third round to Seles, who is still performing well and is at the top of the rankings. In New Haven I lose in the quarter-finals to Jennifer Capriati, who's now ranked No. 2 in the world and is a grand slam champion. Capriati's comeback continues its rapid rise. She thunders ten aces at me and she is hitting the ball cleanly. I am playing well but she's just a bit too strong for me.

Then, finally, we are back at the US Open, and without my father behaving like a drunken maniac it's perfect here in New York City. We settle into our room at the InterContinental. I pick up the newspaper at breakfast and don't read about my 'tennis dad from hell'. Mum and I walk Fifth Avenue without a care. I saunter through the players' lounge without the worry of what I might be about to be involved in. That my father might orchestrate an embarrassing scene. No doubt everyone else is happier when he is not on tour too.

I cruise through the opening rounds, just doing my thing, playing tennis. I defeat Arantxa Sanchez Vicario in the third round but lose to the world No. 1, Martina Hingis, in the fourth round. But there are no tears this year. A fourth round at the US Open is a solid effort.

From this US Open, I start a rapid rise. Mum and I are on a hectic travel schedule involving dozens of flights and three continents and I don't mind the whirlwind. I just want to be away from him. I first head to Brazil, where I make it to the final of a tournament in Bahia, losing to Seles, 6–3, 6–3. And I win my second title – in Tokyo, where I bring down Kim Clijsters and Aranxta. This sends me into the top 10 for the first time.

Only a few months ago I turned eighteen and I'm in the top 10 in the world. I am over the moon. My father doesn't praise me. There are no proud words for me for achieving this impressive ranking. Nothing changes.

I head to Europe and play in Leipzig. I then catch another two planes to play in Moscow, where I win my third career title by bringing down Elena Dementieva.

At tournaments in Zurich and Linz I make the final and face Lindsay each time, but she gets the better of me in both. I also win the doubles title in Linz with Nadia Petrova.

Whatever happens on the court, I don't mind. I don't care because I feel free. I walk onto the court with an air of lightness. I train hard. I play. I win. I might lose. I know I have done my best and that when I walk off the court there will not be hell to pay.

I do 'normal' tennis things like hang out with other players in the lounge. I am in a really good headspace.

My rankings sees me get into the year-end championships in Germany, where I reach the quarters.

Even though he calls through all these tournaments, it is nowhere near as scary or as stressful as when my father is physically in front of me. I have had the best results of my life, playing the best tennis, without him around.

It's been an incredible second half of the year: this is the right environment in which to play tennis, a focused and calm one. I am actually rising fast without my father around. I finish the year in the top ten – No. 8, to be exact.

12

Enrique, 2002

I start 2002 in the States as my father's said there is no way I'm playing at the Australian Open. For once I agree with him and am okay not to go as the backlash and pressure could be ridiculous. We release a statement saying that the event is too far away. I am fine to stay away from any drama.

I leave my father filming a car advertisement near our home in Saddlebrook. It's for the South Korean car company Kia and in the ads – he films a couple – he's poking fun at himself and his aggressive behaviour court-side. They've turned some of the worst moments of my life into comic advertising. How humiliating.

In one of the ads he holds a plate of salmon, 'I have been in places where they charge for excess like this.' In another he says with a smile, 'Some people say I am never happy, but who is happy when you have to pay too much?'

Kia's marketing gurus came up with the ideas. They say they have picked my father to front their campaign – which, to make the whole thing worse, runs on Australian television during the Open – because 'There was much more to the hot-tempered, sometimes drunken Mr Dokic than had so far been publicly presented,' as my father is a 'warm and friendly guy'. It's offensive to portray him as harmless. There's nothing funny about anything he has done.

It's strange watching him playing this version of himself. It couldn't be further from his true self. He's never light-hearted and silly; he's the one who has us walking on eggshells every day. And now he is making money out of these terribly embarrassing incidents. These moments, nightmares for me, have been made into a joke.

But, like anything to do with him these days, if I can physically get away from him it doesn't matter so much. Accompanied by my mum, I leave our home in Saddlebrook and start up my hectic tennis schedule again.

At the Paris Open indoor tournament in February, I play well. I win against Elena Dementieva and in an incredible match I beat my childhood hero, Monica Seles – the first time in five meetings – to make it to the final. It's a really tight match. We have similar games. We are both aggressive players – we take the ball early and hit it well off the ground. I serve well in this match and manage to keep the ball deep. I use the court well to move Monica around and hit some unbelievable drop shots. I can't believe it when she hits a shot wide at match point and I've won. I leap around the court in joy.

My joy is cut short, though, when I realise I've torn my right adductor and have to pull out of the final, which was to be against Venus Williams. A scan shows a five-centimetre tear. I can barely walk. It hurts like hell.

I rush into rehab and try to repair my injured leg, then get on a plane for Antwerp, Belgium, where I play Patty Schnyder in the first round. I can barely get on to the court. I'm walking gingerly and wincing with pain. I muster all my strength and with sheer grit manage to win the first set 6–4. By the second I can't move my right leg. It's like a dead weight I am dragging around. I get to the third set, but I have to quit. I never quit but this time I have to. The scoreboard reads 4–6, 6–4, 1–1. I shouldn't have played in Antwerp but my desire to be away from my dad overruns good sense – I should have rested my leg.

I take four weeks off to do rehab and get ready for Indian Wells and Miami. I play okay at both tournaments but am unsure because of my adductor. Still, I continue to practise and work hard. By Sarasota my body is better and I don't drop a set to take the title here. I am enjoying this life of just my mother and me on the road. It feels right, and my happiness with this arrangement shows in my results.

But at my next tournament in Amelia Island my father decides to join us. It's near our home in Saddlebrook, just a few hours' drive away – too close for him not to come over. I steel myself and do well here despite his presence. I push through, beating Mary Pierce and Elena, and then face Justine Henin in the semis. But I have to retire at 6–2, 4–1 because of gastro.

My father also decides to travel to Charleston. The peaceful atmosphere I was enjoying is broken: he goes crazy when I lose in the first round. We tear straight back to Saddlebrook down the highway, he's driving like a maniac, yelling at me in his 'angry voice'. By the time we get home it is past midnight.

I'm exhausted but as soon as we walk into the house my father takes me aside. 'You are going running,' he says. He takes a place on our front step and lights up his pipe. 'Off you go. I want you to do laps.'

He sends me off into the black night to loop around the streets of the resort. I run through the night fighting off tears. I run past mansions, past the plush fairways. The multimillion-dollar sports complex – the place dead and silent except for the sound of my tired legs pounding the pavement. I hope like hell no one sees me. I soon give into my sadness and start crying. Wishing I wasn't in this situation anymore.

When he's around, every minute of my life is full of tension. It's only been two weeks but I am back to living on the edge. I am back to my good old living hell.

We stay in Saddlebrook for a week so I can prepare for the clay court season. I count down the days to us leaving for Europe. I can't wait.

My mother accompanies me to Europe again for another lot of tournaments. I go to Hamburg first, win against Justine Henin, and make the semis. In the semis I retire with a slight hamstring strain. We travel to Berlin after the tournament. I beat Mary Pierce, then lose in the third round.

I get a chance to focus on my fitness when my trainer comes over and I train intensely for five days in Berlin.

⊙

I meet Enrique Bernoldi in a Berlin hotel lobby. He's a charismatic Brazilian Formula One driver, a man who risks his life weekly and, I guess, usually gets what he wants. He's good-looking, all floppy dark hair and soft eyes. He's five years older than me and he wends his way over while I wait in the lobby for my mother. We start to chat. There's a players' party the following night, at which he appears again. We exchange email addresses. I'm wary but Enrique pursues me.

I have never had a boyfriend. I've never been allowed to really talk to guys.

Lately, I have been thinking about leaving. I can't stand the abuse, the public embarrassment. I have been wondering what it would be like to speak my mind in press conferences. To make my own life decisions. I'm sick of being put up to things by Dad. I want to take ownership of my life. I want to live a quiet and normal life on the tour and off it. I just want to do my own thing.

Enrique has walked into my life at the right time. I'm starting not to care about the ramifications and when I meet him I can see he could be an escape from my hell. He's charming, funny and a little bit cocky. He's sure of himself but he seems kind. He makes a real effort to get to know me. I'm flattered and delighted – it's so good after the years of not having any close friends take an interest in my life, not having anyone to really talk to or confide in. In the coming weeks we start to message and email each other. We talk on the phone. It's a warm feeling to know that someone, no matter how far away they are, is thinking of me. In Rome he takes me out for dinner.

My mum is okay with this. She doesn't say much about it, or stop me from going out for dinner with him or calling him up. But she indicates to me that she doesn't think it is particularly serious. However, things do get more serious after the French Open. Enrique knows my father is difficult and controlling; he understands I can't change my travel plans and escape for three days on a whim because my dad will find out and there'll be hell to pay. So it is he who moves heaven and earth to be with me. Every spare weekend or day he has, he comes and sees me in Europe.

In the meantime, in the last couple of months I have continued to play well – I make the semi-finals in Hamburg, beating Justine Henin. I get to the final of Strasbourg in France and the quarters of the French Open. I lose in a tight match to the eventual champion, Jennifer Capriati. My good results maintain my top ten ranking and get me closer to the top five.

In June I win at Birmingham, beating nifty Russian player Anastasia Myskina. I've now won a title on every single surface, which feels like a fantastic achievement. Enrique is still doing anything he can to be by my side and I enjoy his support. My tennis is on the rise, my personal life is suddenly good. But even though Dad isn't travelling with me on tour I know shit is going to hit the fan soon.

It doesn't take my mother long to change her mind about me seeing Enrique when she realises that I'm starting to have deeper feelings for him and that he's coming to spend time with me more often. She likes him but she's worried about the ramifications for me, and her, if my father finds out. In brief moments I'm also concerned, but most of the time I ignore it. I choose to live in the moment, which I know won't last.

During Wimbledon Enrique and I have a long conversation about life, sport and, of course, my father. His controlling ways. For the first time I trust someone enough to tell them about the abuse. He listens intently, wide-eyed, and he doesn't ask many questions, but he seems to understand, to get the situation I've been in all my playing life and remain in now. Rather than peppering me with questions about the frightened state I live in, he seems to want to get me away from it. But ... I don't think he fully understands my situation and what my dad is like, what I am dealing with day to day. He grew up in a completely different environment from mine.

He knows I will have to go back home for a training block soon so he gives me a mobile phone to ensure I can communicate with him.

⊖

My father is busy setting himself up back in his homeland. For now he has rented a house in Belgrade. He rings me up and orders me over, tells me I will do my three-week preparation for the American hard-court season there. I obey. I've become used to upheaval, moving around, leaving places and people behind and never questioning him or his moves. As usual I am just trying to survive day to day, keeping myself together mentally, living under these crazy rules.

When we touch down in Belgrade I call my father to ask where the house is. He's spiteful. 'You played pathetically at Wimbledon, you made only the fourth round,' he shouts. 'You are not to come to our home – you and your mother can stay somewhere else. But don't come home.'

Here we go again.

I am livid. I am in the top ten. *Top ten*. One of the best tennis players in the world, and he's behaving once more as though nothing is good enough. It makes no sense and I am sick of it making no sense. I know he is damaged and has got serious issues but anger is growing inside of me. *At the end of the day, what would you have without me and my tennis career?* I think. We'd be living on social security in government housing with no money. On the verge of poverty. We'd have no cars, no real estate, no great hopes. He wouldn't be able to buy the big houses, the fancy cars … all the things he likes to spend my money on. And he is telling me I can't come home, the home I am paying for?

My mother and I check into a hotel and make ourselves comfortable. Yes, I'm furious, but we're fine with not having to go home to him. We have been lounging around for a few hours when the phone rings. 'You can come home,' my father says.

I feel like screaming. He makes us check into this fucking hotel room and then demands we come home. He couldn't have done this three hours ago when we landed back in Serbia? I hang up and look Mum in the eyes. She's endured years of this nuttiness. She's been mentally broken by him. She's a shell of a person, without a shred of self-esteem; she has no voice, receives no love from him. Like me, she has constantly been told she is a 'pathetic cow'. Yet she loves my father – she will never be disloyal to him. But now I'm starting to think that with Enrique by my side, this could be my chance to get away. That I finally feel I could leave.

Meeting Mum's gaze, I ask her if she'd come with me.

We talk it through and debate how we could do it. In the night? How would we buy the plane tickets without him knowing? Could we hide our escape plans? Where could we seek refuge?

But it's all just hope with no hope. My mother doesn't have the courage – and she doesn't have the courage because he has made her feel like she is a worthless human being, that she needs him, that she can't live without him.

We pack up our things to head to our new rental home in Belgrade.

⊘

Enrique likes to text me all the time and for two months we have been in touch almost every hour of the day. It's only when I am sleeping he doesn't text or call. But now I'm in Belgrade I can't do this – Dad is circling, watchful, and he knows nothing about my boyfriend. Enrique is confused as to why the communication has dropped off so sharply. He knows my father is unstable, he's seen the bad press, he's heard my horror stories. Still, I know it's hard for him to properly grasp why he can't reach me whenever he wants to, the way he has over the past two months when I was on tour. In fact it doesn't help that Enrique is also quite possessive. 'Why can't you use a phone in front of your dad?' he asks. 'Why don't you just say you are texting your friend?'

'Because I am not even allowed to have a friend.'

So I have to hide again – this time with my secret phone. I hide in all different corners of the house. The garage, toilet, garden. I also hide the secret phone – under my bed, in corners of my cupboards, anywhere away from my dad so he can't hear the incessant beeping of the messages Enrique is sending. For three weeks I'm racked with nerves as I simultaneously try to text my boyfriend and hide the phone. I'm extremely careful and my father doesn't suspect a thing.

I think I'm falling in love with Enrique. He's witnessed the claustrophobic hell I have been living over the years. He wants to help me and says he will do anything he can to make my life better. But as we grow closer, I know something is going to have to give. We can't hide forever.

We start the US hard-court season in Stanford, where I make the semis. Mum and I go to a tournament in San Diego and Enrique joins us. It's there that I beat Jennifer Capriati for the first time, as well as Myskina and Kournikova, which feels fantastic. I'm playing well, with the right attitude, and my groundstrokes are humming. I make the final. By making the final and beating a number of top players, I will be top five when next week's rankings come out – No. 4 to be exact. My great form continues. I am facing world No. 2 Venus Williams in the final, her sister Serena is No. 1 in the world; they have become the dominant forces in tennis.

In the final against Venus, having played a lot of three-set matches, I'm fatigued. This week I have played back to back and I can feel it on this hot day. She gets the better of me over two sets. I am not too disappointed with losing the final. It's been a terrific tournament.

We go out to celebrate that I made the final, and over dinner Enrique presents me with a beautiful diamond ring and asks me to marry him. I find myself saying yes, but somehow feeling under pressure to, worrying what would happen if I said no. For some reason I'm uneasy about this proposal. Yes, I think I love Enrique, but at this stage I can't imagine being married to him … But I say 'yes' to buy time – it's not like we have to get married on the spot.

Also, right now I don't want to have tension and fights and I'm almost 100 per cent sure he has done this because things have become tense with my father. I'm beginning to realise that Enrique likes control. Perhaps he feels that by proposing to me my father might calm down and accept us as a couple.

No one is supposed to know we are planning to get married but I don't know how we're going to keep it secret.

Yes, Enrique has been sweet, attentive, but he's become more and more anxious about not being able to see me or contact me whenever he wants. Yes, I think he loves me. But I'm not entirely sure about his intentions.

My gut feeling is that he has proposed to me for the wrong reasons.

⊘

I am world No. 4 in singles and No. 9 in doubles – both career-high rankings. They should be reasons to celebrate. A time for praise? Forget about it. In our phone call Dad barely acknowledges the achievements. Of course I am not exactly surprised.

My mother isn't happy with me either. While she tolerated Enrique's presence at the start, she's now worried that it's almost constant. She knows we are playing with fire. It's not helped by the fact that Enrique doesn't seem to give a shit about hiding his affections. The more I urge him to be careful, the more he seems to do the opposite. He will do whatever he wants and I don't like this. He leaves to go racing again.

I love Enrique but he doesn't seem to understand who my father is, appreciate my situation at home. He thinks that simply by getting engaged we have fixed our lives. That everything is sorted. He doesn't seem to grasp that when our engagement is exposed, our lives will tumble into chaos.

He has constantly been asking me to tell my father that we are together and we're getting married. He keeps pushing and pushing. I have been afraid to do that because I know the fallout will be a nightmare. I try to explain how angry my dad will be but Enrique doesn't seem to want to listen or understand why I want to keep us private for now. He thinks that if we are seen together, our relationship and engagement will be made public, so my dad will find out through the press. Enrique naively thinks that Dad will leave us alone when he finds out. No matter how hard I try to explain to him how crazy my dad will go when he discovers we are engaged, Enrique simply doesn't seem get it. 'He can't do anything,' is his brash answer.

He doesn't know my father.

After San Diego I travel to a WTA tournament at the Manhattan Country Club in LA and have a smooth run to the semi-finals, where I face the American player Chanda Rubin, ranked world No. 22. I'm warming up before the match when my mother comes over to me looking anxious. She sits me down. Someone from the Serbian media has called my father and told him I have a boyfriend. The reporter has seen Enrique in the stands supporting me at various tournaments. He has photographs of Enrique wearing his 'I HEART JELENA' t-shirt at Formula One races.

My father is on the phone and he fires off endless aggressive questions, calls me a 'whore', and before long I'm in tears, denying everything. Mum picks up the phone and backs me up. 'It's nothing like what they are saying. This guy came to a few tournaments but they are just friends. Nothing happened. He was just there.'

My survival instinct is to deny everything, as is my mother's. At this moment I know my match is dead in the water. I am in a mess mentally.

I get back on the phone and try to talk him down from his crazed state. I'm due on court in just a few minutes and he's ranting and raving. Television commentators on their way to my match, and fans, have seen me crying.

The phone call, the realisation that I can't hide Enrique forever leaves me in a state. I'm wiping tears away as I head to the court to play Chanda. Now I am afraid he will turn up to a tournament somewhere. While I can usually temper my emotions, today it's impossible. I walk onto the court visibly upset. The crowd cheers excitedly as my name is announced but I don't feel as though I am present at the Manhattan Country Club. It's more like I'm having an out-of-body experience. There's only so much I can take, and I have been subjected to constant physical and emotional abuse for nearly fifteen years of my life. I am breaking apart. All I want is freedom. All I want is to be happy. I do love Enrique. I want to be with him but I also want peace. *Let me be in peace and play tennis.*

I turn out one of the worst performances of my career. It's the first time ever I have literally not been able to compete. People aren't even clapping on points because they can see this is not a contest. Some boo. I manage to win two games. Afterwards Chanda remarks in the press conference that I slipped into 'semi-tank mode'. I tell two reporters I was feeling poorly because of a stomach virus – anything to hide what really is going on.

When I find Mum, she's terrified. 'If he finds out that I've lied for you, he will kill me,' she says. It's true – he would go ballistic. She tells me I have to decide. 'You need to tell him the truth, or finish your relationship with Enrique,' she says. 'Don't forget, your father can just turn up at a tournament at any time.'

She's also angry that it's come to this. She'd prefer me to break up with Enrique and keep our lives as they have been.

But me? Suddenly I have the desire to tell my dad, for him to know I want to be with Enrique.

I head to Montreal, play strongly and beat Martina Hingis to get to the semis. Enrique arrives at the end of the tournament and we go to New Haven but I withdraw because I pulled my hamstring in Canada in the semis and don't want to risk a severe injury.

In the US Open I make the second round.

⊝

In September I return to Belgrade for a three-week training block. While I am there, Mum decides to reveal to my father that I am seeing Enrique. Incredibly, my father doesn't lose it. He has a proposal instead. He calls me into our living room. His tone is serious, it's like we are having a business meeting about my life. This is what he puts to me. 'No problem if you want to have a boyfriend. But you are going to sign everything over to me,' he says. 'All the money you have earned up until now and a big part of your future earnings. Then you can do whatever you want. No problem, you can go.'

I'm sure he thinks I won't agree to this. He starts dictating more terms of the deal. He's calm. Not screaming. Just telling me how he will control my finances. 'Your mother will continue to travel with you, and I am staying home; you will have a credit card for your tournament expenses, flights, meals, accommodation,' my father says. 'But everything you earn is mine.'

I don't give a shit I am giving it all away. All I can think about is being free with Enrique. But I'm fairly sure that my father thinks we are not going to last long, that he's just demanded this so I'll be back in a few months.

I take the deal. I just want a life. I want a life without fear. I want a life with Enrique. I want love and peace not chaos. Not craziness. Not hell.

From here I play tournaments in Brazil, Tokyo and Germany, and I do pretty well – I make two quarters and a semi. And Dad? It turns out that signing the papers does not stop him wanting to control my life. He is ringing me all the time. His phone calls can go for hours. I might have signed that financial contract in the hope of a life without fear, but the verbal abuse is more intense than ever.

'You are disgusting whore,' he screams. 'A disgrace, an embarrassment to our family, a slut.'

One particularly nasty phone call comes after I lose in the semis of a WTA event in Japan and I think after it, *I've had enough*. Enrique and I have a talk. He sees that my family situation is destructive and unhealthy. 'You need to leave home and come with me,' he says one night in our hotel room.

I know he is right. I will never have a real chance to grow with my father around and nor will our relationship. I agree. It's time to go.

13

Leaving, 2002

I start writing my mother a goodbye letter in Moscow in early October 2002. As I put my pen to paper tears splash onto the notepad.

'Please forgive me that I am leaving you, but this is something I have to do.' I write these words knowing the pain that my father is going to inflict on her. I am positive that she will bear the brunt of his rage. Chances are he will blame both her and me – but she will be the one to deliver the bad news. And I'm filled with sadness knowing I am leaving behind her and my dear Savo. I feel horribly confused as I write, wondering if I'm really doing the right thing. In one sense I'm still the little girl who wants to please her father. On the other hand, I am nineteen and I have realised life doesn't have to be like this.

Enrique has decided we should make our escape late in the night. He books a taxi to the airport for 3 am for our three-and-a-half-hour plane trip to Monaco. There, I'll move into his apartment.

I don't sleep. Waves of anxiety and doubt continue to wash over me. At 2.55 Enrique takes my hand as we leave our room. On the way out I slip the letter under my mother's door. My heart breaks. Guilt haunts me on the drive to the airport and I'm in shock that I have actually done it. *What will happen next?* I wonder. *Will he call? Will he come and find me?* I know my father, his dogged determination, his obsession with my career and me. The thought of him hunting me down terrifies me. But I also feel a strength and determination not to live this wretched life under his thrall anymore. I reason with myself there must be something horribly wrong if I never want to go back home or see him.

I settle myself in Enrique's apartment but we have to leave almost immediately for Germany, where I'm to play the Porsche Grand Prix event in the southern city of Stuttgart.

The situation I am now in is utterly foreign. Enrique might be by my side but it's the first tournament I have gone to without my father calling the shots, whether from behind the fence or thousands of miles away. Am I going to make this work? Am I going to be okay? I'm not sure. I can't help picturing my mother handing my dad the letter. I imagine the rage spewing from his mouth, him calling me and my mum whores, the fury he will unleash on her. These thoughts keep cascading through my head but I try to refocus and head out to the court for my first-round match. It is after I have warmed up for my match, against Russian Tatiana Panova, that a WTA official comes and finds me in the locker room.

'Jelena, your father is here,' the official says. 'He's trying to find you.'

Although I have told the WTA not to let him near me, no one has been able to stop my dad buying a ticket to the tournament like any other fan. I have no option but to go out and play. I walk to my court with my head down. I can't bear to have a confrontation in public with him. I get on the court but it's hard to focus, my mind isn't on this match at all. Minutes later I see him out of the corner of my eye, standing with arms folded over his burly chest. He is looking angry and he has Savo with him. Savo gives me a small wave. It breaks my heart. I want to cry when I see Savo. My father knows my little brother is my Kryptonite. There's only one reason Savo is here and that is to pull at my heart-strings. The crowd cheers heartily but I hear nothing.

In between points my mind wanders. I am a traitor, I say to myself. I have betrayed them. I should just go home to them. The guilt swarms over me again. *Maybe I have done the wrong thing. Maybe I shouldn't have left? Maybe he knows best. Why have I left? Was my life so bad?*

But the fear hits me. No. No way can I see him and talk to him. There's no way I can face him.

With my head whirring with negative thoughts and him as an unwelcome spectator I lose, of course: 1–6, 6–4, 6–1. I rush back to the locker room. He hasn't tracked me down to talk me out of this decision to leave – yet.

In my hotel room with Enrique, the phone calls start. 'We are in the lobby, Savo and I, we just want to talk to you,' my father says. 'Come down and talk.'

'No,' I say. 'No, Dad, I can't.'

On no account will I go down there. He calls again and again but I refuse to budge. As much as I want to see my little brother I can't risk it. Eventually they leave, having rattled me to my core.

I arrive in Zurich, Switzerland, strung out and scared, always looking over my shoulder. In the first round I somehow beat Iva Majoli but by the second round I am emotionally unravelled and I lose. By the time I reach my next tournament, in Linz, Enrique thinks something radical needs to be done to keep my father away from me. At his urging I meet with the WTA and ask them to ban my mother and father from all tournaments. While they can still buy tickets, they are now prevented from accessing family accreditation passes.

My parents go on the publicity offensive, assuring anyone who's listening that all is fine between the three of us. 'It's all lies, I don't know where it's come from,' my father tells a Serbian radio station. 'I am not fighting with the Formula One racer, [the stories] are not true. But I think he is her biggest mistake.'

He even has a shot at Enrique. 'Brother, I drive faster than him,' he says.

$\ominus$

Each morning I look out from the balcony of Enrique's luxurious apartment at the twinkling harbour peppered with yachts. A few weeks since leaving, and the peace I thought I might feel after escaping my father is just not there. I am sad, mainly because of my brother. I miss him so much. My dad's words ring over and over in my head. 'You are a whore and a traitor.' *I* am *a traitor*, I think. I convince myself I have let down my family. There's nothing good about me.

This guilt is eating away at me; my mind is sliding into a pit of sadness. But as bad as I am mentally, I have to go and earn a living. My father has cancelled my credit card, and because of the contract I signed in Belgrade I don't have a cent to my name.

While I may have legally given him everything I have earned so far in my career, I now give him extra money; money that's not in our agreement. My hope is that giving him more money will buy me some peace.

I pick up my racquet bag and head down to the courts with Enrique to meet with a possible new coach. Heinz Gunthardt is a former coach of Steffi Graf. He lives in Monaco and has agreed we could work together. Today we have a solid training session and I think we could be a good fit, but I don't decide on the spot.

I focus on putting in a hard training block of ten days with Heinz before I head to LA for the WTA season-ending championships. Once in LA, my hopes of doing well in this tournament, and in the process earning some money, go wrong in my first practice session with Justine Henin. I sprain my right ankle. The pain is wretched: the ankle swells to an enormous size. The next day it turns blue and purple and I can't walk on it. The physios go to work as we have three days before my first match; they consider injecting it but in the end they tape it up. I'm determined to play, and within 24 hours I can walk on it, gingerly.

Prior to my first match I think, *Just walk on the court, try to play*. I don't want to default. To be frank, I can't afford to. I have to pick up the prize money.

My opponent is Anastasia Myskina – not someone you'd want to be playing on one foot. But I have no choice. After I warm up for my match – I can hardly move – there is no option but to go out there and hit the hell out of every ball I can get my racquet onto. Due to the state I'm in I have no option but to go for full-on winners. I take the court and I also go for my serves both first and second. To my relief, everything I hit is going in and Myskina isn't playing her best. I win the match almost literally on one leg, 6–3, 6–4.

The win sees me financially secure for the next few months. But in the next round is Serena Williams. The world No. 1. I haven't taken a set off Serena in all our meetings and today I'm not even sure if I'm going to be able to walk out of my hotel room let alone onto the court. I'm on painkillers and still hobbling. I muster all my mental and physical strength to get out there.

I can barely cover the court. Somehow I manage to get to a tie break in the first set, but I lose it 7–1. My ankle gets even sorer in the second set and there's no way of stopping Serena – I don't win a game.

It's been a tough week and year but I'm happy, and I have won $US100,000, which will help pay for my travel and coaching.

Enrique and I fly to Honolulu to try to forget about the state I am in and to have some time to ourselves.

⊖

Enrique and I go to his hometown of Curitiba, Brazil, at the end of November for Christmas and the New Year. His parents are lovely, charming, kind people. They welcome me warmly into their home on the outskirts of town, though he and I stay at his apartment in the city centre. His parents know a little bit about what I have been through – Enrique has told them – and they do all they can to look after me.

On the surface Enrique and I seem like a happily engaged couple. But to my distress, things aren't that great in Brazil. It's mainly because I feel as though I've gone from being the only woman in the world for him to seeing him flirting with other women and becoming more distant with me. It's hard to ignore the tension rising between us. We continue to play the happy couple in front of his parents. But marriage isn't on the cards for now. I know this because we don't talk about getting married, we don't have any firm plans or a set date. I hope our relationship will get better.

Enrique's family has a beach house and we decide to stay by the ocean for a few days. His fitness trainer accompanies us too. This will be good for us both, and the trainer's a nice guy. Enrique and I work out together but we also fight – I don't think he fully understands the difficult decision I have made to be with him. Or that he appreciates how much I feel I've let down my family, particularly my brother, by

195

leaving. I don't get the sense he understands how much pain I am in and how broken I am.

We also argue about his wandering eye. He is commenting on other women more and more – particularly here in Brazil. One day we descend from bickering about these subjects into a full-on shouting match. The tears start rolling. The fitness trainer remains silent. I can see he doesn't want to get involved. I walk away from the confrontation.

Enrique doesn't apologise. He spends the rest of the day carrying on as though nothing happened. He doesn't bring it up again and neither do I.

Days out from Christmas my father does another outrageous media interview, which I read on the internet. 'I couldn't stand it if Jelena turned out to be [a lesbian],' he says in the article. 'I'd kill myself.' In the same interview he says he doesn't like Enrique and that it will all end with him soon. 'She didn't tell me about it and when I read about it in the newspapers I didn't believe it,' he says. 'I don't like him. I hope the relationship doesn't last long. I don't believe it's a serious relationship anyway; if I did I'd do something about it. I hope they split up soon.'

Normally I would roll my eyes at his words but after our huge row I wonder whether his prophecy that Enrique and I will split up could come true.

We celebrate New Year in Brazil and head back to Monaco a few days later. I hope that in 2003 I will be able to figure out my situation.

⊖

Nothing changes in the New Year. In fact, it gets worse. It's January and under the beautiful chandeliers at Monaco's Le Métropole shopping centre I break down into inconsolable sobs. I am gasping for breath and trying to make sure people don't see me losing it. A darkness firmly grips me. Enrique consoles me but I can see he doesn't get what is going on. Breaking down has started to become a regular occurrence for me. Every few days I suffer an uncontrollable and unstoppable stream of tears along with a chunk of bad, dark thoughts. It can happen anywhere: at the courts, watching television, out on our apartment balcony. And now here, at Le Métropole, where I have come to try to distract myself by window shopping.

While Enrique no longer races with Arrows – the team went broke – he's joined World Series by Nissan and there are periods where he has to travel for work and I am left alone. But even when he is here, our relationship continues to unravel. Since we battled I have emotionally declined, distance has grown between us. He gives curt, unhelpful answers in my times of need. I know he thinks I should just get on with life. He's said it before. He claims he knows I am having a hard time and says he supports me, but his lack of engagement with me and my emotional state tells me that he doesn't care that much.

I think he thought that when he got me away from my family all my problems would be fixed. I would be his happy fiancée. What I have recently concluded is that he wants to have me to himself. As I have now learnt, Enrique always likes to get his own way.

⊖

I'm only handful of spots from the world No. 1 ranking and I have a pressing issue: I need to formally appoint a coach. After meeting with Heinz Gunthardt in Monaco in October I decide to go with him because he has a solid coaching resumé, but the downside is he can't travel full-time, so we agree to a six-month trial period.

In late January Heinz and I spend a week together and then he is off with commentary commitments, though we continue to communicate on the phone. I head to Japan on my own. I walk into my hotel room and it is deathly quiet. No father, mother, little brother, no Enrique. It's just me. It's strangely peaceful but as soon as my head hits the pillow, it hits me with force how sad and terribly lonely I am again.

Despite my flat mood I manage to get to the quarter-finals in Tokyo, and at Paris's indoor tournament afterwards. But by the second week in February, in Antwerp, Belgium, my bad headspace is on full show. I have a shocking day and lose in the first round.

My confidence is slipping away. Not only that, but within weeks I realise that Heinz probably isn't the coach for me. We just don't click. He's not someone who can help me when I'm in the state I am currently in – vulnerable and anxious. He's clinical in his approach and of course not available full-time. But right now there's nothing I can do – I really can't look for someone else at this stage of the season; nor can I stand the possibility of having no one with me while I am competing. I can't stand being alone. I try to make it work.

Meanwhile Enrique and I travel together to a tournament in Scottsdale, Arizona, where we continue to bicker more than talk. After a long day of practice, in our Scottsdale hotel room we descend into another huge argument and this time it is about Enrique being jealous.

My mind spins. I've got to get out of this. But where the hell will I go? I have nowhere. I have no one. I am definitely not going back to my father.

Unsurprisingly I lose my opening-round match at Scottsdale. On the court these days I find I have no confidence when it matters. The combination of not having a team, a steady coach, plus my disintegrating personal life is badly affecting my tennis. In Indian Wells I lose in the first round. But in Miami I manage two wins before meeting Alicia Molik in the round of sixteen. She's all blank stares and silence – it's a shame we don't even say hi these days. I beat her 6–1, 6–4 to book a spot in the quarters, where I lose to Kim Clijsters.

In Sarasota Enrique is rude and calls me names, putting me down all the time. A coach, who is a friend, observes it. This man is someone I really like and respect, and he confronts Enrique, telling him never to talk to me like that again. He adds that if he does so, Enrique is going to have to deal with him. It's such a relief having someone stick up for me. I might be mature as a tennis player but I'm a person who doesn't really know how to make friends. To be honest, I'm disturbed by the thought of even trying to make friends because I still feel like most people will reject me. Often I'm positive that because of all that's happened to me in Australia, I must be thoroughly unlikeable. When I add up the bullying I experienced in the school playground, the rejection from fellow national players and my father's treatment of me, it's hard not to feel really quite worthless.

In a completely unexpected way, especially considering how desperate I was to get away from him, I'm feeling lost without my dad. You couldn't question the results I had in the years he was with me. For all his faults, he was organised. There was military scheduling around practice times and even what I ate. From the age of six, I trusted every word that came out of his mouth about tennis. I executed everything he told me to do with precision. Was I talented? Yes. Did I want to work and compete? Yes. But he helped me get there. He knew what he was doing.

Enrique joins me in Warsaw, Poland, and despite my patchy form I do well and make the semis. I go to Berlin, Rome and Strasbourg where I play average.

By the French Open, I'm well and truly fed up with the situation with Heinz. After my loss in the second round, when I ask him for feedback, I don't feel he tells me anything useful.

This makes no sense, I realise. *I can't work like this.*

I have been paying Heinz thousands of euros a week to have him turn up every few weeks and tell me jack shit. He's rocking up to the practice court and then he is off for a week. His TV commentary commitments seem to take priority over my tennis career. Although he comes to tournaments, he leaves a couple of days in, not even finishing the week. My results are better when he hasn't been able to make the tournaments.

The next day, when I tell Heinz that this isn't working, strangely, he seems shocked. 'Are you sure? Think about it. I could come next week and help you out before Wimbledon?'

My mind is made up. 'No, we are over,' I tell him.

At Roland Garros I run into Borna Bikic. He's shown interest in guiding me before – we had a couple of casual conversations about it in Amelia Island and Berlin earlier this year. But now we sit down and seriously discuss the possibility of him formally coaching me. He makes a strong pitch, although he's coaching another player at this point. He's extroverted and friendly; however, he comes with barely any coaching experience. Up until a few months ago, when he started coaching this other top 100 player, he's never been on tour. He's also Croatian, a Catholic – a fact that would send my Serbian father berserk. I sit on the decision and tell him I will let him know.

With my confidence waning I start to think about Australia again. I have no bad feelings about Yugoslavia at all, but I find myself going back to the fact that I never agreed to, never wanted to leave my home in Australia. It's not just about playing for Australia, the country that embraced me, supported me before my father made me turn my back on it, it's about where my heart is. Even though I was born in Yugoslavia and respect my background and heritage, I feel a pull back to Australia.

I speak with Australian Open tournament director Paul McNamee, a man I trust, and talk through my feelings and worries with him. 'I feel like I am Australian. This is what I want to do. But I am scared. I am scared of the reception that I am going to get, not only from the crowd, but other people in Tennis Australia.'

The purpose of the conversation is not to make a firm decision on whether I will return; just to see what Paul thinks. Paul is always supportive and excited for me. He has always understood it was Dad's decision to leave.

After the French Open I return to Monaco for a week to train and finally make a decision about my coaching predicament. I'm going to employ Borna. I've decided to take a gamble. Yes, he's only worked with one other player on the tour. But he's nice, an easy-going guy. I am up for someone who's going to be there by my side at breakfast, lunch and dinner, who will accompany me to practice and hit with me. It's not just about having a tennis coach – if it were I wouldn't hire him, based on his experience and credentials – it's about finding someone who will make my life easier and less stressful. It's about having a true friend. A companion who can stop me from slipping into this terrifying sadness I have been experiencing.

I need someone to help me survive – that's what's important now.

14

Borna, 2003

Enrique and I meet Borna in Vienna for the next tournament, and Enrique is on edge. He and Borna have met before, earlier this year, but now that Borna's my coach, Enrique seems grumpy. In Vienna I'm introduced to Borna's brother, Tin, for the first time. He's a quiet guy, subdued, nothing like Enrique or especially Borna. He attends my matches and training a few times. I like his personality – there's a welcome calmness there.

Enrique leaves Vienna after a couple of days and goes to a race; I get to the quarters, then Borna and I travel on to Eastbourne and Wimbledon. Borna hasn't got a grip on how severe the rift is between my parents and me: he wants to reach out to them in the hope of some kind of reunion. I tell him it's useless, that because he's Croatian they're even less likely to want to talk to him, but he goes ahead. Of course they rebuff him, saying I have to come home and that's all there is to it.

Despite my new coach – a new injection of support – I'm still feeling flat. I don't win in Eastbourne and the press write that I look 'listless' in my first-round win over Britain's Elena Baltacha at Wimbledon. The truth is that not only do I look listless, I feel listless. On the court I am confused. My confidence is still in shreds. Once your confidence is low, you have no trust in your shots, your game, your ability. You start to doubt everything. So I'm tentative on the court. My head and heart are not in it. Off-court events, everything that has happened in the last eighteen months, are taking their toll. I am the eleventh seed here but I only just manage to beat Elena.

I walk back to the locker room feeling hollow. I manage to make it to the third round before I lose to a sixteen-year-old Russian girl called Maria Sharapova. Again, post-match reports describe me as seeming 'out of sorts'.

Borna and I arrive back in Monaco for a training block and it's obvious that Enrique doesn't want him there. After our first training session Enrique is boiling with annoyance, critical of my decision to hire Borna. 'He's inexperienced and young,' he says, steaming around the living room. I know a lack of credentials isn't the real issue. Enrique's jealous.

'I have no one else,' I say. 'It is what it is.'

The fact I have employed Borna having barely consulted Enrique has also made him angry. He doesn't like it when I make decisions for myself. Enrique likes things his way. Since my move to Monaco into his home, almost a year ago, his control of me has extended. He has started to tell me what I should do with the money that I earn. Yet he's still looking at other girls, admiring them in front of me. He's also started talking about me, disclosing intimate details of our life to other people. Word sometimes filters back about his disrespectful talk and it saddens me he is treating me like this.

For being in the top five in the world I've been given a Porsche Carrera 4S at a tournament at Filderstadt in Germany that's sponsored by the car maker. It's a beautiful silver vehicle that I've driven a handful of times, a lovely car, but I'm not really interested in that kind of thing, and I know that Borna will need one while he's in Monaco so I offer to let him use it while we are training there.

When I tell Enrique, he's visibly annoyed – he loves the Porsche, though he has his own car, a BMW M3.

'He can take my car,' he says. I know why: there's no way in this world he will have Borna driving a better car than he has.

Borna's downstairs, so down goes Enrique, reluctantly, to hand the keys over to him. But rather than giving them to him, Enrique throws the keys 30 metres into the bushes and storms off.

Over the coming days Enrique continues to brood. He's icy.

It gets to the point where I know we are not going to work as a couple anymore. I confide to Borna that I want to split from Enrique, that we're unhappy. Borna agrees to help me move my stuff out that afternoon. After practice, while Enrique is out, Borna and some friends of mine who live nearby meet at my apartment and help me pack up some of my belongings.

They drop me and my bags at the apartment of a friend; Borna is also staying there. Enrique calls non-stop. He is shocked that I have moved out and pleads for me to come home. 'I'm staying here for the night, I'll call you tomorrow,' I tell him. The phone calls don't stop the next day. He is adamant I should come back, and eventually he convinces me to. 'I will change,' he promises.

Within hours of my return, everything goes wrong. When I get to the apartment we start to argue again. He screams at me until I gather up my racquet bag and weakly walk out the door.

On the street, I ring Borna. Briefly I tell him what has happened, that I'm not going back up there alone, and ask could he come and help me pick up the rest of my things. Within minutes he arrives and we both go back up to the apartment. I tell Enrique I need all my stuff, that we are over for good.

Enrique starts acting like an idiot. Throwing my belongings around the apartment. A trophy smashes into a wall. Then shoes. Clothing. He's lost his mind. I manage to pack a bag with some possessions.

Borna pipes up. 'Listen, man, just leave her alone; leave it all alone. It's done,' he says. 'Just let her go to a hotel. You guys should cool down for a few days.'

Enrique doesn't respond well to the suggestion; if anything he amps up his madness and the wrecking continues.

Casting around for ideas, I spy his computer on our marble coffee table. I pick it up. Hold it above my head.

'Listen, if you throw one more fucking thing of mine,' I say. 'I will break your fucking computer.'

He stops. The rage seems to drain from his face.

'You're an asshole,' I say. Borna and I leave.

Even though the situation was frightening, Borna and I can joke together with our friends, who arrive to help me with all my gear for the second time in 24 hours, that we should open a moving company.

Borna and I check in to a hotel in Monaco. We decide to stay in adjacent rooms so he's near me as I'm feeling a bit scared of Enrique.

A few days go by. Again Enrique calls and begs to see me. I soften and agree to meet him. He suggests a time in the evening on the promenade down by the harbour. It's a dark place by the water's edge, which worries me. What if he throws me over the wall and into the sea? Borna suggests he comes with me early and hides somewhere in the bushes so he can secretly watch us.

He conceals himself as discussed; I breathe easier. Unfortunately for Borna, a stinking dead cat makes his viewing spot very unpleasant, and he has to endure it for about half an hour while Enrique and I talk. Borna daren't move away in case Enrique sees him. Enrique has no clue.

I tell Enrique I'm not coming home for now. That I need some time to think about it. But I know there really is no chance of me ever going back to our apartment.

⊖

Several evenings later I'm out with Borna, some friends and Tin having dinner at a restaurant down by the water. Tin has just arrived from Croatia for the week. There's a light-hearted vibe at dinner – free of tension and argument. Yachts bob on the harbour. It's an idyllic, peaceful setting. For the first time in days I'm feeling slightly relaxed. We are nearly finishing our main courses when the peace is broken by a car screeching up to the front of the restaurant. As does every other diner, I turn around, wondering, *What's going on?*

It's Enrique. He gets out, leaving the ignition running, and storms up to our table. If he could blow smoke out of his nose right now I swear he would. 'You need to come with me,' he says. It sounds like an order. He stands by our dinner table, waiting for me to get up and leave. Mortified, I say, 'You guys stay, enjoy the rest of your dinner. I'm sorry about this. I have to go or there will be a huge scene.'

I follow him to the car, get in next to him, and he smashes his foot to the floor, hurtling out onto the road as though he were competing in a race. Driving like a madman he floors it past the restaurant strip. More diners crane their necks to see what is going on. The wheels screech around the corners and at times we are flying over the bitumen.

Somehow I manage to calm him down. He agrees to drop me off at my hotel, and when he pulls up out the front we speak for a few minutes in the car. He's going off to race the day after next. Luckily, I convince him to leave things as they are for now.

The following day Borna and I are parked out the front of the hotel, readying ourselves to get out, when a vehicle nudges the back of our car. Shocked, we look back and see it is Enrique. We get out.

I go over to his car window. 'We are over; don't ever call me again,' I say.

He leaves for his race the next day. That is it. I need to focus on my health and wellbeing. I have had enough trauma already.

$$\ominus$$

My heart aches. All contact with my little brother has been cut off by my dad. I miss Savo so much and wonder how he fills his days. I wish I could see him.

My parents and I don't speak.

For now I have neither a management company (my father severed ties with them after I left home) nor a true home; I am on the road and living out of my suitcase. Everything is up in the air. I am twenty years old with no idea what the future holds.

Borna and I head to the US for tournaments in Stanford and San Diego. I get to the quarter-finals of Stanford and manage a win at San Diego. Then I lose in the first round of LA, and manage one win in Toronto and New Haven respectively.

Off the court my life might be untidy but there's a shining light in the form of my newfound friendship with Tin Bikic.

On the last day in Monaco before Borna and I leave for the hard-court competition season in the States, Tin puts his number in my phone. 'If you ever want to talk, call me,' he says. 'If you are having a hard time, call me.'

I text Tin first a couple of days after we arrive in the States. We have friendly conversations, just general chit-chat; he's chilled and fun to talk to. We talk about tennis. He's concerned for me after my break-up with Enrique. We call and check in with each other.

Enrique and I haven't spoken for weeks then one day out of the blue he calls. It's obvious he isn't coping with the break-up, the rejection, the loss of control. My mobile phone starts bleeping with missed phone calls from him.

Two weeks before the US Open he calls again and this time I finally answer.

'I am going to come to New York and see you,' Enrique says. 'I want to see you. I miss you.'

Has he forgotten everything?

'Don't you dare,' I tell him. 'Listen, you are coming for nothing.'

I don't need the drama.

Most of my possessions fit into a large black suitcase, which sits in my hotel room at the Le Méridien in Manhattan. I am back here for the US Open. I love New York and always have, but as a professional athlete; and in the past with my father supervising me, there has rarely been time to see the sights. Usually I am focusing solely on tennis, but now I am trying to sort out my private life, and I'm feeling off as preparations for this grand slam are ramping up.

Here in my fancy room I'm staring at the suitcase, mulling things over, when my mother phones me.

'We need to meet,' she says. 'I have some things for you to sign.'

It comes as a complete shock that she is here. The last time I saw her I told her to sleep well then I disappeared into the night with Enrique. Ran away. I escaped. But in her eyes, I betrayed her.

I agree to meet her at the entrance of Flushing Meadow and I get her accreditation. She looks older, angrier and she is more distant towards me than ever before. After I get her the US Open accreditation and we're sitting together in the players' lounge, she straight away shoves a bunch of papers my way. They're filled with legal jargon. She's officious, which is unlike her.

'You have to sign over the Saddlebrook house, Jelena,' she says coldly. 'You are wrong to have left. Look at you. Why have you done this?' She is on-message from my father.

'I couldn't live the way I was living anymore,' I answer. 'Nothing was ever enough. I couldn't take his abuse anymore.'

Her blank face reveals that she doesn't understand me or my reasons for leaving. She has chosen to stay.

I glance through the documents and do as she asks: I sign the house in Saddlebrook over to them. I have signed over millions of dollars worth of assets and money so far.

She gathers up the papers, cold and angry. I see no love in her eyes and that really hurts.

Despite all this she stays on in my room – for three days – sleeping in a separate bed. She meets Borna, to whom she is aggressive and dismissive of. Her attitude fuels tension between us. Despite this I try to keep things civil and arrange for us to have dinners together. Away from Borna she continually tells me I'm making a mistake, that Borna is the wrong coach and that I should 'come home'.

I go to practice to prepare for the US Open and in the afternoons I return and face her campaigning for me to go back home to Serbia. 'Your father is unhappy and angry with you,' she says. 'You are doing everything wrong. You must come back home.' I tell her I can't do that, but she knows life for her would become better if I did. As I knew he would, my father has been blaming her for me leaving, so she persists. I know he's putting her through hell and I feel so guilty about it.

Sometimes, when I need a break from the pressure, I phone Tin to talk it through and he is incredibly supportive and kind.

One day when I return to our hotel room after calling Tin, my mother asks me where I have been. I tell her I've been on the phone but she refuses to believe me and launches into a tirade. Sounding just like my father, she accuses me of sleeping with Borna and my mixed doubles partner, who has been staying in a room near me and Mum.

I am appalled at her aggression and bizarre accusations. My mother, the woman who once loved me dearly, a constant in my life until a few months ago, has become a stranger to me. We are further apart than ever before and the way things are now, I'm not sure if we will ever be okay again. In tears I leave the room and call Tin, who calms me down. Then I go and see Borna, who says he'll talk to my mother. But his attempts to reason with her fall on deaf ears. 'How can she even think something like that?' he asks.

She leaves the next day. I am reeling from what she has said, so hurt. I try to understand how she can be so hostile towards me. Then again, over the years she's been horribly abused herself and, I think, brainwashed by Dad. Presumably she still loves him. For me, I know he is my father but it's very hard to love him after what he has put me through.

I'm in this awful emotional state and the US Open is a day away. Somehow I get through to the second round. Tin phones me after the loss. I tell him I am not feeling very good, the disappointment I am feeling in tennis and in life.

He wants to come to my next tournament, in Bali, which I think would be great – I'd love him by my side. I like his calmness and how he seems to really listen to me when I talk. I hear no jealousy in his voice. In his character I see absolutely no hint of anger. I like having him to talk to about my day. The fact is, right now I really can't be alone. I love talking to someone who actually, I think, understands me.

Tin's kindness has won my heart.

15

Bali, 2003–4

Tin is a respectful, kind, quiet soul. His background is athletics – he was an impressive sprinter for Croatia who had the potential to go to the Olympics but was stopped by injury. Athletics is not a big sport in Croatia; thanks to the turmoil of war, over the years a lack of facilities and finances has made it hard to break through, another reason he had to give it up.

We get along on many levels but one of the reasons we have a deep connection is his real understanding of what it takes to try to be the best you can be as an athlete. Then there is his demeanour. Conversations with him are relaxed and sane. He is a positive person, always seeing the best in every situation. He also makes me feel safe. He's the opposite of Enrique.

I know I don't need to jump into a full-on relationship right now; then again, because of the wretched state of affairs with my family, I feel as though Tin is exactly the type of person I need in my life.

Borna and I are on our way to Bali. Tin is to meet up with us at Singapore's Changi Airport, from where we will all go on to Bali for the next tournament. I spy him at the gate and from the moment I see him standing there waiting for me I know I am developing feelings for him. I feel calm. He embraces me and kisses me on the lips. I know from that kiss that we might soon be more than friends.

We touch down in Bali and I turn on my phone as we walk to the carousel. My heart sinks when I see there are chunks of text and notifications of voicemail messages from Enrique.

'Jelena, I really need to see you,' reads one SMS.

Then my phone starts ringing. Enrique's name flashes up. I quickly move out of earshot of Tin and Borna to take the call.

'How are you?' he blurts.

'Good, yeah, fine.'

Over and over he tells me he wants to see me, and he sounds serious; there's a neediness in his voice.

After trying to reason with him for a while, eventually I hang up. I feel that he might be in Bali – it is something he would do. Given his desperation to see me in New York, something tells me he could well have taken the long-haul flights from Europe to be here. I try to put the call out of my mind, and I hope like hell he isn't here.

In Bali, Tin and I share a nice villa. I spend my days practising hard for the tournament and at night we relax. A few evenings later we're watching a movie when someone starts knocking on the door. The knock turns into a BASH, BASH. My heart's in my mouth – I know it is Enrique.

'That's him,' I whisper. 'It's certainly not room service.' I jump off the bed and start searching for a place to hide. I run to the palatial bathroom.

'I'm not here. I'm going to hide in the toilet,' I hiss at Tin. 'Tell him I'm not here.'

Tin starts laughing. 'How come you're not here?' he says. 'He's going to know me from Monaco. He knows I'm Borna's brother.'

'Tell him I'm not here now.'

I squish myself into a corner of the bathroom and Tin opens the door. Enrique's face falls. He is standing there with a huge bunch of flowers.

'I am here to see Jelena,' he says.

Tin, still calm, tells him I'm busy.

Enrique hands over the flowers to Tin and walks off into the night.

Tin comes to find me in the bathroom. We are in disbelief about what has happened. He calls Borna, who's a few villas away, and tells him to come over to our room straightaway.

What I find strange is that Enrique reacted so calmly. It's so un-Enrique.

Then I hear BASH, BASH, BASH. He's back. I knew it. I open the door. His calm facade has dropped. He's the more familiar, angry Enrique.

'I told you not to come,' I say. 'We were done three months ago.'

He pauses. He looks confused, like he's searching for something to say.

Then he blurts out, 'Give me back my ring.'

I roll my eyes, go find the ring and give it to him. 'You can go fuck yourself and your ring,' I say as I hand it over. I also throw the flowers back at Enrique. He starts screaming and insulting me.

At this stage Tin interjects and tells Enrique to back off. Tin pulls me into the room and closes the door. Borna arrives.

Enrique has a female friend with him, a Balinese actress who is there for moral support, and it was she who managed to find out my room number. As Enrique, Tin and Borna continue to argue, she calls out, 'You are all going to disappear.'

Now Tin and Borna become extremely angry. Enrique tries to

play down the threat made by his Balinese friend and the pair walk away. Then Enrique gets offensive and aggressive again and Tin and Borna, both in boxer shorts, chase him out of the resort.

The next day I have to play my first-round match and as expected my head is all over the place and I play horrendously. I lose in the first round.

⊘

Borna's an attentive coach at the very beginning. At practice he helps me all he can. He's making an effort and doing his job. His lack of experience is clear, which doesn't bother me at this stage because I'm so in need of a friend – in a fragile state – but as he and I continue to work together my tennis career starts to slide. It's a subtle decline, but I notice it. Still, I'm willing to give him a chance to learn.

Tin continues to travel with me and we get along really well. It turns out that Enrique called Dad after our Bali encounter to tell him how much he still loves me, how I've left him, how he went to Bali to try to get me back, but now I'm with a Croatian guy *and* a Croatian coach. Of course he knows how much that will piss my father off. He asks my dad, 'How can you let that happen? Aren't you going to do something about it?'

In Shanghai I beat Jelena Jankovic; in Leipzig I win the first round, but then lose to Kim Clijsters. I know I'm not playing to the level I used to and I worry I've become accustomed to scraping through matches – I feel like I am all over the place on the court.

In Leipzig I meet Tin's father for the first time. He comes to visit Borna and Tin and he watches my matches. He's like Tin – quiet, polite, incredibly nice.

A week later I'm back in Moscow and Filderstadt. The tournament in Moscow marks a year since I ran away from my family. I stay in the same hotel and there are reminders of my escape everywhere. I can't even think about tennis as bad memories come flooding back.

My thoughts are clouded by memories of the escape and the chaotic past year.

In Moscow I begin falling into a deep, dark, depressive hole. On the court I can't summon any form or fight. I crash out of the first round of the tournament but I don't care. All I want is to go back to the hotel, crawl into bed, pull the covers over my head and hide away from the world.

For the first time in my career my ranking goes south. I can't defend the points from the year before. I was top ten in 2002 and No. 4 by July 2002 and now here, little more than a year later, thanks to my fraught off-court life, I've got no direction on court and I'm only just inside the top 30.

In Filderstadt I play dreadfully, another first-round loss, but somehow I manage to find form in Zurich. After failing to win consecutive matches for three months I get it together and make it through to the semis. I face the world No. 1, Kim Clijsters. She flies out of the blocks as our match opens and is up 3–0 within 15 minutes. She takes the first set 6–1. I manage to pull it together and I start the second set off well. I hang in there with her and win the second set to even it up. In the third set I save a break point and steady myself to stay on course for victory. Eventually I beat Kim, 1–6, 6–3, 6–4, to make the final of the Swisscom Challenge. For the first time in months I'm smiling in a press conference because when the match was on the line I won it. It's my best tennis in twelve months.

'Even if I lost I wanted to go off court knowing I had given it everything,' I say. 'I haven't had a great time but now I feel I have got my head together and got my tennis together.'

My fighting words aren't enough to prevent a loss to Justine Henin in the final, 6–0, 6–4. Mentally fatigued from the whole tournament, especially from the match against Kim, I just can't trouble Henin from the first point of the match. Today is not my day.

⊘

Even though I really, really like Tin, I worry about us. It could be happening too quickly. Everything feels problematic; I'm carrying a lot of baggage from my relationships with my father and Enrique.

I get to the quarter-finals of Generali Ladies Linz, even though I'm not playing to the level I should be. I narrowly lose to Japan's No. 1, Ai Sugiyama.

Right now there's a lot of anxiety about my life off the court. From the second set against Sugiyama until the end of the match I cry and cry and cry. It has nothing to do with tennis. Mostly it's because I want to be with Tin, who's a really lovely guy and totally different to Enrique, and I can't help feeling there are going to be problems. Based on his past form – and intuition – I figure that my father is going to have another insane reaction when he finds out about Tin.

Soon after, it hits the Serbian press that I'm dating Tin Bikic, a Croatian, and sure enough within hours my father's name lights up on my phone. I don't pick up.

Dating Tin. Coached by Borna. Everything raked over and amplified in the media. The worst things I could have done in Dad's eyes. He would probably rather I dated a terrorist than a Croatian Catholic man.

When he leaves a voice message, I brace myself and listen to it. 'You are nothing but a whore. You have betrayed us. You are a stinking, awful whore,' he screams. 'You are with the enemy. You've brought shame on me.'

Again he calls and leaves another vile message.

Sometimes I answer his calls. It's brutal when he puts Savo on the phone. This breaks my heart. It pushes me to the edge. This is the brother I have adored since before he was born. Even when Mum was pregnant I begged her to have a boy, so badly did I want a brother. When he arrived, I peered into his crib at the hospital, looked at his squashed-up newborn face and asked, 'Why does he look so red?' She laughed at me. I insisted on carrying him out of the hospital, in a cane basket, and ever since I have wanted to be his protector. And as our home environment became more and more chaotic and violent, I felt the need more urgently. But now I can't even talk to him, let alone protect him. I worry he might think I have abandoned him.

Despite the emotional abuse I am now receiving in the form of phone calls and voicemail messages I continue to send my dad money. Every couple of weeks I make a wire transfer of around US$200,000. I send the money in the hope of peace. I send the money in the hope that he finds some happiness. But instead he keeps ringing and continues to make my life a nightmare.

$$\ominus$$

It's December and Borna, Tin and I arrive back in Monaco. We're in the lobby of the hotel where we are staying – I still don't have an apartment here – when Borna shows me a piece of paper. We've been working for the last six months without a contract. That's not unusual in tennis. But now Borna wants one. I am currently the No. 14 women's player in the world and he's written that if I get into the top ten, his pay doubles. His percentage of prize money also doubles, though he's getting paid well, especially for someone with so little coaching experience. I read on and his demands seem ridiculous. He appears to want to control every aspect of my life, including when Tin can come and see me.

I tell him I won't sign it, that I can't agree to any of it now. But if I do get into the top ten next year, I'll consider the money part. We leave it at that.

A few days later Borna goes to Zagreb, where his family live, to spend some time with them. Tin and I stay for a couple more days in Monaco, then join Borna and the Bikic parents for a week in Zagreb before starting the off-season. It's lovely to meet Tin's mother. She has a tougher exterior than his father, but she is also warm and kind. Both Tin's parents are extremely accommodating and supportive. I note that their home environment – the gentle chatter, kind conversation, warm atmosphere – is radically different from the one I've been used to and grew up in. The Bikics are close, they joke, laugh; the coldness and clinical conversation, the fights, the tensions of the Dokic household are a world away.

We spend a week in a rented Zagreb apartment and I meet Tin's friends and socialise with them. We all get along well. It's strange to be in Croatia. The last time I was here I thought I would be back in two months' time, and here I am thirteen years later. But it's good being there and having a 'normal' time. The last eighteen months have been traumatic. It's such a relief to find myself taking a breath and not thinking about tennis – just being.

This interlude with Tin in Zagreb makes my feelings for him grow significantly. We have the same outlook on life, the same morals. He is very rational and calm in all situations. And I find myself falling in love with him. I have no doubts that he is the right person for me.

We decide to go to the Slovenian mountains to train at altitude for the upcoming season. It's beautiful there. Because it is winter we train indoors, and it's a productive few weeks. After a month we head back to Monaco to set up a new base before my first tournament next year. Borna and Tin want me to feel like I have a home, so we find an apartment. It is good to have a proper base after almost a year, even if I sleep there for only one night before we head to Tokyo.

Tin and I feel strong together. But the worry of my situation with my family won't recede; I'm still weighted down by our estrangement. As the weeks pass, it seems more and more as though Tin alone is keeping me together.

16

The Fall, 2004

Even though my confidence is low, I am now ranked eleventh in the world. In Tokyo, a month into 2004, I get through some testing three-set matches to make the semi-finals.

Though I might look like I am keeping it together, the reality is that I have no idea what I am doing on the court. My self-esteem is shot. It feels as though I am making things up as I go along. On the eve of my first match in Paris at the Indoor Open, my father leaves another horrendous voicemail message. 'You are a whore,' it begins – his phone messages always start like this now. 'A cow. A fucking bitch. A traitor.' Without fail within seconds of his phone tirades I will have tears streaming down my face.

Does he actually think these calls will bring me home? Or does he just want to grind me down? If that's the case, it's working. The calls rot my confidence. So when I walk onto the court in Paris, where I'm playing Russia's Elena Bovina, I am not there mentally.

Our match starts well for me and I win the first set, 6–4. At the end of the second set we get to a tie breaker and soon I have match point. My backhand down the line just catches the net. I don't convert the match point. The match slides out of my control. At the change of ends I put a towel over my head and with that unwillingly surrender. I don't want to give up but somehow I know I have. In fact, I have a similar breakdown to the one I had in Linz. I can't stop crying. I can't focus. If one point or one game doesn't go my way, the rest of the match seems to fall apart. What's happened to my resilience and determination? My trademark fight has diminished. Life has diminished in me. I am not the player I used to be – I am mentally fragile.

I lose, 4–6, 7–6 (5), 6–0.

The match shows up all the cracks in my current situation.

⊘

My father threatens to kill Tin – the Croatian man who has 'brainwashed' me and stolen my heart needs to die; the life of the only person keeping me together is now threatened. Tin, the ever-calm Tin, handles the chaos perfectly. While everyone else seems to take from me, he only wants to care for me. He's measured and respectful, even in the face of these maniacal threats, which he refuses to be cowed by. He even remains positive that my father might come to accept our relationship; that one day his harshness will fizzle out and we will all get together and get along fine.

Personally, I find it appalling that my father is literally waging a war against Tin. Hanging on to this sort of discrimination is so unnecessary. I don't care if someone is Catholic or Orthodox, Croat or Serb. All of us need to move forward. There needs to be more tolerance. I hate the estrangement that results from differences of religion and nationality. Can't we just live in peace? Tin and I are in love and that's it.

In fifteen years of playing tennis I have never broken a racquet. Now I break them all the time. I smash them into the ground. My composed personality has been replaced by crying and tantrums. I kick wildly at racquet bags, the net, the fence, whatever is nearby. I have gone from being calm to going crazy. And my mental state is reflected in my tennis. Three–two in the first set? I give up when I'm behind. My competitive spirit has been zapped.

I'm in really bad shape when I play Nicole Pratt in the first round of Doha. I can't win a game in the first set. Partly I put this down to complications caused by my racquet – I've changed manufacturers twice in eight months, getting through three different types of racquet. My latest is wreaking havoc – it doesn't suit my game. So now I don't have confidence in my game or the racquet or myself. Still, after a terrible first set I finally manage to pull out some of my trademark determination and get back into the match to beat Nicole, 0–6, 6–3, 6–4. There's no warmth between us, which is a shame – I wish it wasn't the case with the Australian players, especially those I played Fed Cup with.

During my second-round match I have a fight with Borna. I am down in the first set 3–0 and he starts to get annoyed I am losing. He's pissed off – I can see it when I look up to him in the stands. I can't contain my aggravation. I look up to his seat and say, 'You can fuck off with that attitude.'

I turn up to Indian Wells and Miami in a terrible state, though I win a few matches. By Amelia Island I'm over this tennis life. I want to go home – wherever that is. What I need is to stop and reset and try to find my confidence again. I tell Borna none of this is working, that I don't feel good, that we should go home. Again, he's annoyed. He's set on going to every single tournament every week. 'Why should we go home when we are getting in the main draws of tournaments?' he asks irritably.

It's a ridiculous reason. I know Borna gets a buzz out of tournaments, the social life, but I'm getting a buzz out of nothing right now. Yet I can't fight him – there's no fight left in me. I know it's wrong to stay, and I feel as though he has no idea how to help me fix things on and off the court. I'm clearly not doing well emotionally so I feel weird and a bit freaked out by his attitude.

I call up Tin, who is back in Croatia, and tell him I want to take a break. Of course, he gets why I want to leave the tour for a period.

'I want to find a way to figure things out,' I say. 'I am not dealing with all my issues. It will only get worse if I keep on playing. I can't deal with my crap while I am playing on tour.'

We forge on; nothing changes. But I can see something is off with Borna in Amelia Island. After I lose in the first round, we decide to spend a week practising there before we go to Charleston. And all of a sudden he is nowhere to be seen, apart from coming to my practice sessions. I don't see him at dinner or lunch. I don't see him in the gym. This is weird for someone who has been wholly invested, and it's very weird for a coach to turn up just to practice sessions.

Then one day my hitting partner tells me that Borna's been hanging out with another girl on tour, the Croatian player Karolina Sprem. He's watching her matches. My first thought is, *What the?* Then, I wonder, is this because my results are bad?

That night we are meant to go out to dinner – me, my hitting partner and Borna. But Borna has another idea. 'Why don't we go and watch Serena play?'

Immediately I suspect something. I'm pretty sure his eye will be on Serena's opponent – Karolina Sprem. Sure enough, from the moment we take our seats Borna struggles to take his eyes off Karolina.

The next couple of days he continues to hang out with her and her team – a lot. My sense is that it's more than just a friendship.

When we get to Charleston I manage to win a match, even though I am playing horribly. Borna's concentration and attention continue to wane. The night before we're supposed to fly back to Europe, my hitting partner and I can't find him, so I return to my room and get on with packing. Then my hitting partner informs me that he's found out Borna has been with Karolina and her team all afternoon, and has spent the evening in her room.

We fly from Charleston to Athens for the Fed Cup play-offs. Tin meets us in Athens. It's been seven weeks since we've seen each other, and I'm so glad he's here. We've been on the phone a couple of times a day but it's just great to have him physically by my side once again. A sense of safety and relief washes over me whenever he is near. His company gives me confidence, emotional confidence; confidence.

For the first time I am to represent Serbia at the Fed Cup. I don't have anything against the country, but it feels strange representing it after being on Australia's team just a few years ago. I am not sure if I am ready to play for Serbia, but Borna and Serbian Fed Cup captain Biljana Veselinovic convince me.

I win two singles matches – both in three sets – but have to withdraw from the next match because of my strained hamstring. Serbian team management is annoyed. My teammates go out for dinner and they don't ask me. It shocks me. No one says goodbye to me at the end of the week. Because of an injury, something out of my control, I feel as though I've become an outcast.

Players never pay to go to the Fed Cup – the country's federation always pays for our trip and expenses. But Serbian tennis officials have told me they have no funding so I've paid my own way for this Fed Cup. I've also played for no fee, even though the ITF gives money to tennis federations towards our Fed Cup wages. I decided to play despite the lack of financial reward. I am not annoyed by the financial aspect, I am more annoyed by the treatment.

So I have given in more ways than one. The unfriendly reception by my Serbian teammates and officials is doubly disgraceful. I leave Athens feeling pretty let down. Neither the Fed Cup captain nor the Federation gets in touch with me and discuss any of this.

By the time we reach Berlin Borna and Karolina's relationship is becoming annoying because my coach's attention is on another player. Yet again I have told Borna I want to go home to Monaco but he was insistent I stay. So he annoys me the most out of everyone. I spend a lot of time in my hotel room and less time on the practice court.

One day I'm napping when my hotel phone rings. It's reception letting me know I have visitors. Suddenly I am listening to a familiar voice.

'Hello, Jelena, it's your mother. I'm here to see you with Savo. Can we come up?'

My heart leaps and then sinks. Why are they here?

'Of course,' I respond. But I feel considerable trepidation about this sudden visit. I open the door and when I see Savo's face I immediately start crying. I haven't seen him for almost a year and my sense of betrayal of him hits me like a freight train.

'We're going to stay here,' my mother says. She wears a tough expression on her face, there's no warmth – I can tell she has come on another mission from Dad. My guess is that he's told her again she needs to get me home. She calls up my father while I am standing with her. He starts instructing her over the phone what to say to me.

I become guarded. With my dad on the phone, she gets to the point. 'You have to leave Tin,' she says. 'You have to come home. You must come with us.'

Shaking my head I tell her this just can't happen. 'What are you thinking?' I ask her. 'Why would I subject myself to more pain?'

My little brother Savo looks fixedly at the floor as I dissolve into more tears. Shortly after I start crying they leave. As the door closes I collapse onto the floor in a heaving mess of sobs and pain.

Following this ill-fated visit the phone calls from Dad resume. He floods my phone daily with abusive messages.

The visit from my mother and Savo triggers my slide into darkness, and eventually my breakdown. After this I am not fine for an awfully long time.

⊘

Karolina is smiling my way when in the past she's barely acknowledged me. It's weird because we don't even know each other.

After a practice session one day, Borna says he'll be staying at the courts. While we're waiting for our transport back to the hotel, I ask Tin, 'What's going on with Karolina and Borna?'

He's silent, looking at the floor.

'Listen – what the fuck is going on?' This time I almost yell.

'They're together,' Tin eventually says.

That's it, I think – *Borna won't be my coach for much longer*. I tell Tin as much. 'Why?' he asks.

'Don't you realise what a conflict of interest it is?' I say. 'He's watching and spending time with another player. You cannot be dating one player and coaching another.' I can't stop my stream of thoughts. I am yelling now, throwing out what has been brewing in my head.

'I'm fragile,' I say to Tin, almost pleading. 'I'm playing like shit and my results are shit. Borna's my coach and he is not here for me. He's watching her practise, he's at her matches and he's giving her feedback. I can't even find him to go to the gym with now. We should just go home and let them be.'

Tin tries to be a peacemaker. He's very fair and realistic with all of us. I know it must be a difficult balancing act for him with his girlfriend on one side and his brother on the other, and I admire how somehow he manages to remain loyal to both of us. Because to me it's unquestionable: Borna's focus and concentration are gone. He's started to turn up late to the transportation, the practice sessions. I am doing my fitness sessions with Tin because his brother doesn't bother to put in an appearance anymore. Within a few days, I am starting to notice Karolina's team is also annoyed with her new romance. You can see that everyone knows now. When Tin tries to go and talk to Borna, to get him to refocus and reset, he finds out the pair are sharing a hotel room.

I feel extremely let down in this situation when I am not mentally strong – and Borna knows that. Of course I am fine with him having a girlfriend, but a girlfriend who is a direct competitor is a major conflict of interest. It's very hard to handle. What I need is someone I can trust, someone who has my back. The thought that someone close to me might not be fully on my side, and is distracted, leaves me feeling even more unstable.

I lose in the first round and play terribly in Berlin, but at least there's no chance I'll have to play my possible second opponent, Karolina. What a drama that would generate.

My mind is not, of course, on my tennis. It is on everything else.

⊝

I decide to seek some professional help to deal with the fallout with my father, and I try a succession of psychologists. I sit on their comfortable lounges and they listen. They nod, scribble down notes on their clipboards, smile sympathetically as I unload about my life. I tell them about my father, of the pain in not having a family around me anymore. How my dad makes me feel as though I have betrayed my family. I search and ask for answers.

One psychologist says, 'Oh, he will come around.'

I think, *What a ridiculous thing to say. That's one thing that's not going to happen.*

I see another who is equally positive. 'It will figure itself out. In ten, fifteen years it will be okay.'

I have to live for the next ten to fifteen years with this?

They obviously don't have the least understanding of Damir Dokic. They don't understand his stubbornness. The psychological torture he likes to inflict on me.

I walk out of these appointments sadder. I feel totally misunderstood and even more alone. It makes me think nothing can be fixed.

I'm still hearing death threats from my father: he's threatened to kill Tin several times by now, and it's become so worrying that we employ a security guard. He is not 'coming around'.

Tin and the guard board a flight to Italy for our next tournament, the Rome Masters. I am to get a flight with Borna around the middle of the following day.

At nine the next morning our transport to the airport is due and I'm standing in the foyer waiting for Borna so we can head there. There's no sign of him and he's not answering his phone.

At 9.15 I call Tin. 'He's not here. It's getting late.'

Then, just as I hang up, I see Borna emerge from the lifts and casually stroll across the foyer to the restaurant. *He's going for breakfast? What?* I think.

Confused, I storm across the hotel foyer to confront him.

'I slept in,' Borna says.

'Listen, we're going to be late for our flight. If you're not here in ten minutes, I'm leaving.'

He looks flustered, says he will grab his bag. We just make the flight.

Once we land at the airport in Rome Borna is constantly on his phone checking the score in Karolina's match while we are waiting for our luggage to arrive.

At this moment I want to fire him. But it's not that simple. He is Tin's brother, for one thing. But really the bottom line is that at this point of my life I can't cope with someone else leaving, and what are Tin and I going to do alone on the tennis tour? And I'm sad because I feel as though my friendship and working relationship with Borna have shattered. I would be okay if he'd said, 'I have a new girlfriend, I can no longer coach you.' But he is not so upfront. The secretive way they have started their relationship, the disappearing, the lack of communication – it's all unnerving me.

With the death threats against Tin, and Borna's behaviour doing my head in, I'm in no good state to play. I'm up against a local girl, Maria Elena Camerin, who's here on a wildcard. She's 78th in the world and I am playing like I don't even deserve a ranking. My concentration is not helped when I look at Borna and can see Karolina has turned up and is sitting just a couple of seats away from him. This all feels so weird and wrong. This is a workplace, not high school. With my mind a muddle of worry and mad thoughts I play pathetically. My serve is terrible. My shots are off. The racquet is still giving me grief. I played better when I was ten years old. I look up at Borna and feel nothing but rage. Inwardly I curse myself. *Why am I still letting him coach me? This is not a normal situation.*

The Italian crowd is delighted with Maria's rise through the match. The underdog is beating the star. I didn't know I could play as badly as I am. I'm shanking groundstrokes now. I may as well never have turned up.

After surrendering the first set, in the second I manage to pull a couple of points together and I get up – 4–1. But I relinquish my lead and soon Maria has four match points. With some heavy hitting I save them all and level it at 5–5. But after another awful service game I hand the lead back to Maria. She serves out the match, 7–5, 7–5.

Borna and I have a huge fight afterwards. He has little productive feedback about my game. His lack of interest in me is obvious.

In Paris for the French Open I decide it's time to try to try to clear the air. Karolina and I go for ice cream; my hope is she'll be upfront about what is happening between her and Borna. But Karolina doesn't say anything. And really I know I should be having this conversation with Borna.

My tennis nightmare continues at the French Open. I lose in the first round.

My mental breakdown is in full swing now and by the time we hit the grass court season in Birmingham, the atmosphere is so ugly between Borna and me, and I'm so bad mentally, that I look as though I'm tanking, though I'm certainly not. But every tournament I'm getting worse. In Birmingham I lose in the first round and the same in Eastbourne. Every match is a slide down further into some abyss. I am not practising as much. Borna continues to watch Karolina's matches and is nowhere to be found. I swing from sadness to anger to disappointment to a sinking sense of betrayal. *Everything is going against me*, I think. My thoughts wander back to the days when I was a junior. Days when it was normal to train five to six hours. Training in 40 degree heat. As a junior there was no one training as consistently and as intensely as I was. Today I'm a shadow of that, doing the bare minimum – about 30 minutes a day of hitting on court. I know the minimum is not enough, but I've lost my way. It's as though I'm frozen by trauma and disappointment, and I can't pick myself up, even with Tin by my side.

My tennis horror show continues at Wimbledon against Argentine teenager Gisela Dulko. I walk out and I know I am going to lose. I shank literally every ball. I start to think about digging a hole right here on court and climbing down it and disappearing. Up in the stands, I catch the eye of Lesley Bowrey – she always comes to Wimbledon. Seeing her, I feel even more ashamed of my performance. I wish I could turn back the clock; I wish she could be here with me now.

During the breaks in play I sit on my seat and start to shake. I can't control these tremors. I am on the edge of tears, embarrassed that the crowd is witnessing this. That I am not performing my best for them. I used to enjoy the Wimbledon atmosphere, the crowd. They like me. Now I am dishing up this crappy tennis I feel nothing but shame. I want to get off the court and go back to the hotel as soon as I can. I lose against Dulko 6–3, 6–3. The Wimbledon crowd claps and cheer Dulko for causing this upset. I feel like they're all staring at me and judging my terrible performance. I imagine them whispering, 'Can you believe this is what Jelena Dokic has become?'

To try to distract myself from my plummeting career Tin and I go sightseeing in London, but Big Ben, London Bridge and all London's other impressive historical buildings can't take my mind of my messy life.

After Wimbledon, Tin convinces me to take a break. We choose the Canary Islands for some peace and sunshine. For ten days we lie on the beach and I don't think about or care about tennis. I can't shake off my sadness, but we have a good time – he manages to get my mind off things for a little bit. But when we get back to Monaco and I see my racquet bag sitting in my apartment, my heart sinks. 'Fuck, no. I can't practise,' I tell Tin. I don't train for a week.

Since it's obvious I don't have the mental strength right now to confront Borna with my frustrations about his coaching, his inattention, his being caught up with Karolina rather than helping me, Tin has some words with his brother. 'Jelena needs to take a break; she needs to get off the tour.' He practically begs Borna to take the rest of the year off. Borna gets angry. 'You are stupid,' he tells his brother. 'You are not being rational. She needs to play.'

I am at a low, low ebb, even starting to think it would be better not to be alive. *Would that just be easier for everyone?* I ask myself. I am starting to have these thoughts more and more. I tell Tin I want to die. He knows the depths of my darkness. I tell him I feel like it is no use going on living.

Every day the threats come via phone calls and text messages. My father leaves half-hour-long voicemail messages. I can tell from the slur in his voice that he is drunk. He says the most vile and disgusting things that I can't even bring myself to repeat. His words pummel my soul. Tin sees my pain and decides to act like a human shield between my dad and me – he takes over listening to the messages so I don't have to endure them, and he deletes the hate-filled texts my father sends.

We go back to Zagreb and I train sporadically. Borna's parents again are really hospitable, always looking after us. They also have some concerns about Borna dating Karolina while he coaches me. They are supportive of Tin and me, as well as Borna, so it's a difficult situation for them, a tough balancing act. They always look out for me – not because I'm Jelena, but because they love me. They are wonderful parents to their boys.

I miss all of the US hard-court season because I can't face the tennis. The off-court turmoil has derailed me and I turn up to the US Open basically on a wing and prayer. I play okay against Frenchwoman Nathalie Dechy but I lose, and in a heartbreaking way – on a let. I go down 3–6, 6–0, 7–5. The next day my body is full of aches and pains – the lack of training has wreaked havoc with my fitness.

A few weeks later we go to Beijing and once more I am bundled out in the first round. I decide to finish the year there – enough is enough.

⊖

Borna bills me every few months and I pay him without going through the bill in detail because I trust him. It turns out my trust has been misplaced. When I get home and study some of his calculations, it dawns on me that for the last twelve months his pay has been significantly higher than we agreed – it has doubled, in fact. I confront him about it.

'Well, we have a contract. Remember? I gave it to you twelve months ago,' he says blithely. He goes and gets the piece of paper, the unsigned handwritten contract.

'I never signed this,' I say. And yet he's been charging me this amount for an entire year. I'm furious – for a start, he's been absent for some of the year.

I don't ask for the money back but I pay him the regular amount we originally agreed to from now.

17

The Darkness, 2005–6

The wind howls and whips my face but on the inside I don't feel a thing. I feel numb. My soul is at rock bottom. My spirit is almost dead. I have decided it is time to end my life. I'm done with the emotional turmoil and pain. I am of no use to this world, to Tin, to my family. I plan to jump from my balcony on the thirtieth floor of my Monaco apartment building.

I feel as though I have abandoned my little brother, even though I could never have taken an eleven-year-old with me on the tour, an unstable environment. I am questioning who I left him with. It breaks my heart that I can't even talk to him or hear his voice.

I close my eyes, imagine the fall. I don't fear it. I step to the edge, put my hands on the railing and think, *Death is the right thing, there will be peace. I am the cause of everyone's problems. If I die, all the grief I feel I am causing will disappear.*

But something stops me and I let go of the railing, I walk backwards off the balcony and click the door shut. Back inside my apartment I sit on the couch in a numb state for hours on end. Yet again.

A couple of times now I have walked out there and considered jumping. As my passion to play tennis has disappeared, more worryingly so has my passion for life. I am sleeping for eighteen hours at a time. When I'm awake I barely talk. I am close to catatonic. Not only have I thought about jumping off my balcony lately, sometimes I think the easiest way of ending things would be to shoot myself. I wonder how I would get my hands on a gun.

My suicidal thoughts highlight my need to find a solution to this terrible state of mind – this situation of not being able to fix my relationship with my family. I am a daughter who desperately wants a civil and loving bond with her parents. I feel I must still hold out hope. Somehow I want to bring my shattered family back together; I want us to be normal. And I desperately want to talk to Savo – I miss him terribly. I want to see if my father will change his mind and ways.

'I need to figure it out,' I tell Tin. 'I want to see if I can work something out. I'm going to go and see my father in Serbia.'

Tin looks crushed. 'You're going back to stay?'

'I have to figure something out. I can't go on like this. We can't go on like this. I will meet you back in Zagreb in a week.'

Deep down I think a trip to see Dad will probably be worthless.

Tin's forlorn. After the countless threats and abuse he's worried about my safety. But he knows seeing my father is something I need to do. He understands – as always, he gets me. Tin packs his bags and leaves for Zagreb and I head to Belgrade.

⊖

I don't tell my father I'm coming. I drive up the long, winding road to his five-acre ranch unannounced. With the millions of dollars I have earned from my tennis career he has built a sprawling palatial home 70 kilometres out of Belgrade in a village called Vrdnik. The house, which he says he helped to build, has six bedrooms, five bathrooms, a sauna, gym, billiard room, three garages and three terraces. There is also a pond, tennis court, a 40-metre wine cellar and stables. The grounds encompass forest and orchards.

I walk up the grand front steps and knock on the door. He answers, and it's like nothing has happened. Like the thousands of vile phone calls, the death threats, have never occurred. But my father doesn't like to discuss things, he never has. I am here, he welcomes me into the house, he doesn't hug me. It's as if I've just popped out to the shops to grab some bread and milk and now I'm back. I'm here and he seems fine with that.

Mum's happiness is evident. Her face is beaming.

We sit around and talk a little about nothing in particular.

My wisdom teeth have been bugging me and on the second day I have to go back into Belgrade to have them out. My mum and Savo have an apartment in the city, near my brother's school. I want to stay there with them after the procedure. I'm thrilled to see Savo – it's been a couple of years and he's really grown up. It's so sad to have missed that.

After I've had my teeth out I call up and tell my father we'll be back in few days.

'No, you are to come home,' he says. 'You have to come back here now.'

'But Dad, it doesn't make sense. It's just easier to stay in the city.'

'No, you are to come home,' he says, his voice growing louder. 'You need to be back.'

As usual everything is on his terms. My father's domineering control is evident within less than a day of my arrival.

I agree. I hang up the phone and turn to Mum. 'Here we go again.' I am so pissed off: we're back to the old days. He still doesn't get it. I am not even allowed to be in an apartment with my mother and brother away from him. It reminds me with a jolt of why I left.

I get back to the ranch swollen, numb, sore, spitting up blood, go to bed and sleep like a log on painkillers.

The next morning I wake up and my father tells me the media is coming in thirty minutes. The media circus. He hasn't even asked me if I would be willing to do any media. My face is swollen and bruised – I am really not up for this. Yet he has contacted every Serbian journalist he knows and in no time they are out on the terrace setting up their cameras and microphones. He wants to spread the message that I have come back to him. He steers me out to front them and throws his big arm over my shoulders. My face is sore and throbbing. Horrified and incredulous, I just want to hide away in my room.

The cameras and journalists are in my face and we pretend the four of us have been happily reunited. There are no hard feelings between us, I tell the press. Dad says the same. And, yes, we might start working together.

It feels all wrong – especially when my father and I haven't spoken about anything. Enrique, Borna, Tin – none of them have been raised. The death threats haven't been mentioned. So infuriating.

You think we are a happy family? I say to myself as the news is broadcast.

In the following days nothing changes. My father continues to refuse to talk about any of our issues. And it doesn't take me too long to work out that he assumes I am back because I think I have made a 'major mistake'; that I regret leaving. He is so wrong.

A week after the press conference I decide to leave again. This is not my home. I can't cope with my father's coldness, the fractured family we remain. But most of all I can't deal with him. I pack my small bag of things and go out to the lounge.

'I have to go to Monaco and do some business but I'll be back in a couple of days,' I tell him, nervous about what he could do if I tell him the truth, that I am leaving for Croatia to be with Tin.

Although he's not happy he doesn't try to stop me. 'Make sure you send me $200,000 tomorrow.'

'Fine,' I say. 'I will send it to you.'

Which I do.

He doesn't say goodbye as I leave the house. My mother and brother hug me and a friend of my parents takes me to the airport. As we drive down the long driveway I'm crying. The emotional pain hits me. The darkness creeps up again. I rest my head against the window and wonder, why can't we work it out?

The visit has actually made my emotional state worse. It makes me think that maybe nothing *can* be fixed between us. I've tried for my family. I know I can't do it on my own, but I feel so guilty not being able to make us work. I blame myself.

My former management company, Octagon, calls me when I am in Belgrade and about to fly to Tin in Zagreb. They're managing Karolina, and they have a concern.

'The situation is unclear,' the manager says to me. 'We're confused and we thought we should give you the heads up. We know Borna was your coach, but we don't know if he still is, because he is in Zurich with Karolina Sprem at a tournament. What's going on?'

I'm confused. I try to set things straight for the Octagon manager. 'No, no, no. Borna is my coach. He's her *boyfriend*,' I say.

The woman is silent on the phone for a few seconds. Then she says, 'But apparently Borna is her coach and ... he has been with her in Moscow and Zurich, and is going to Linz ...'

I hang up.

⊘

Reunited with Tin in Zagreb, I find I'm having trouble breathing sometimes. When I get this checked out, I'm told my septum is badly deviated and I need my tonsils out.

I undergo surgery in November 2004. I ask my mother to come – I really want her support, her care after the surgery. She thinks about it but decides no. I'm sure it's because my father won't allow it. Once again, it is wounding that she doesn't have the courage to make her own decisions, which she surely should when it comes to her kids.

The surgery takes several hours and the recovery is intense. My throat and nose are full of pain and my face is black and blue. Several days after the surgery, discharge is still coming out of my nose, I'm spitting up blood and can barely talk. One evening Borna arrives at our apartment. I assume he's here to check up on me. He sits on the dining room table. 'I think it would be better if I coached you both – you *and* Karolina,' he declares.

Is he for real? But when I look over his shoulder Tin is nodding too. He adds uneasily, 'It's the best thing for everyone. Have a think about it.'

'How can you suggest this?' I whisper, my swollen airways and face throbbing in pain. 'You are not going to coach two players while you're dating one of them.' We still haven't had a conversation about his relationship with Karolina. He won't talk about it, doesn't seem to think it's necessary.

I look to Tin. You know it's wrong. How can you even think I would go along with Borna's plan?'

Borna starts to backtrack. My reaction has worried him. He must know he has painted himself into a corner. For now I kick him out of the apartment, but still I don't sack him. Even though he is doing so much shit and is hardly around, Tin and I feel safer like this than alone. We're young, inexperienced and not ready to take on the tour as two 21-year-olds with meagre experience. We're holding out hope that Borna can try harder to be the coach, the leader, the big brother we need.

⊘

I can't shake my desire to return home – to my real home, Australia. After sitting on the matter for what already feels too long, I call up Paul McNamee, whom I know I can always trust. We have a long conversation and try to figure out if we can make this happen. But in the end my fear and memories from when I was last in Australia, being booed in the Rod Laver Arena, help me decide not to take it any further this year.

Borna is cranky. Ninety-nine per cent of the reason why is because he won't be spending five weeks in Australia with his girlfriend watching her play at the Open. These days he is distracted all the time. He's constantly on the phone to her or rushing off from my practice sessions to talk to her.

Tin confronts him about not being focused but he's unrepentant. 'I could have been – and should have been – at the Australian Open with her,' he says. Tin is mad at him but at the same time he is trying to handle the situation diplomatically.

At the end of January I head to Thailand with Borna – Tin remains home. In the second round I have to retire in the second set against Ukrainian Alyona Bondarenko with a hamstring strain, having lost the first in a tie breaker.

Then we head to Hyderabad in India, where I don't make it past the first round. I also lose in the second round of Indian Wells – I can't even manage to win a game in the second set.

We stay for a few more days in Indian Wells and the situation with Borna comes to a head. I have to get treatment from the physio and as I'm waiting for my appointment I see from the players' lounge that he is getting into my rental car – with Karolina. That means that I have to wait for a bus, not that I mind catching the bus, but I can't believe he's taken my car – the car that I'm paying for – without telling me and left me to make my own way back.

I call Tin in tears and we agree I'll return to his side in Zagreb and try to figure things out. But Borna informs me there are no seats on the flights out of Palm Springs back to Europe and we'll have to stay on for another four days. On the day we leave I discover that we could have made any of those earlier flights, but Borna wanted to stay around with Karolina a bit longer.

The day after we arrive in Zagreb he says he has to go to Germany for 'personal reasons'. Twenty-four hours later Octogon calls me and informs me he's in Miami with Karolina.

I call him. 'We're done,' I say.

$\odot$

So now it's just Tin and me on the tour, hoping for the best. Our first tournament as just the two of us is in Estoril, Portugal. We book all the accommodation, flights and arrange practice. Tin is doing everything he can to make my life run smoothly but the bottom line is he's not a qualified tennis coach. Still, he tries so hard to help me.

I am now ranked 450th in the world. It feels surreal that I was No. 4 only a few years ago. In the first round of the Portuguese clay court tournament I lose in three sets. It's my thirteenth loss from my past fifteen matches. In the press conference I speak openly and tell the media I need to completely overhaul my game. 'I need to start at the beginning, like I did when I was fourteen or fifteen,' I tell them. 'At this stage, I need match confidence.' I tell them there's a mountain of work to be done if I ever want to be a force again. At the moment I am up and down; I had my chances and I didn't take them – I beat myself today. I know at the end of the day that this is not about tennis, it is about off-court issues.

In my next tournament, in Morocco, I have to punch my way through qualifying to get into the main draw. I beat a Brazilian ranked 973, another ranked 199 and finally a player without a ranking; I push my way in – and make it to the round of sixteen by beating Slovakian player Dominika Cibulkova. I lose just before the quarters to the No. 1 seed, Chinese star Li Na, 6–0, 3–6, 6–2.

Tin and I are actually in a good place. We are solid as a couple. But my form on court remains flat, my confidence zapped and I simply don't know how to get either back. There must be a way to work it out. I mean, I am a person who was playing 30 tournaments a year, competing nine months of the year, training every single day. I spend hours ruminating on why it is all going wrong for me on the court. *Why am I so broken? Why can't I compete?* Sure, there are some wins here and there. But it's the talent I have that gets me to victory. If I were able to work as hard as I have in the past, I know I'd be doing a lot better, but, I conclude once more, I am not mentally fit to work to my full potential.

Little changes during the rest of the year: I lose in the first round in several ITF tournaments – in Prague, Fano and Cuneo in Italy, and in the third round of qualifying in Pétange, Luxembourg.

Around this time I have to meet with Borna to work out the money I owe him for our last few months of coaching. And something is not right. This time it's to do with 'miscellaneous' items on his bills, to the tune of tens of thousands of dollars. When I ask him for receipts he is unable to produce them.

'Like, what is "miscellaneous" for? Coffee?' I ask.

Borna starts to laugh, but he's flustered. He tries to brush it off but I'm not letting it go. 'You can't just bill me tens of thousands of dollars for miscellaneous items. For what? I don't understand.'

He can't explain a thing.

⊘

My mother has been reaching out to me. In August, at the Martina Franca tournament in Italy, Tin and I decide that she can come see us. She stays for the week and watches me bash my way through to the final sixteen. A great feat after getting through three rounds of qualies. Although this time she doesn't push so much for me to come home, she goes on and on about everything she's thinks is wrong in my life at the moment. Tin is extremely nice to her; he couldn't be more of a gentleman. He tries to explain to her that I'm emotionally broken. With me by his side, he says I need some support, and support from her would help a lot. Tin tells her that I'm very depressed and struggling.

As Tin talks my mother's expression is cold. She is defiant in her response. 'She was never mentally and emotionally broken when she was with me and my husband,' she says pointedly. She also says that my dad's being tough on me was 'normal'. 'He is her father,' she says. 'It is fine.'

When Tin again raises the subject of my depression, Mum repeats her answers: 'Well, with us she wasn't depressed. With us she was winning. With us she was so happy. She has become depressed since she has been with you.' We listen in shocked silence, blown away by her comments. With her, like it is with my father, it seems it's all about results and money. It's all about winning, not about my emotional welfare. It's about being with 'them'. Controlled by 'them'.

Instead of showing concern as a mother, she asks for more money. Since I left home she has constantly been making requests to me to send money to my father but I'm ignoring them now. I start to see it is stupid sending him money. I've given him millions over the last few years. The money I've made has paid for things like my father's ridiculously large ranch and his luxury cars. It's like burning money, giving it to him.

Anyway, the cash is no longer dropping into my bank account. I would be very well off financially if I hadn't given him everything; as it is, I have hardly anything for myself now.

Mum returns home after a week. Once again we are left bitterly disappointed by the lack of reconciliation and support.

Back in Monaco, my thoughts return to Australia. The pull home is constant and I decide it's the right time to call Paul again. I tell him I am ready. I want to come home to play at the 2006 Australian Open. He's really pleased and starts making plans for my return.

Although I might be ready, my body isn't. My weight is about 10 kilograms heavier than when I was at my best. I cut the sugar and the crap from my diet. I start to run. I start to train harder.

In December 2005 my plane hits the tarmac in Melbourne. I'm back in Australia a shadow of the player and person I used to be, still fragile, but determined to make things right in my homeland. With Tin by my side I ready myself and walk into the Arrivals hall to face a bunch of TV cameras and journalists who have a sense of what a moment this is. I smile nervously for them, offer polite hellos and tell them I will speak to them at Melbourne Park.

Paul has asked me to attend the training camp that is held at Melbourne Park before the wildcard play-off. It starts in a few days.

Today I'm elated yet fearful – worried about the public's reaction. Tennis Australia has organised a press conference, which they think I should do before the camp and my first practice session. When I arrive at Court No. 5, where the conference is to take place, I am incredibly nervous. Never have I seen so many journalists and photographers in my life. Their eyes are on me; they are silent. The only sound is of the distant trains rattling down the tracks to and from Flinders Street station. I am thinking, *Oh my God*. I know that turning my back on Australia was a grave mistake, but I am here to right my wrongs.

'I was seventeen at the time,' I explain. 'Even now, I don't know much about life – a little bit more than then, but that's why I came back. I want the people to understand what happened and hopefully I will get that message across. I felt Australian then, I still do, and I want to play for Australia again. I think I deserve that.

'I regret the way that I left. Hopefully [Australia] can understand me and what happened. I'm looking forward, not going back to what happened, and hopefully [people] can start to love and support me again like they did before.'

Then, for the first time in almost five years, I get on the Rebound Ace. It feels so good to hit a ball back on Australian soil. Relief washes over me.

The media attention I receive at the Australian Open play-off is the equivalent of what I've experienced in the past at a grand slam. Reporters are everywhere, filming me at practice, in matches, after matches. A huge number of people have turned up to watch me try to revive my waning career. They cram in around the small courts where the play-off matches are taking place. Even though my ranking has plummeted, there's an expectation I should be winning these early matches even if they're against girls ranked higher than me. So pressure is huge, *but* everything feels right. Coming back has been exactly the right thing to do. Tin and I are so happy to be here.

Lesley Bowrey has agreed to be back by my side – to coach me and be there for moral support. She's more than happy to help me in training and at matches. And that's a good thing, because over the week, if I'm to win a spot in the main draw, I have to play double the amount of matches I have this year. It's a daunting prospect but I set to work. I have a new hitting partner, Duje Kuvačić. He's from Melbourne and has a Croatian background; Paul McNamee suggested him and he's great. We soon become friends, and he and Tin get along well. He is very supportive and comes with me to my play-off matches.

I defeat the local girls easily. Actually there's nothing exceptional about my tennis but anyway I make it to the final, where I beat Monique Adamczak in three sets. I have proved my worth and attained a wildcard into the Australian Open. Paul hugs me after the victory. His faith and confidence in me have been rewarded; it's his victory as much as mine. Geoff Pollard also congratulates me.

The Australian tennis fans' support for me appears to be strong. A group cheers loudly for me in Auckland, my first WTA tour match since last May. Lesley isn't able to make the tournaments before the 2006 Australian Open so we have parted ways. It's been fantastic having her back by my side, but it's not the same as it was years ago – this is a different situation from when we worked together when I was kid.

I face world No. 81, German player Julia Schruff, in Auckland, with the letters AUS after my name. I win the first set 7–5. But the same old problems rear their head in the second. It's 6–5 as I serve for the match. Victory is close. But my nerve goes. My serve lets me down. I swear at myself, openly annoyed and tell myself off. All of a sudden Julia and I are in a tie breaker and I lose it, 7–3.

I lose the third set in just 20 minutes – 6–1. My cheeks are bathed in hot tears, my fragility on show.

To make things worse, some bitterness from Australian tennis players trickles out in the press. A week or so before the Open, I pick up the paper and sigh deeply. 'Angry Stubbs depicts Dokic as abused and abusing,' reads the headline. The journalist has interviewed Rennae Stubbs. My former doubles partner says she saw the bruises on my body and knew of the physical abuse I was suffering. In her view I need to be on my 'best behaviour' at the Open. Although she claims to support my attempt to get my career back on track, she adds, 'All those people who put so much time and effort into her, she'd better not let them down again. If Jelena doesn't want anybody to think, "You've just come back here for the money," then she'd better show it, and she'd better not go running off when things don't go so good. She has to grow up a lot and put her best foot forward, and I don't think that's going to be easy for her.'

I'm really disappointed. What Rennae and many others don't realise is that I have not been offered a cent and nor do I want money. All I want to do is play tennis for Australia. I don't have any financial motivation.

Tin tells me to let it go, but it bothers me; I can't help it. 'I think it's hard for people to grasp that I just want to be back here and play for Australia,' I tell him. 'It's easier for them to think I am here for the money and not for the country.'

Rennae, who witnessed a tiny part of the terrible pain I went through in Canada, can't seem to find any understanding for my situation. She has admitted to seeing the bruises. She has admitted to knowing about me being physically abused. *Is money or your personal view on it more important than someone's wellbeing? You saw the effects of physical and emotional abuse on me when I was a kid – but here you are discussing funding issues?*

The article reawakens painful memories – of being left out on team tours, teased on the bus, having things thrown at me, being told I couldn't sit next to my compatriots, couldn't go and hang out with them in their rooms, told to 'go back where I came from'.

I throw away the newspaper. Tin reminds me there are those at Tennis Australia who are supportive of me, that the Australian public supports me too. Paul McNamee is on our side, always kind and accommodating. As usual Tin encourages me to focus on the positives.

⊖

It wouldn't be an Australian Open without my father making himself the screaming headline of the slam. This year he does from his Serbian ranch. On the eve of the tournament he tells the *Daily Telegraph* that I paid him nearly US$1 million last year. My father dubs it a 'divorce-style settlement'. He adds, 'She didn't call at Christmas or New Year. We want her to call. She can't go on like this.'

The report doesn't bother me so much. It's the truth, although I have signed far more than that over to him. As for him wanting me to call? I really don't think he does. He wants me back to control me; and he wants his ATM back.

It's five years since I've played in the Australian Open, six since I've had an (AUS) beside my name. Yet when I wake up on the first day of the tournament, I find I'm not nervous. As 349th in the world I simply want to put up a decent fight against Frenchwoman Virginie Razzano, who's 54th. It's going to be tough. I walk out onto Margaret Court Arena and the crowd roars; it's incredibly loud, the place is vibrating with support for me. *They are on my side, they are really on my side*, I think. It's a dream-like reception. I look up to the stands and take in the green and gold. 'Aussie, Aussie, Aussie,' goes the chant. They are waving flags and banners in support. I am back and it feels like I never left. I never would have imagined the crowd would be so supportive. I am so grateful.

I win the first set 6–3. We go to a tie breaker in the second and I have two match points. I lose the first match point. But the second match point is contentious. It rests on a line call. I think the ball, my shot, went in. But no, it is called out. The crowd starts booing at the call and for me everything goes downhill from here – I start to lose my mind. Razzano takes the match 3–6, 7–6 (8–6), 6–1.

After the loss I break down in the hallways underneath Rod Laver Arena. Tin holds me as I cry. I was so close. I am gutted about losing, but I couldn't be happier about the reception I received. In fact, afterwards I even wonder if perhaps the match goes down as a highlight of my career because it showed me people understood that leaving all those years ago wasn't my decision and they wanted to support me.

Borna appears in the hallway. He's here in Australia as Karolina's boyfriend and coach. He approaches me to offer his commiserations. 'I'm sorry you lost,' he says.

I look up. Red-eyed.

'Get lost,' I say. I don't want to speak to him. *Where were your apologies when you weren't around for Tin and me? You should apologise for that. Not for the match.*

I stay on for the doubles and my father shows up in the press again. The next day at breakfast I see his face splattered on the front page of the newspaper. The Australian media have picked up a Serbian report in which he says he wants to kidnap me, and has threatened to kill an Australian as revenge for me returning here. He adds that he wants to drop a nuclear bomb on Australia, and he accuses Croatia *and* the Vatican of influencing my decision to quit Serbia and return to Australia. It's a step above his usual level of crazy, and when I read it I actually can't breathe, I'm so horrified.

I look around the breakfast room. *Are people looking at me?* I wonder. *Oh, there she is, the girl with the deranged dad.* I head back to my room to hide. The embarrassment crushes me and what's as bad is the hopelessness I feel. There's nothing I can do but get angry. Angry that he has set my relationship with the Australian media on a rocky path again; angry that even without him in my daily life I still can't shrug 'the daughter of the controversial father' tag; angry that he so determinedly refuses to give up his 'crazy father' role.

I cancel practice and barely move from my hotel bed all day. Later, I put out a statement. 'This has proven to be yet another unfortunate distraction around my return to Australia and competitive tennis. I have spent my life recovering from events such as this.'

I sometimes wonder if I will ever recover.

18

The Struggle, 2006–8

I return to Zagreb with Tin and within days the darkness starts eating at my soul again. My resurgence of form, the weight loss, they're obliterated by the misery washing over me once more. And I just can't be bothered hitting a tennis ball. When I try to train, I give up a few minutes into a session. Soon I can't even look at my racquets. Within days I don't have any energy to get up. Instead I lie in bed with tears drenching my pillow. I cry until I have no tears, then I do nothing but stare into space. I will myself to sleep so I can get away from my reality for a few hours. Tin tries to coax me out of bed and into the day but I can't budge.

During these hard times, he's my rock and companion, stoic through them all. He tries to find solutions as I am overcome by misery, and he wipes my tears away. He comforts me, and he's always there for me.

Some days I sit in a darkened room watching television, and I turn to food. I start eating sugary snacks, chocolate bars, lollies, whatever will make me feel better for a few minutes. Within weeks I am out of shape again and my athlete's body disappears. The pain of losing my family is terrorising my thoughts again every day. And this pain is compounded when I call home to speak with Savo. My father answers.

'Hi Dad, I would like to speak to Savo,' I say.

'No,' and he hangs up the phone. I try again but he won't let me talk to my brother.

I know he thinks by denying me a relationship with my little brother, he will force me back. He wants to ram it home that I might be able to play tennis without him but I can't live without my family. It's a ploy aimed at hurting me. And it does. The pain of not having spoken to my brother properly in years is tearing at me. I long to ask him, 'What have you been up to? How's school? Who are your friends? What do you do with them?' I haven't seen him grow up in the last few years.

The suicidal thoughts begin again. They're in my head every day. About how I'm going to do it. Of course, I have stood on a balcony and considered jumping. Again I think the quickest and easiest way would be to get my hands on a gun.

In these despairing, lowest moments, the only people stopping me are Tin and Savo. I couldn't do it to Tin, and as for Savo – I have always promised myself to try my best to look after my brother. So I think of these two and I am sure there's got to be a way out of this misery. I have reasons to stay in this world. There are bigger things to do, not for myself, but for them.

All this time, when I'm not practising and when I'm fighting myself to stay alive, I don't even think about quitting tennis, because, really, it's the only thing I know and, to be honest, although I don't want to play now, it's partly keeping me alive. Still, I have no coach.

A couple of months into my relapse into depression Tin manages with his kindness to encourage me to play again. He convinces me we should try to play some ITF tournaments in April. Zagreb doesn't have the tennis facilities we need so we decide to head back to Saddlebrook. Not to the house that I gave to my dad – we stay in the resort. And there we attempt to resurrect the remnants of my wayward career.

I train with whoever's around and do plenty of fitness work. I hit a lot with the best hitting partner in Saddlebrook. A couple of days into our stay, Borna and Karolina arrive. The situation is awkward and weird, especially when Borna approaches the tennis manager at the resort and says he needs my current hitting partner for her.

'He's booked up now and is with Jelena most days,' the manager says.

'I don't care about Jelena,' Borna retorts.

I overheard this entire conversation, not that I confront him about it – I just don't have the energy. It's hard to hear these words from someone who I once considered to be a true friend.

Next thing, my fitness trainer tells me that Borna has asked him if he'll work with Karolina. My trainer said he could but she would have to work around my schedule a little bit. According to my trainer, Borner says, 'I don't give a shit about Jelena and her schedule.'

When did this become so ugly? It's so hurtful.

After the training block in Saddlebrook we're off to Europe, where I take my place among the journeywomen, the fighters, the juniors, at the Open de Biarritz. There's no glamour playing in some of these ITF tournaments. There are no courtesy cars, no all-day buffets, beauty salons, free massages or physio, as there are at the majors and big tournaments. The prize money is paltry – you get just over US$50 for turning up. It's a tough atmosphere. It's a slog.

My first opponent is an Italian girl ranked 678th in the world. She's never won a match, and in four years I have fallen from world No. 4 to 446. Really I should win if I were blindfolded.

I lose.

My game is ugly. My serve is awful. *This is a fucking disaster*, I think to myself. My Italian opponent beats me 7–5, 7–5. It's such a bad performance that I feel at this stage I don't even know how to play tennis. Everything is wrong.

The only thing that has really stayed strong is my relationship with Tin. But he can't compensate for me not being able to talk to my brother or the terrible relationship I have with my parents. I am missing things no one could give me. At this point, nothing is going to change those feelings and problems in my head. It's plain and simple – I am sad. Depression has hit me hard. I realise I need to deal with these issues if I am to live a normal life. And I'm not trying to get better to play tennis well again. I just want my mental health to be right. This is not about tennis anymore. This is a question of being able to live a normal life.

At the moment, I wake up every day feeling an enormous weight on my shoulders. On top of depression I have developed crippling anxiety. I am having panic attacks when my heart rate goes up, I get short of breath, I feel hot. It can happen anytime, anywhere, sometimes in crowded places; indeed, I start to feel uncomfortable in front of crowds, which obviously makes it difficult when I am playing at tournaments. When I have this anxiety, my thoughts go out of control and I imagine awful scenarios. I catastrophise – I picture scenes where I am dying, say, in a car accident, or a plane crash. I've developed a fear of flying, something I used to love. The depression is the worst, though. I feel like there is no way out of what seems a never-ending sadness. As much as I want to I just don't have the will to live.

On top of this I'm dealing with a sizeable financial burden. As this financial year draws to a close, I'm left with a tax bill that adds up to a couple of million dollars. Even though I have barely seen a cent of my money, the authorities are asking me to pay tax on it. My money has always gone to my dad, yet I have to shoulder the responsibility for the taxes on it. And the issue is turning into a battle as I literally can't pay the bill. So I am also spending hundreds of thousands of dollars on lawyers.

In the meantime Tin and I amp up the search for a coach, and a few weeks after my crushing loss I am introduced to a local coach in Zagreb. He's an upbeat guy. He agrees to coach me for a few weeks in Zagreb before I try to qualify for Wimbledon.

I fail to qualify, losing to Alexandra Stevenson in three sets. Actually, in my bad form, with zero confidence, I am buoyed by the fact I'm still able to play a three-set match. A few weeks later the coach and I travel to Darmstadt in Germany for an ITF tournament. I start strongly and qualify for the tournament with three gutsy victories. The coach and I take heart from my renewed fight, and then I win my first-round match. Could it come together now?

After the match the coach praises me, then he breaks some difficult news. 'I have to go home right now – I have personal problems,' he tells me.

Within a few hours, he has packed his bags and off he goes back to Zagreb. I am alone again, and I'm terrible when I'm alone, on and off the court. I am sad this happened. I win the second-round match 6–4, 6–4, but by the quarter-finals I'm a mess. Anxiety and depression fill my head. I feel like I am losing my mind in my hotel room by myself. By the time I get on the court for my quarter-final match I'm in no state to play and although I fight hard in the first set, in the second set I lose all my concentration.

For three months I don't touch a racquet. Then someone tells me about Nikola Pilic Tennis Academy in Germany. Tin encourages me to do a stint there, so I go over in late October and work with an Austrian coach, making strong progress. I work harder than I have all year. Three weeks into the tough stint, the coach suggests I go and play an ITF tournament in Germany.

'It's too soon,' I say. 'I haven't played for three months, and I've only trained for three weeks.'

The coach points out that if I lose the first-round, it doesn't matter. Why not play qualies. Get some match practice.

I decide to go. I decide to put myself out there.

⊘

I have become *that* player on the tour. The one who everyone thought could have been a grand slam champion. A promising athlete who is lost and burnt out. The player with the tennis father from hell, whose career fell apart. Lowly ranked players now get a buzz out of beating me on the back courts of small cities and towns.

Anyway, the coach and I go to the ITF tournament in Ismaning in Germany, where I make it to the semis from qualifying. I receive a small pay cheque.

After my mild success in Germany the Pilic academy offers me a contract to train there. But when I read the fine print I see that every training week will cost a few thousand euros and the academy will take 40 per cent of my prize money and of any sponsorships. It also stipulates I must pay all my expenses, as well as coaching expenses if a coach travels with me. My immediate reaction is not to sign it, but first I try to negotiate – I tell them I can pay when I am here and when the coaches come with me to tournaments. We don't reach a deal – they're asking for too much money.

By the end of the year I am ranked 621. I have become, basically, a tennis nobody. I now doubt I will ever be good again. I sit in my darkened bedroom in Zagreb and once more think it would be easier to give up on being alive. The suicidal thoughts return. I start sleeping sixteen hours a day and once again I am profoundly depressed. When I'm in this state I feel like there is no way out. To make matters worse, I'm bankrupt. There's no cash flow. The tiny pay cheques from my ITF tournament appearances don't make a dent in my debt.

I have no management, no coach, no parents, and no money. No brother to talk to or see; this stings me the most.

Tin says it's time to let tennis go. 'We need to get you well enough again so that you can end up living a normal life. Forget about tennis and competing for a while. If you continue like this you won't live for much longer.' I can see he is really concerned about my wellbeing.

There follows a very quiet time for us. We hardly ever socialise. He understands that all I want is to be by myself, just being. He coaxes me to the coast for a short visit a few times but mostly I prefer to be in our apartment, quiet.

More weight creeps on my frame but the silence, the solitude, the days filled with nothing start to heal me. Then a phone call from my brother lifts my spirits. Now he's no longer a child, the truth of why I left our family is, perhaps, starting to dawn on him.

He tells me that, incredibly, my mother has split with my father, and she is living with Savo in Belgrade at present. My father kicked her out of the Serbian ranch. I'm sure it's because he's never forgiven her for me leaving; he blames everyone else for bad things happening. It's never his fault.

Despite this development, my mother and I haven't reconciled. When we speak she never shows remorse for her harsh ways over recent years. A few months after moving to Belgrade she returns to Australia – back to an apartment in Fairfield and away from Savo.

With these changes in my family set-up and an opening of the lines of communication with Savo, my passion to play tennis returns. Tin and I decide to do a long training block in Australia leading into the 2007 wildcard play-offs for the Australian Open. I train hard for two months at Melbourne Park, feeling better and better on the court. The weight starts to drop off. My mind is sharper. I am 24 years old and I will try to take on the tour again.

I decide to compete in the play-offs for an Australian Open wildcard. In December I give an interview to the *Sun-Herald* and tell them that I'd like to think I could be somewhere in the top 50 by the end of 2008. That I know it's a goal I can attain. But I know it is going to be tough.

I win three matches in the play-offs to get to the quarter-finals and then I'm felled by an injury: my hamstring goes in the second set against seventeen-year-old Olivia Rogowska. I have to retire at 6–3, 3–1. Fortunately there are a few weeks until my first tournament at Hobart and I train hard at Melbourne Park.

Not everyone at Tennis Australia welcomes me back with open arms. We're standing around after another torturous, hot training session at Melbourne Park when a coach tells me about a conversation he was privy to between some Tennis Australia coaches. Apparently one of them said that if he'd been making the decision, he wouldn't even have let me come back to Australia, let alone play for wildcards. He says he wouldn't allow me any chances at all.

The news shocks me and the people close to me, who find the coach's words confronting.

'It's pretty brutal,' says the coach. 'Why are they like this?'

The coach's words remind me of the time my father said to me, 'They don't accept you and they never will.' For a moment, I think coming back here perhaps wasn't such a good idea.

But there are also some good people on my side. People like Tennis Australia's Craig Tiley, who wants to help me out. He helps me try to find some quality people I can work with. He gives me some advice. Darren Pearce is incredibly nice, too.

I start working with coach Chris Johnson in Hobart before the tournament there and we get on well. He's a lovely, understated guy.

I know the work is paying off when I slay my opponents in three rounds of qualifying for the Hobart International. In the first round I face world No. 54 Martina Mueller. I win the first set but then I lose the second. I am down in the third set but I keep fighting and I manage to turn the match around. Where recently I have been falling apart in the crunch moments, here I pull myself back up and manage to win in the final set, beating her 6–4, 0–6, 6–2.

This is a major win for me – psychologically as well as on the circuit. It proves to me that some of my mental strength has returned; that I am fitter in all ways.

Next up in Hobart is world No. 39 Italian Flavia Pennetta. This march won't be easy and unfortunately an ankle injury, one which I sustained in qualifying, stops me in my tracks. At 0-5 I have to withdraw from the tournament.

In the qualies at the Australian Open, with the hot wind whipping through Melbourne Park's back courts, calls of 'C'mon, Jelena' echo through the grounds. I've won through the first round of qualifying but I don't manage to get past the second round. Still, I have worked hard, won some really good matches in the past few weeks. Are there grounds for me to have been given a main-draw wildcard? Absolutely. Feeling emotional and disappointed that I wasn't given one, I tell the press, 'The issue is who they [TA] gave it to. They didn't even wait to see how I would play in Hobart. The wildcards were announced after the first day of qualifying in Hobart, so I was disappointed they didn't even take me into consideration.

'I definitely think I deserved a wildcard into the main draw, I think I've done more in one week and had more big wins in one week than some of those girls have in their whole careers.'

In my mind, there is a greater issue at play – something that has always plagued me. *Here I am again*, I think. *I am always on the outer*.

Doubts float around in my mind. The words of the Australian coach saying I shouldn't even be allowed back in the country echo over and over. I know there are members in the Tennis Australia hierarchy, selectors, who don't want me in the country, let alone at Melbourne Park. Missing out on a wildcard, I don't think it has to do with my form. There are some forces always moving against me. Not everyone has my back. This is not about money. I am not getting funding anyway, though everyone seems to think I am. No, that couldn't be further from the truth that I am getting funding. I am not being financially supported by Tennis Australia. Even if I were offered financial help, I would not take it. All I want is fairness and to be given a chance on the court. A chance to compete. I just want to play. I am fortunate, though, that I can use the Tennis Australia courts, facilities and coaches if they have the time for me. Bernie Goerlitz and Chris Mahony help me out on court whenever they can.

This situation is reiterated a few years later, when I am again passed over for a wildcard at one of the grand slams, having won a whole lot of matches, including three ITF tournaments in a row in the lead-up to the grand slam. A player confirms to me in a private conversation that she knew she was getting a wildcard months out from the event. This is even though the decision is not supposed to be made until much nearer the tournaments, and players are supposed to demonstrate their form in the weeks leading up to them.

At any rate this time it feels like nothing can dampen my spirit or fight because I have played some of my strongest tennis in ages, and I'm in the best shape I've been in for a while. The darkness is lifting and I'm starting to realise that while I've had some tough situations and life hasn't been easy, I am still very fortunate that I am healthy, and the two people I love – Savo and Tin – are healthy. Everything else can be worked out.

All this adds up to a switch being flicked inside me. My fight is back. But I'm still struggling financially. I'm forced to sell my apartment in Zagreb right after the Australian Open to finance my career, which I'm more determined than ever to kick-start. The money I get from the apartment pays for airfares, hotels, food, coaching expenses and salary.

Back in Zagreb, Tin and I meet up with Borna, and despite our history I soften and decide to give him another chance. Because of my terrible finances, I can't afford a big-name coach. Tin encourages me to give Borna a go. Again. The truth is I am utterly desperate for a coach and he is here, available. So he walks back into my life.

Even though we haven't spoken in ages I manage, after much effort, to reach Savo via phone. I invite him to come to Fes, Morocco, to be with me at the tournament. He's due to arrive around midnight and I have arranged for transportation to bring him to the hotel because I have to play the next day. I wait for him but I fall asleep. When I wake up and look at the clock it is 12.30 – and then I notice Savo sitting on the bed next to me in the shadowy light. 'I didn't want to wake you,' he says shyly.

I'm over the moon to see him, and hug him with all my might. It's the best thing to have my baby brother here, though also I'm a bit nervous. It's been years since we spent much time together – in fact, we've never spent time together alone as adults. Still, his presence gives me a great boost. We don't talk about our father, our parents' separation. What we try to do is simply reconnect our relationship without bringing their destructive force back into it. Tin is still in Zagreb but Savo gets along well with Borna. And I'm very attentive, constantly checking my brother is okay. I just want him to be happy here and I'm worried about whether he will accept me, whether my father's opinions have created the wrong picture of me.

After I'm done with the tournament – I win through three rounds of qualifying but fall in the first round – Savo leaves us and heads back to Belgrade. It's been a fantastic week. For the first time in years, I feel like we've moved forward and got some of our closeness back; it's a relief.

⊘

As the year progresses, I'm winning at tournaments but my serve has become shambolic. I struggle with my ball toss; I can't figure out how to get my motion right. Even in my winning performances I'm serving like a beginner; I am just trying to put the serve in, taking a lot of pace off it just so I can start the point. In Darmstadt I'm so flustered I consider serving underarm at one point.

The serve is the most complicated shot ever and Borna, unsurprisingly, has no idea how to fix it. I hit fifteen double faults in one match although miraculously I still manage to win. I am playing three-set matches purely because of my dreadful serve. By the second half of the year my double fault count goes through the roof. I'm doing 25 to 30 a match. Everything I'm doing is wrong: how my feet are set up, my ball toss. My motion is all wrong. My left arm is going all over the place. Even my service grip is wrong.

I decide I need to make a radical change. Since Borna won't try to fix it I turn to a tried-and-tested fallback: YouTube.

I pore over YouTube videos of 'Serena Williams' serve' and study the method of the woman with the best service game in the world. I replay slow-motion videos of her serve. It's hard to see exactly what she's doing with her grip but I figure out it's quite similar to mine. Then I look at her feet. Her motion. Her ball toss. I copy her serve as closely as I can. I memorise her movements and then I practise them straightaway on the court.

I win three ITF titles on the clay in Europe combined with a couple of quarter-final appearances. Savo continues to travel with us more and our relationship is getting stronger. It is making me happy that we are developing a bond again without any other influences. My coaching situation with Borna is not good. Tension is growing between us again. We decide to do the off-season in Germany. I end up taking over my preparation and dictating the drills and schedule. But anyhow the confidence I have gained this year, the ITF titles, my ranking is up to 178 with only nine tournaments behind me, mean I am feeling better.

By the time I arrive in Australia in December 2008, my confidence has risen and my faith in my own decision-making is the strongest it's been in years. And I'm fit. I've managed to shed nearly 20 kilograms. That said, I lose in the round robin of the wildcard play-offs. Two years ago that would have thrown me into a spin and I probably wouldn't have been able to mentally regroup. But now I win the rest of the matches in my group as well as the quarters, the semis and I make it to the final.

The day of the final it's stinking hot, all dry heat and baking winds. I am taking on the player who beat me in the round robin and we are burning up on the Melbourne Park court, both sweating like crazy, trying our best to keep hydrated in the brutal temperatures. I stay resolute, despite the conditions, and manage to defeat her 6–7 (3), 7–5, 6–3. The wildcard is mine! I am extremely relieved and happy.

While my tennis is improving, my relationship with Borna is not. It all comes to a head once again a couple of days before we go to Brisbane, where I have also been awarded a wildcard. At a practice session at Melbourne Park he has me hitting straight down the middle of the court. There's no purpose in doing this drill, no goal in practising like this. He does this every day. Unless I push to do certain drills, and practise my serve (which he doesn't think is necessary), we don't do anything that makes me a better player. Today I've had enough. 'Say something, Borna. Communicate to me properly!' I urge him.

He responds with a blank face.

'You're not saying anything, you're not fixing anything; you're just standing on the court and not talking. You have no idea what you are doing. You are not even booking practice. I'm doing it all. It's been like this for months.'

Still he stands there expressionless and wordless.

'Get out,' I tell him. 'Leave the court now. I am going to do it myself. I am going to continue my session with my hitting partner.'

He won't budge. He still doesn't say anything. He remains on the court in silence for several minutes.

'Leave, Borna,' I say. I stand one metre away from him and feel my grip tightening with frustration around my racquet. I'm so angry I smash the racquet into the ground until it crumples and bends. After that one is messed up I chuck it away, go and get another from my tennis bag and hack it into the blue court surface. Then I find my third racquet and smash that into the ground. I grab my fourth spare racquet and break it. Finally, I crack the fifth one into the ground and break it, too.

Even on my worst days a few years ago I would have never done anything like this. With my realisation that he is useless, my anger is growing more and more every day. This has been going on for too long. After breaking all the racquets, I sit on the chair, pissed off and upset. Borna is making me nervous and tense; I am unhappy with him around – especially on the court; and I know that my tennis is suffering. Every time he is not as involved in practice, I am much happier.

We are on the phone to my racquet sponsor over the Christmas and New Year break trying to get new racquets. I call them and I fib, saying my racquets have been stolen. They are sympathetic and say they will try to get some shipped in. Because of the summer holidays in Australia nothing is happening quickly. But my racquet company manages to get me a few racquets for the Brisbane International.

By the time we get to Brisbane, Tin is trying to smooth Borna's and my working relationship by telling his brother he must start offering up feedback; that it is troublesome for me when he's so passive.

Going into the first-round match to play top 20 player Amelie Mauresmo I am nervous. It is a high-level match. In the end, I lose a quality two-set tie breaker to her. The loss tells me everything. The way I have had to structure my practice sessions, alone, shows me that I am doing the right thing.

Now I just need to get the consistency over the next twelve months.

19

Australian Open, 2009

The passionate crowd's cheers boom in my ears when I walk into Hisense Arena in the first round of the 2009 Australian Open. My stomach churns, my hands are shaking. The adrenalin is firing. I haven't played on a big court like this for a while and I'm extremely nervous, but I have a little confidence because of my recent form. I'm not thinking about winning. I'm not thinking about my chances. All I want is to play well, to give 100 per cent.

First I am up against Austrian player Tamira Paszek. Her No. 80 ranking belies her ability – she's a tough competitor. I have never played her before, but I know she runs well and gets a lot of balls back. I take the first set easily but she comes back at me like a freight train to win the second. It's clear the match could go either way and my nerves start to kick in. I start to have doubts, and do everything I can to shove them to the side.

I manage to get a break in the third. That's great, of course, but also makes me incredibly nervous because I feel I could now win this match. Soon I have a match point. We play a long rally until I hit a forehand cross-court winner, a shot I don't mean to hit so close to the line, but it is in.

Elation.

I climb into a golf cart to make my way back to the locker rooms, then to the press centre, where I reflect that whoever wins this tournament cannot be as happy as I am now. I can't believe I have won the first round of a grand slam. In my heart, it's just as if I have *won* a grand slam – that's how huge this feels. It's been some years since I have won a WTA match.

The media scramble to talk to me. For the first time, I open up, but there is only so much I can explain. *If only they knew*, I think to myself. If only they knew of this hellish journey I have been on. I choke up when I'm asked what the win means to me and tell them it's a miracle I'm here.

The tears are also because of my coaching situation. If only the press knew the fights I'm having daily with Borna and how I feel all but alone, coaching-wise, at this tournament.

A wave of support grows for me following this victory. I am almost mobbed at practice sessions; wherever I go people assure me they are behind me. It feels like everyone I meet wants to tell me they are on my side.

My second-round match is scheduled on Rod Laver Arena. I haven't played there in eight years – it was back when my father was wreaking havoc. And of course the last time I was in the arena I was booed. It is exciting but I am also feeling incredibly nervous to be here on Rod Laver Arena. I am having flashbacks to that 2001 Australian Open; of people jeering and the horrible situation orchestrated by my father when he made me switch nationalities. Regardless of the result, I want to enjoy the atmosphere, the crowd, because I know this time it will be a vastly different experience.

Tickets for the match sell out when it's announced I will play the No. 17 seed Anna Chakvetadze. The fans squeeze in to the garden square outside the stadium to watch me try to bring down the talented Russian. Once again, my nerves are running high before this match – even more so than in the first round. I stand in the archway ready to walk out onto Rod Laver, taking a peek outside shortly before I'm called. It's jam-packed out there and the sight lifts me. Then I hear the stadium announcer, his rich voice stretching out the syllables of my name. 'From Australia, Jelena Dokic'. A roar rips through the stadium. I've never had a reception like this – and what a big contrast to when I was last here. No matter what happens tonight, I've won already.

I give the fans what they want – a tense and entertaining battle against the Russian, which to my joy, and the crowd's, I win, 6–4, 6–7 (4), 6–3.

This is big. I throw my fist in the air in victory. Borna and Tin embrace in the stands. I shake Anna's hand and then, in tears, raise my arm to acknowledge the crowd. My voice wavers as I thank them for supporting me – this level of support has been beyond anything I could have hoped for. To be honest, as happy as I am – to be in the third round, to win again on Rod Laver Arena – what has moved me the most is the incredible support I have received from the fans tonight. The crowd was absolutely amazing.

Mentally, I feel stronger by the minute. When I face Caroline Wozniacki, seeded 11, I feel nervous but confident. Caroline is on the verge of breaking into the top ten, has had a fantastic year and is the most consistent player I have faced this slam. But I walk into the match feeling no pressure. I am positive.

I have six break points in the first set and convert none of them – she comes out all guns blazing and outplays me. By the end of the first set, even though she wins it, rather than feeling down and negative, I know I can make an impact in the second set. I get straight into it and am able to hold my serve and stick there with her, get a break and that is it – it feels as though the match has turned. I am playing really good, smart tennis and I think I'm the better player on the court at this stage. Perhaps this helps me to break and get on top of her in the third. I am aggressive and serving well. All the way through the third set, my elation on the court is obvious. I shout, 'C'mons' at Tin. Excitement is pumping through my veins. I can feel victory is close. Caroline is playing better but she can't keep up with me as I get stronger and stronger.

After a long rally there's a forced error from her and the match is mine. Everyone else appears stunned. I've won, 3–6, 6–1, 6–2. *I* am shocked. The Rod Laver Arena crowd roars, screams and cheers. The atmosphere is electric. I am heaving with emotion and so are they. It's the crowd, the sound of the crowd, that lifts my spirits more even than the fact I've got through to the fourth round of the Australian Open.

Beating someone like Caroline, who has been a really strong player over the last couple of seasons, is a massive win. Again I feel incredibly emotional as I thank the crowd. And then I apologise to Tennis Australia, for, I say, 'being a pain'. I've already apologised to Craig Tiley for my outburst about not getting a wildcard over a year ago. And now it seems important that I say sorry publicly to him and Tennis Australia. Of course I know that several people in Tennis Australia didn't support my return, they've made that clear behind the scenes. And, yes, I was hurt by that. But I remain incredibly appreciative of what TA has done for me, so I want to acknowledge this on such a special night.

The press starts to write about my team and my career resurrection. They mention the people behind me, and put Borna and Tin down as the reason for my successful comeback. Certainly I owe everything to Tin for getting me here. But not Borna; neither do I mention him publicly as the reason I am doing well. Yet as the press don't know the truth, they assume he's also helped me resurrect my career.

My next match is against a Russian girl, Alisa Kleybanova, who is the 29th seed and nineteen. She and I have been practising with each other up in Brisbane before the Australian Open and these are always terrific sessions. But they've left me with no doubt this will be a difficult match. And it is: from the very beginning it's tough. I win the first set in a very tight contest and even though I'm playing pretty well in the second set, she has lifted her game up a notch and I start to struggle towards the end of it. Alisa performs better and better as the minutes roll on. Mentally, I am tiring. I lose the last two games of the second set and Alisa is looking very strong now. She's hitting the lines and serving well.

By the third I am really down, and soon I'm trailing 3–1. I can feel myself checking out of this grand slam. It is 15–40 on my serve (1–3). Then from nowhere I regroup. I have no idea where it comes from; I don't even know how I hit four straight winners to get to 3–2. My fighting spirit is back. I manage to break her and all of a sudden we're at 5–5. It is then that I fall. I twist my ankle. The trainer comes out, the match is stopped for about five minutes. My ankle isn't too bad and I can continue to play. The joint is a little sore and swollen but I am able to ignore the mild pain. We're set to battle again. I am really trying to hold my serve – it's the main thing I am focusing on. I hold at 6–6. As we sit down on the change of ends at 7–6, I know I must win the first couple of points on her serve as it will put a lot of pressure on her.

I win the first couple of points with some aggressive baseline play and deep returns. After a great drop shot and a strong passing shot, we're at love–40 on her serve: I have three straight match points! The crowd is going nuts. Then Alisa misses her first serve. I step well inside the baseline for her second serve, which she hits pretty short. I hit a great backhand down the line and it's a winner.

It's over. It's taken more than three hours. I break down and can't stop the tears. The emotion washes over me as a passionate roar emerges from the crowd. I have never heard or experienced a crowd like this. The following day, Australia Day, there's a headline in the press that proclaims 'Jelena Day', and my victory is dubbed 'heroic'.

⊖

I'm in the quarter-finals of the 2009 Australian Open. I can hardly believe I've made it this far when a year ago I was grinding my way back onto the tour. Two years ago I was contemplating ending my life. My soul was shattered. Today, I'm so happy as I fight my way through this slam, but unquestionably also mentally fatigued going into my match against world No. 3 Dinara Safina.

We are one set apiece going into the third set and at 4-3 I have a chance to break but miss a backhand down the line by millimetres. Dinara has momentum with her and breaks me at 4–4. From there she serves out the match and wins, 6–4, 4–6, 6–4.

In all honesty I had nothing left to give. Physically I am in good shape but emotionally I have nothing in reserve – and yet I've had the greatest emotional victory at this tournament. Not only that, I'm the first player since Lindsay Davenport to have won four straight three-set matches at a grand slam, and just the fourth wildcard in the Open era to reach a grand slam quarter-final.

My results promote me to No. 91 in the rankings, back in the top 100 for the first time since 2003.

⊘

The day after losing to Dinara I can barely move or think – I've caught flu and it's hit me hard. My great play and results mean I've been included in Australia's Fed Cup team, which is to be played in five days' time. I'm desperate to represent my country for the first time in seven years but a few days later, on antibiotics, I'm still terribly fatigued and feeling dizzy. I go to the Fed Cup coach, David Taylor, and tell him I need a day or two off to try to get over this illness.

I travel to Perth and although my throat remains swollen, my nose blocked, it feels terrific to be part of the team. But I can barely train. I can't seem to shake the infection, can hardly breathe when I push myself to play. When I take the court in Perth I am not myself at all – I'd say I'm playing at 60 per cent of my ability, and because we're facing a different country every day over the next couple of days, I am facing the possibility of playing a singles match every day.

I win all my singles matches, and so does Sam Stosur; the team wins the doubles matches as well, so we qualify for World Group II play-offs. It is great to play Fed Cup for Australia, and in Australia – an awesome feeling. We celebrate with a team dinner but I am feeling flattened. Something isn't right.

20

Exhaustion, 2009

A week after the Fed Cup I continue to struggle. Possibly it's because I've played ten matches in three weeks. Still, I don't take a break. I accept the wildcard offered to me into qualifying at a tournament in Memphis in early February. I get through two rounds and then lose in the first round of the main draw – I'm extremely fatigued.

Borna has some visa issues that mean he can't come with me to the States, but because I'm an IMG client – I've been with them for over a year – I have access to the Nick Bollettieri Tennis Academy, which is now owned by IMG. It's an exceptionally well-equipped and organised facility. I'm able to use its coaches and fitness trainers, excellent hitting partners, and Nick himself is on the court for a few sessions a week and helps me out.

Despite all this, I can't train the way I have over the last year. The energy that helped propel me to the Australian Open quarters has all gone. Mentally, I am on, I want this – I want to keep on improving. But I am plain tired.

The next tournament is Indian Wells. We arrive four days before the tournament begins but I can barely get out of bed. I start sleeping from 10 pm to eleven the next morning. The fatigue causes me to sleep long hours and cancel fitness sessions. Tin and I start cancelling my practice sessions too. I haven't been like this since I was depressed. And I am not depressed. I hit once or twice for a handful of minutes. But I only want to sleep all the time. I am napping for one to two hours at time. Nothing is quite right.

We go to Miami and I feel a bit better. I get through my first round but I lose in a tight three-setter to Wozniacki.

We go to the next tournament in Florida and I have to pull out because I am not feeling good. I head back to Zagreb, try to train, barely train and board a plane to play Switzerland in a Fed Cup tie in Mildura, Victoria. I'm exhausted by the end of a 24-hour plane trip and then another short flight to Mildura from Melbourne. Still, I win my match, we win the tie and I head back to Europe immediately. The trip does nothing for my lethargy.

Then I hit the clay court season. Though I'm training nowhere near the level of 2008 I manage to win three matches in Bucharest, but can't win one in Warsaw.

⊙

All hell breaks loose in May. I do an interview with Australian magazine *Sport&Style* in which I open up more than ever before. It touches on my father's history of physically abusing me, taking my earnings, and how I fled my family to escape what I call 'the situation'.

With my father you never know how he will react – I know anything can happen and I'm always wary about how much to say. This time he responds immediately. He grants an interview to the Serbian newspaper *Blic* in which he does not deny the beatings – 'There was no child that was not beaten by parents – the same with Jelena' – and he threatens to blow up Clare Bergin, the Australian ambassador in Belgrade, unless she puts a stop to the reports of his abuse.

It's been many years since I stopped reading newspaper reports of all the demented shit he says. Apparently in one interview with Serbian television he said that talented children should 'always be forced ... There are no limits.' But this incident is off the scale; I can't ignore it.

'I'm a war veteran and I'll kill her [Bergin] with a hand grenade launcher in centre of Belgrade,' he says. 'I know Serbian police could arrest me because of this words. However, I'm not afraid as this is the only way to stop the journalistic scam from Australia.' He claims he's got an 'arsenal of weapons' in his house.

The police investigate and find that for once he is telling the truth – they uncover seven hunting rifles, a hand gun, bullets, and two bombs. He's charged with threatening to harm Clare Bergin and possession of illegal firearms and explosives.

The trigger for these big, explosive outbursts from my father is a feeling that people are against him. He's gone way too far this time, and he's actually facing jail time. A judge orders that he's held in custody pending an investigation and his lawyer applies for bail for him. He has to start taking responsibility for his words and actions. I am all over the place because Savo is in Serbia dealing with this mess and I wish I could be by his side to help him.

All this is happening when I draw Karolina Sprem in the first round of the French Open.

I knew this day would come. When Borna and I have fought in the past I have put this very scenario to him. I find him at the courts and when I break the news to him, the blood drains from his face. I look him straight in the eye. 'See what happens?' I say.

In the lead-up to the match he is tense. So am I. I have never been this nervous going into a match. In my head, I am going through all the times he let me down. It brings up those feelings of hurt, anger and disappointment I had around that time in my career.

As the match opens I'm on edge and it shows in my tennis. I literally can't put a ball in the court. Karolina wins the first set. Going into the second I psych myself up. I tell myself; *I just have to get it together, don't think about the past, focus on the tennis and concentrate on my game plan, this moment now on the court.* I manage to break her early on in the second set and from there I take control. I win the second set easily and the trend continues in the third, which I race through as well. I win the match 3–6, 6–1, 6–2. I'm unbelievably happy and relieved as Karolina and I shake hands.

Next up in Paris is world No. 4 Elena Dementieva. I haven't lost a match against her since the Sydney Olympics. I walk out onto the No. 1 Court and from the opening game I dominate. I win the first set 6–2, playing incredible tennis. Hitting with great depth and using my angles, serving and moving extremely well. In the second set I am up 2–1 and she's about to serve. On the second point in her service game, I go to return one of her serves when I feel an incredibly sharp pain in my lower back.

I try to take a few steps but my legs literally won't move. I can't walk – I'm stuck in the middle of the court. Panic fills me and I look to my box. Crying in pain and shock, I manage to get to my chair. But it hurts too much to sit down properly so I have to use my hands to prop myself up and hover over it. I still can't move my back. I am stuck and my back is spasming.

The physio and a tournament doctor carry me off court to a

facility underneath the stadium, where they lay me on the floor on my stomach so they can have a good look at my back. I am wondering, if I get down on the ground, will I be able to get back up? The pain is so intense. The physio tries to work on it but this doesn't make too much difference. In the end, in my stubbornness, I tell them that I want to go back on court. The physio looks at me like I'm mad, but I want to give it a go.

I get back out on the court. Elena wins her service game and we get to 2–2. Somehow I manage to hold mine. At 3–2 my way Elena is serving and now the pain is getting worse. I really have no chance of getting to the balls. I can't serve at all. After we play an especially long rally I feel another incredibly sharp pain in my back and am forced to retire.

I'm heartbroken because I really think I would have beaten her and my hopes of going into the third round of the French Open are dashed, as are those of beating a top five player at a grand slam.

The doctors think I might have slipped a disc in my back. That night I go to sleep with a huge belt strapped around my middle and three pillows stacked up under my legs to help support me. I can't get a wink of sleep in this position even though I'm on heavy painkillers and muscle relaxants. An MRI scan the next morning shows that it is not the disc. Finally, they figure out it's a nerve spasm.

Because of the injury, I don't train for two weeks. Slowly, however, my back releases, gets better and I start to walk again, but the injury means I miss Birmingham. And at Eastbourne the previous problem rears its head again: fatigue. Once more I am sleeping sixteen hours a day. I find sunlight unbearable so I stay inside. When I am in my hotel room I draw the blinds to block out the light. For fifteen minutes a day I walk, and that is all I can handle. After my short walks, I go back inside, with the blinds drawn, watch television and sleep.

Along with fatigue there is the distraction of Dad, who has been sentenced to fifteen months in jail for his threats to kill the Australian ambassador. He's lucky, in fact: it's far less than the maximum eight years he could have been handed.

My father is a mess. Whether he has been threatening to kidnap me, the US government, the Australian government, whatever, he has never shown any caution about saying these awful words. It has finally caught up with him. But at the end of it all it is sad that he has to go to prison.

My brother and I continue to build on our strong relationship. I am happy to have him in my life.

⊝

The bone-aching fatigue I am living with causes all sorts of chaos for my tennis. I pull out of Eastbourne but I am determined to go to Wimbledon, though I've prepared for it on a mix of sleep and shade. I've turned into a tennis-playing vampire.

It's a bright, sunny day when I walk out on the court at Wimbledon to play German qualifier Tatjana Malek. For all the rainy, grey days I have played here, today there is not a cloud in the sky. Normally I'd love these conditions, but today the blazing sun has me feeling weak. Still, I manage to win the first set 6–3. Then I start to break down. The sun hurts my eyes. It seems as though the light and heat are zapping my energy. At a change of ends in the first set I can hardly stand up anymore I'm feeling so dizzy. I play two points and my pulse rate shoots up. My head spins again. I feel like I might vomit or faint. It's no surprise I lose, but I still manage to make it three sets.

The doctors I consult suggest a battery of blood tests and after a few weeks I learn that I came up positive for the Epstein-Barr virus, which causes glandular fever.

I try to remain positive as I lie bedridden in our Zagreb apartment. I still can't stand the sunlight. I watch movies, crap television, reality TV – endless episodes of *Real Housewives*, *Desperate Housewives* and *Gossip Girl* fill my days. It's so frustrating that my ascent has been halted, especially when this year I've moved up the rankings with minimal training and a coach whose commitment I still question. The depression isn't creeping back, thankfully, but I don't want to *watch* tennis. I am just eager for this fatigue to disappear so I can get back to playing and competing.

By September I'm feeling much better, and decide I'll try to play the US Open. Borna is unable to get a visa to the States, so Roger Rasheed says he'll help me on the court at Flushing Meadow. He gives me great advice and direction. He's coaching Gael Monfils, but in any free time he comes to my practice sessions, and even watches some of my matches. He knows so much about the game, about the fitness levels required to excel, and is very professional. I have a lot of respect for him.

In New York, even though I haven't been able to practise much in the past month or so, I play a solid opening match, but I lose in the first round.

Because I am so rusty after my convalescence, Borna and I decide it would be a good idea to undertake some intense training and this time we choose the Mouratoglou Tennis Academy in Paris. Patrick Mouratoglou has an impressive reputation as a coach – a few years ago he was with Marcos Baghdatis, and since then he's brought up some other great players. It's a nice quiet place with amazing facilities. It seems the perfect venue for me to train in after everything that's happened in the past months. When we arrive, we find Patrick is accommodating, generous and a particularly nice guy.

The time there is really beneficial – I feel far stronger after a couple of weeks and immediately after we leave I take out an ITF title in Greece, then get to the final at a tournament in central France, Joué-lès-Tours, and win another big ITF title at a tournament in Poitiers. It's a tremendous boost to win a lot of matches on the ITF circuit to end the year and although it's been a tough one for me with injury and illness, I'm sorry the season is ending.

After taking two weeks off in Zagreb, Borna and I disagree about how to approach the off-season. He is pushing hard for us to go with the program the Mouratoglou Academy offers, when a big group of coaches and players spend ten days in the Alps and three weeks in Mauritius. It's tempting but my preference is actually to spend the time working solidly one-on-one. I'm quite concerned that in a group environment, as the Academy's will be, Borna will lose focus, because he's all about having fun and socialising.

We fight about the options. Eventually I relent and agree to go with the Mouratoglou program.

At Val d'Isère in the Alps we do group fitness training, working hard in the thin air. By the end of the fitness preparation, I know it's the wrong decision to be here training like this – in a group environment – and when we get to Mauritius, as I predicted Borna switches into holiday mode. Once again we don't work on anything specific. There is no plan. There are no goals. I'm baffled that Borna thinks what we are doing is useful; I strongly believe we should be concentrating on drills, patterns, tactics on the court, my serve.

We board the plane for our trip from Mauritius to Australia and I turn to Tin just before take-off. 'This was the worst-off season ever,' I say. 'You are aware that with what we've just done there will be no results.'

I rest my head back and go over it in my mind. I feel like Borna has been on a three-week vacation.

This is no way to prepare for a grand slam, I think.

21

Fighting, 2010

It should be exciting to be back in Australia after leaving on a fairytale high last year. But I know in my heart that this year the Open could be a tennis horror show. Why? Well, my confidence is shot and my coaching situation is a mess. Borna and I have gone from bickering in training to full-scale warfare here in Australia. We shout. I feel like I am pulling him along on the tour. The situation is incredibly distracting.

We get to Brisbane and I play okay despite feeling like shit. Although I lose in three sets to Ana Ivanovic, it's not my worst tennis.

In the southern tip of Australia for the Hobart International, miraculously, I win my first match against qualifier Elena Baltacha. Even though I win I feel like I didn't deserve it. And my second match is horrendous. I can't put a ball in the court.

Borna and I fight in practice, after practice and before and after matches. It's the same old stuff: he's not giving me any advice on my serve, my shots, tactics, basically anything and everything to do with my tennis. There's no 'Good work, Jelena.' 'That is right or wrong, Jelena.' It's silence, just the pop of tennis balls, me sighing and looking at him for advice every few minutes.

Why do I have this guy here? I ask myself again. At any moment, it feels he could slip off and be gone. Whenever he is in my life I always feel like he is on the cusp of letting me down.

On the plane trip from Hobart to Melbourne our preparation for the Australian Open spins into a mess off the court as well. We board the Jetstar flight and I take my seat beside the window. Tin is beside me, with Borna next to him by the aisle.

Fifteen minutes into our flight a woman sitting in front of Tin starts complaining. She turns around and says tersely to him, 'You're pushing my seat with your leg.'

Tin looks at his legs, which haven't even grazed the back of her seat. It's a ridiculous accusation. We almost start laughing. Are we being *Punk'd*?

'What's she talking about?' I whisper to Tin.

The woman has stood up now. This time she raises her voice. 'They're pushing my seat, he's pushing my seat ...' She's almost yelling. Tin's leg still hasn't even brushed her seat.

She says, 'She thinks because she's a tennis player she can do whatever she wants,' and she calls over a flight attendant to protest.

'She's pushing my seat.' Tin looks at the flight attendant and points to me, not even sitting behind the woman, and to his legs, which aren't touching the seat.

'This is how I'm sitting,' Tin says.

The flight attendant asks him not to push at the seat. Tin is incredulous but just nods. We sit still, staring at the ground, hoping this will stop. People are looking over at us.

But the woman responds by getting louder and more aggressive.

I whisper to Tin, 'Look, just don't say anything. Just let it go. Just sit how you are sitting. If you're not doing anything and she keeps on saying you're pushing her seat, people will see you are not the one who is doing anything wrong.'

Tin agrees. But the woman is now demanding to be moved. The flight attendant comes back and Borna decides to interject. Tin's demeanour is like a calm, blue ocean where Borna has a temper, and in this case he loses it. He says loudly to the flight attendant, 'If the woman complains one more time I'm going to break her. I am going break her arm, her leg, if she doesn't shut up and sit down.'

The flight attendant hears Borna's threats loud and clear, and she says she's going to call the police.

Appalled, I'm looking out the window wishing I was somewhere else. This is not good.

The flight attendant gets on the plane phone and calls Victoria Police. I hear her describe Borna as 'aggressive'.

By the time we have touched down at Tullamarine Airport in Melbourne other passengers have hit their phones and are on social media broadcasting the news of Jelena Dokic and her entourage being involved in a mid-air drama. The police are waiting for us. They question the woman, and then me and the Bikics.

Borna admits to the cops he was hot-headed. 'Yeah, I did say a few words. I didn't mean it but she was getting really loud and aggressive.'

The woman retracts her complaints. It is all cleared up within five minutes. But the damage has been done. It's all over the Channel 7 news. There are fevered 'flight drama' stories that claim there's chaos in my camp on the eve of the Australian Open.

There's chaos, all right, and it's not going away.

I spend a lot of time trying to fix the fall-out. Naturally Jetstar, my sponsor, are unhappy with the incident. IMG explains on my behalf exactly what went wrong on the flight and the sponsorship is saved, but it's a really embarrassing incident that was easily avoidable. Nor does Borna ever apologise for any of it.

⊖

At our first practice session on Rod Laver Arena Borna and I have another blazing fight after a shocking practice session. I am left sobbing to Tin. Once again Roger comes to the rescue. I ask him if he'll do a few sessions with me, and they make me feel so much better. When I tell him my concerns, he straight away knows exactly what to do. Tony also comes to some sessions to give me advice and feedback. It's so nice of him to help me out, too; he's a great man, someone who always makes me feel calm.

On my home soil, the grand slam scrutiny is intense. A *Herald Sun* photographer snaps my fight with Borna and subsequent meltdown. 'Jelena Dokic Wilts Under Open Pressure' the *Herald Sun* writes. 'Jelena Dokic was reduced to tears in practice yesterday as her troubled Australian Open preparation plunged deeper into crisis ...' If they only knew the real story.

This year I don't get past round one. I've gone from the tennis fairytale princess story of 2009 to a total disappointment. I am flat in my match against Russian 27th seed Alisa Kleybanova, who feels powerful against me, and gets me in straight sets, 6–1, 7–5. As I exit Melbourne I am left soul-searching all over again. The only reason I am working with Borna is because Tin has over and over again asked me to give him a chance. But these days even he is realising Borna is not a good person to have around me.

After the Australian Open we return to Paris to train at Patrick's tennis academy. And it's here that I finally accept I have to let Borna Bikic go. Tin completely understands my decision, in fact encourages it.

Borna and I talk and I tell him we're done, immediately relieved as I say the words. He's disbelieving at first, but he accepts my decision.

In the subsequent weeks the feelings of freedom and relief are always there. I play in Monterrey, Mexico and Indian Wells, and even though I have no confidence or form, at least I'm not unhappy, stressed, tense every day. The burden of an impossible situation is finally gone.

$\ominus$

Even though I am happier, I'm in a jam because I don't have a coach and it takes time to find one who is available or suitable; it's even harder to hire at short notice in the middle of the season. I head back to the Mouratoglou Academy to try to make a plan.

One night after training Tin and I brainstorm about the coaching conundrum. He knows I am dreadful by myself. I really need a coach if I am going to make my tennis career work. We discuss doing at least a few weeks or months with Borna – until we find another solution. Even though I know it is wrong to work with him again, it's almost like I really want to confirm this time, not just to myself but to everyone else, that Borna can't lead me back up the rankings and be supportive.

Tin talks me around to re-employing Borna within a few weeks of sacking him – we feel we have to be pragmatic and take the only option available to us because the French Open and Wimbledon are just around the corner.

We do a passable ten days' training in Paris. I am not at my best, my form and confidence are low, and inevitably Borna doesn't bring any guidance to the table. A few days into our Paris training block, he announces he has a new girlfriend. I am fine with it. I don't care.

But Tin is pissed off because Borna is distracted again on my time and money and we are due to leave for an ITF tournament in a few days. I make it clear to Borna that what he is doing is not right. Just before we're all supposed to leave for the tournament he tells us that actually he is going back home with his girlfriend. I knew this would happen – and two weeks before a grand slam. Tin is mad, I am sad. I tell Tin to let it go but he has really had enough because we have given Borna so many chances.

We go our separate ways at the end of our stint at Patrick's academy.

It couldn't be clearer that our relationship with Borna is over. Tin and Borna are barely on speaking terms. Almost estranged. We are both very hurt.

After this enormous coaching crisis, my form and confidence are at an all-time low. Nonetheless, I make the quarters in Prague. Even though I have no help on the court and we know it is going to be a tough few months, I have more hope now. Tin and I are doing great and are stronger than ever. I am putting in more hours on the court; I'm slowly starting to feel better, but my head is still a bit of a mess due to recent events.

Two thousand and ten is a tough year for me. I under-perform in the next two grand slam tournaments: I'm underprepared going into the French Open and lose in the first round; I'm still coachless as Wimbledon approaches, and lose in the second round of qualifying, after having a match point. It's a tough loss. To clear my head I go for a walk and end up sitting in the middle of the Bank of England's cricket ground in floods of tears. A press photographer captures the moment. Horrible.

The load of the last six months has caught up to me. Mentally and emotionally, I'm drained. How am I supposed to get through the ITF tournaments in Europe I have committed to? Perhaps I should take a few weeks off and really figure out what to do next. I need to make a radical change.

Tin suggests going to Switzerland to work with reputed Dutch coach Glenn Schaap, who has coached some top players like Nadia Petrova; he's a man known for his tough training methods and great tennis knowledge. Over the past twelve months we have been talking with him about working together on a part-time basis – he works at an academy in Switzerland and is currently working with another player, Andrea Petkovic. It is an excellent opportunity but I'm so tired from all the crap that has happened with my coaching situation with Borna this year that I'm not sure if I have the energy to go. Because my faith has been lost, I don't know if it is a good idea to even try out Glenn as my coach.

Tin and I discuss it and he tries to convince me to phone Glenn. Although I practically have one foot on the plane to go home, I change my mind at the last minute.

I have nothing to lose anyway, I think.

Glenn's pleased I've called. He's at Wimbledon for another week, but says I should go to the academy in Switzerland, where another coach will look after me for a week until he arrives.

We arrive at the academy in Bern and I practise with a coach who is a former top 30 male player who owns the academy. They also give me a fitness trainer who does daily sessions with me. It is tough and well run and awakens me with a jolt. Straightaway I realise what I've been missing out on for a long, long time. Guidance, hard work, support, positivity, discipline. Glenn is not even here yet, and I know when he arrives it will get even tougher.

When Glenn arrives we do an unbelievably gruelling first session. I can sense from the outset he is trying to test me. And test me he does. His fitness and training sessions are total punishment. Sprint after sprint after sprint. Boxing and then more sprinting. We do almost three hours of tennis on the court at a time. I feel like I hit thousands and thousands of balls without stopping. I am constantly left gasping for air. After hours of training I feel almost dead and I want to vomit. But I like it and I like working with him. He soon sees I am not a quitter. I never say 'Stop,' 'I can't do it,' even though I know he is taking me to the edge and testing me to see if I will give up.

At the end of the first week, Tin turns to me and says, 'Fuck, you've been doing the wrong things.'

For the next four weeks Glenn trains me hard – six, seven hours a day. It reminds me of my days running in 40 degree heat and three-hour tennis sessions when I was a teenager in Australia. It's intense. Exactly what I need. My confidence rises. This feels like the best training I have done in years.

After the five-week stay I head to Contrexéville for a tournament, an ITF 50,000, and play the best tennis I have all year. I win it. And then it's on to another ITF 50,000 in Bucharest, a more testing event with high-quality players. After saving match points in the semi-final and final, I manage to win that too.

After less than two months of hard training and competing, I am amazed that I have been able to make this much progress.

Next up it is Canada. There, I win a tournament in Vancouver, so I am now on a 15-match winning streak. But, having not played this much tennis in almost a year, I'm pretty tired, and I fall in qualifying at the US Open. Despite the loss I know I am on a better path now.

To finish off the year I have a semi-final appearance at Joué-lès-Tours. I am ranked No. 135 in the world. This is a miracle for someone who didn't win a match until May, especially considering this year's coaching debacle, and the fact I only played fourteen events all year and only performed well in the last five.

Switzerland has been my saviour, an eye opener. Glenn has been the perfect coach to get me back on track.

After a quick break in Zagreb, I hang at home relaxing with Tin, then return to Switzerland to rip into more training in my off-season.

As 2011 dawns, we head to Australia for the Open wildcard play-off and for me to do a few more weeks of training. I get wildcards into Brisbane, Sydney and the Australian Open. I manage to win the first round of Brisbane but can't get a victory in Sydney.

Glenn is with us in Australia and even though everything is fantastic between us in training, he finds it difficult to be away from home. He's struggling with the travel and the huge number of weeks required on the road. It soon becomes clear that it would be best if he returns home to his loved ones. Certainly there is no fight between us. He is a great guy and I have a lot of respect and love for him. I think he is one of the best coaches in the world. He knows so much about tennis, the way you are supposed to train, and he makes you work incredibly hard.

⊖

In the first round of the Australian Open I have a pretty easy win over top 100 Czech player Zuzana Ondraskova, but I can't get through the next round – it's a close match but it doesn't go my way. Still, even though I lose I am playing solidly.

My next tournament is a big WTA event in Paris. I go through three rounds of qualifying and then in the first round I beat world No. 30 Lucie Safarova in a tough three-set match. I also defeat Nadia Petrova, ranked No. 20 in the world, in the second round. They're my biggest wins since 2009. Even though I lose in the quarter-finals to world No. 2 Kim Clijsters, it's been a fantastic week.

Feeling tired I don't do that well in Dubai and Doha. Nevertheless, Tin and I go to my next WTA event – in Malaysia. In the first round

I draw the No. 1 seed and world No. 5, Francesca Schiavone. It's a tough draw. After losing the first set we have a big battle in the second, which I manage to clinch in a tie breaker to push the match into a third and deciding set. I really lift my game in the third and manage to win the match. It is a huge win – my biggest in almost ten years. I am ecstatic. I continue to play better and better and make it to the final.

In the final I face Lucie Safarova. It was always going to be tough against her. It's been a decade since I last won a tournament – even played in a final – and I'm desperate to win this title.

I don't start well. I lose the first set too quickly and get to 5–3 down in the second. Somehow I summon some fight, save two match points and win the second set tie-break. I am down a break at 3–1 in the third. But again I find a way to crawl back and win the match.

I can't believe it, I think to myself on winning. *I can't believe I have.* I am so happy, the happiest in years. Tin is always on tour with me but Savo has been with us as well over the last couple of weeks, including here in KL, so it is great having him here with us to witness this victory.

Following the title win in KL, Tin, Savo and I have a week of downtime in Zagreb, where we chill out watching movies, go to the cinema, as well as train.

At our next tournament in Miami, and also in Charleston, Australian coach Louise Pleming helps me on the court. I started with her after Glenn went home; she's helped me with a few tournaments and it has turned into a longer-term arrangement. She's fantastic; she does a lot on- and off-court to support me. She has brilliant energy and is so positive and hard-working.

It's in Charleston I notice the chronic fatigue that recurs on and off, ever since I had glandular fever, is starting to creep up on me again. It seems to strike for a week or so at a time. So it comes as no surprise I lose in the first round in a tough three-set match.

Once more the fatigue is debilitating, making training impossible. There is no choice but to withdraw from playing Fed Cup in Melbourne, Australia. I'm also forced to pull out of four more clay-court tournaments.

Even with very little training in the previous couple of weeks, in my first event back I beat Simona Halep in Strasbourg. I lose in the second round, then go on to lose a tight first-round match at the French Open.

Slowly I increase my workload and after a few more weeks I make the final on grass in 's-Hertogenbosch. More good wins follow, including one over top-20 player Flavia Pennetta.

At Wimbledon I lose a tough first-round match. Lou is still working with me, and we decide to meet up at Nick Bollettieri's tennis academy in Florida.

Following Wimbledon I take a week off and Tin and I make our way to Florida, where Lou joins us. At this stage I am ranked No. 40 in the world – my highest ranking in quite a few years. In less than twelve months I have managed to go from barely being in the top 200 to being in the top 40. This is pretty well all due to Lou and Glenn Schaap – even though I don't work with him anymore, he has put me on the right path. I should have done this years ago.

From Nick's academy we are off to my first event on the American hard courts in Washington. All is going well in my first-round match until something snaps in my right shoulder just a few games in. It's a searing pain that shoots up and down my right arm and up into my neck. It feels awful and I am not sure if I can go on, but I don't want to retire. I manage to finish off the match despite being in great pain.

An MRI indicates nothing is broken but that the tendon is inflamed. I'm sent off with painkillers. At this stage I can't even lift my arm past my chest but I throw myself into rehab, and into a pit of worry about whether I'll recover, whether this injury could take me out of the hard-court season.

Our next stop is San Diego, and I manage to get on the court. While I can hit my backhand, I feel pain on my forehand, and it is especially sore on the serve. At times I am forced to serve underarm. There are of course a lot of double faults due to my shoulder but I still almost win the match – that's the most frustrating part.

I call my father twice over the course of this year. We don't argue, but neither do we have much conversation. There's still an iciness between us. My hunch is that he thinks it's all my fault, this chasm. He still doesn't approve of the way I live my life. As ever, in his view life should be lived his way or no way. How can I establish a stable relationship with him? After these abrupt conversations, I put down the phone and don't feel like I have any connection to him. Despite trying my hardest, I just can't seem to have a 'normal' relationship with him; I can't bring us closer.

I despair ever having a good relationship with either of my parents – but thank God for Savo. He is based in Belgrade and has travelled quite a bit of the year with us, joining us in Europe and the States when he can. When we are apart, I am in constant touch with him. To me, my brother and I don't fit in to this 'family' and every day I am thankful we have each other.

22

The Injury, 2011

The pain won't go away. It's deep in my shoulder and shoots up into my neck, then sears down into my bicep. It feels like a nerve, I tell the doctors. But is it a nerve? Nobody has a definitive answer. Every consultant has a different opinion. Some think it is nerve-related. Others think it is a tendon. The treatment I receive assumes a tendon injury. My days revolve around rehab and treatment but hardly any practice. Every few days I practise for an hour at the most.

I'm longing to play in the US Open but the pain intensifies – not only when I serve, now I feel it more and more often when I hit forehands. Every few shots I experience a stabbing sensation. And when I serve I still can't lift my arm higher than my chest before it is filled with pain. Even high forehands become a problem.

Another city, another specialist, and this time in New York. An MRI of the area shows up inflammation in my bicep tendon – apparently the root of the pain could be a weakness in my shoulder or back.

The latest solution is to give me a set of exercises to do every day to try to fix this supposedly dodgy shoulder.

Even though my gut tells me the pain has nothing to do with my shoulder – I suspect it's from my arm or bicep – I do everything that I am told, from rehab to exercises. I am fastidious about my recovery.

In pain and up against it, I try to prepare for the US Open. I manage to complete only a few training sessions and my right arm still hurts a lot. During training I don't serve at all; I try to save my right arm as much as I can.

My goal here at Flushing Meadows is merely to get through a match. My first opponent is Olga Govortsova; somehow I manage to secure a win. Afterwards my shoulder isn't good and when I take the court for my second-round match, again I'm unable to serve or compete properly, which is getting very, very frustrating. What's incredibly annoying is that nonetheless I've been playing well.

I'm well inside the top 50 and on my way to the top 30, but it will be weeks and weeks before I can train properly, thanks to this injury. I have to pull out of all the tournaments I am due to play in Asia and Europe.

Every specialist tells me to rest for a minimum of four to six weeks. So I do.

With time on my hands, I talk with Tin about going to see my father. After barely talking to him for six years, then our brief contact last year, in the last few months I have been back in contact with him a little more. A quick phone call every couple of weeks – just short conversations about how he is and how I am.

Savo and I decide to make the hour-long trip to Vrdnik from Belgrade together. I want to try to get some closure on what has happened to our family. I have always hoped to mend things with

Dad, though deep down I know that unless I'm playing for him and giving him my money, probably there can't be a relationship. But I need to try.

Savo and I spend a few hours talking with Dad at his ranch. After some amicable chat, I tell him he went overboard, that he mistreated me not just with physical but with verbal abuse, like the phone calls, and by freezing out my brother and mother from my life. Once my tears start, they fall thick and fast.

'I know,' he says. 'I agree. I went overboard. I am sorry.'

Even though he is apologising I can feel it in my soul that he thinks he was right.

I also feel like he should have instigated this meeting between us. But deep down, I know that he will always think that the right thing to do was, in his words, 'to discipline me' in that way.

The entire mistreatment of me, his abuse of me as child and teenager, is not a big deal to him. He doesn't see what the fuss is about. He doesn't seem to get that the family fell apart because of him and his actions. I am not sure that he is even bothered by the fact that everything did fall apart.

I ask him if I can spend some time here at the ranch with him and if I can bring Tin as well. I want all of us to be together. I would love that we would all somehow get along.

'Of course,' he says.

My father would rather I was not with a Croatian man. But he has come a long way from saying he wants to kill Tin to saying my partner can come to his house.

Another meeting is arranged, and when Tin walks into the house, my father greets him. He shakes his hand. Over the next couple of weeks Dad and Tin get to know each other a little bit better. Tin and I are staying at Savo's place in Belgrade. There I work diligently at my light rehab training program; the afternoons are free. We all eat some meals together.

We decide, the three of us, to issue a joint statement, which I release via Tennis Australia on their site.

> I would like to confirm media reports that I have reconciled with my father, Damir Dokic. My partner, Tin Bikic, and I have visited my father at his home to finally put an end to our disagreement. I initiated the meeting as I wanted to reunite my family and allow us all to get on with our lives and be happy. This has gone on too long.

Dad calls up and happily gives interviews with the Serbian press. He then calls a heap of TV and print journalists and offers exclusive interviews with me. I am incensed and don't want to be part of this. He arranges interviews without my knowledge and then tells me five minutes before the journalists are about to arrive. Soon my training sessions at a tennis centre in Belgrade are being filmed by news crews. I am being door-stopped on the way to and from sessions. It's too much to cope with. The attention is nuts, chaotic.

I realise too late that my father has constructed yet another media circus. Although I play along, I feel used – used to give him a better image in the media.

⊖

By the beginning of October my shoulder has started to hurt again. I am due to play a tournament in Linz, Austria, but it's six weeks since I've been in a tournament and I'm unsure if I should go. In the end, despite the flare-up in my shoulder, Louise Pleming and I decide I will play. I get through only one set and then have to retire.

And that is the finish of my playing year. I continue with my rehab and exercises, even though it isn't improving my injury. Lou and I plan for me to come to Melbourne in early November.

It's getting time for me and Tin to leave Belgrade and begin my preparations for the new season. I know I won't be seeing my dad for a while so I call him up to tell him I'm going to Australia. When I spell it out to him that I have to go back to Croatia and then on to Australia for the off-season, he is annoyed.

'You should stay here,' he says angrily.

'No, I can't,' I protest, and repeat that I will be going.

It dissolves into an argument. I hang up after the conversation turns into a shouting match. Maybe there will never be peace between us. He is a bit calmer, perhaps because I am older, but he has showed his controlling ways are still the same. He hasn't changed.

$\ominus$

In Melbourne there is no better news; the physios and doctors advise me to continue with my rehab and exercises. For the next couple of weeks, I am only allowed to do fitness training. In the hope the inflammation will just go down on its own, I am not to hit a ball until late December.

The year is drawing to a close and it's been a promising one, despite injury hampering my rise. At the beginning of December Tin and I attend the annual Newcombe Medal, Australian Tennis Awards night. A few days before, I ask the organisers if I can make a speech – I really want to say thank you – and they agree. Undoubtedly, some in the Australian tennis community believe I shouldn't be allowed back in the country, thinking again that I am just here for money, which is grossly untrue. But many others have given me unfaltering support and I want to show them my gratitude.

On stage in front of the 800-strong crowd I thank the Australian tennis community from the bottom of my heart for supporting me from a young age, despite some ups and downs. Among those I single out are Craig Tiley, Paul McNamee, Darren Pearce, Tony Roche, Lesley Bowrey, Pat Rafter, Todd Woodbridge, Lou Pleming and my fitness trainer Aaron Kellett. I thank them – the people who never discriminated against me, instead always helped me and gave me a chance when others refused to.

Late in December I start training very slowly with Lou. To begin with she just feeds me slow and easy balls from the basket. My shoulder doesn't hurt on my ground strokes but still hurts a lot when I serve. All this rest and I feel like nothing much has changed.

Orthopaedic surgeon Greg Hoy helped Pat Rafter and Casey Dellacqua through their shoulder troubles so after recommendations I go see him. 'There's no tear, nothing. You've got a huge inflammation in your cross-section between the tendon and tendon bone,' Greg says. 'You're going to need a cortisone shot, especially if you want to play the summer in Australia in two weeks. That's the best way to get it treated because it hasn't gone down in four months so it's not going down on its own.'

He adds, 'But it's also something that I think we can solve pretty quickly.'

Because of Greg's words I have hope.

He refers me to a specialist to inject the cortisone into my bicep tendon. The specialist's rooms are across from Melbourne Park, so off we go, Tin, me and Lou. They jam a big needle in my shoulder and in goes the cortisone. Fingers crossed.

A few days later, during my first hit since having the injection, everything seems to be going great, but the real test is the serve.

And, unbelievably, my shoulder doesn't hurt when I serve. It's an incredible feeling after month upon month of pain. I know I am under-prepared as I have barely hit a ball in four months. As relieved as I am that I have no more pain in my arm, I know it's going to be a very tough start to the season. A few days later I am due to play in Auckland.

It's no surprise when I lose in the first round but, considering everything I have gone through with my arm, it's a solid match. I win one match at the Apia International in Sydney. I win my first-round match at the Australian Open, which is quite an effort after months and months without playing tennis, but lose in the second round: it's obvious that I am lacking the court time needed to be playing at this level.

A few months on, things get worse. During a regular practice session in Indian Wells, something snaps in my right wrist, and an incredibly sharp pain forces me to stop altogether.

Within fifteen minutes the pain is overwhelming. I can neither move my wrist nor hold anything. Immediately I consult a physio, who isn't sure what is wrong but thinks it might have something to do with my tendon. I try to play my first-round match in Indian Wells but barely able even to hold my racquet, I retire after only game.

Tin and I go straight to Miami for the next tournament; fortunately there's also a respected hand, elbow and shoulder specialist there, so I book a visit. He looks at my injury and suggests a cortisone injection into my wrist tendon.

Unlike my shoulder, the cortisone isn't a solution for this injury. A few days after the injection, not only does my wrist still hurt, it also starts to squeak when I move it and the pain spreads through my hand. My wrist pain is too bad for me to win a single match in Miami. In Charleston I am forced to retire in the first set.

Tennis is off the agenda and we head back to Zagreb, where I consult a hand specialist. Frustratingly, he doesn't have the answers. Nor does anyone else in Croatia. Everyone just says to rest.

Six months on and my wrist is getting worse even though I haven't been playing at all. I decide to phone Dr Alejandro Badia, a well-renowned specialist in Miami, to get advice from him. He says based on what I have told him about my pain it's very likely I'm going to need surgery. I should come over as soon as possible to Miami. Within 24 hours I am on a plane to see him.

According to Dr Badia the tendon has thickened significantly and I need to have it shaved as well as have a tendon reconstruction. This is a complex procedure, not to be taken lightly. I also have three cysts, lodged between two bones, and I need to have them removed as well.

The surgery is scheduled and everything goes according to plan. Afterwards, he sends me home with my wrist in a big cast and a rehab plan.

Over the next six months I do my rehab. My recovery is long and slow. My wrist has no flexibility or strength; it's literally like learning to use your hand again. This puts me in a rough headspace.

I've been out of tennis for almost a year. It's the longest period of non-playing time I have had since I was six years old. Unfamiliar territory.

Six months after surgery my wrist is good, but has only average movement and remains weak: I don't have enough strength and power to hit from the baseline. I've been so long out of the game that if I am to make a serious comeback, it's going to take me at least twelve to eighteen months of tough and consistent preparation.

During the European summer I go to Frankfurt and train at a tennis academy there. My wrist is still not 100 per cent and I find myself thinking that this might be it. It might be over. It feels cruel that I might not get to use the faith I finally found in myself. The last time I played I was twenty-eight, which seems too young to stop.

⊘

As I recover from surgery I decide to visit my grandfather's grave in Croatia. After I make a number of calls I find out through my mother's sisters that he is buried in a cemetery in Čepin. Tin and I drive the three hours from Zagreb.

At his gravesite I lay some flowers, light a candle and place a ceramic angel. Tears run down my cheeks – I miss him terribly. Even though I don't remember his face anymore, because I was eight when I last saw him and I don't have a picture, I carry wonderful memories of this man. Of him being kind and protective. And he brought out the best in my father; Dad never struck me in front of his father – the only family member I can say that about. I used to love to go to my grandfather's place every weekend – it was my safe haven. I loved sitting on his sofa on his lap. It's so sad that I never got to say goodbye all those years ago when the war was erupting.

⊖

Back in Australia for the wildcard play-off I am extremely rusty. I lose 6–2, 6–4.

After the match I say to Todd Woodbridge, 'If they were now to give me a wildcard for the main draw, I wouldn't take it. And even if they gave it to me for qualies, I wouldn't take it. It's not right. I am nowhere near ready.'

Todd has been helping me for a while. He has great knowledge of the game, works incredibly hard on the court. He's an amazing guy, guiding me, giving me advice and direction, and continuing to do so in the coming months, which will be hard ones for me.

It's clear that the amount of time I have had off because of my injuries has taken a severe toll. I face facts. It is going to take an extraordinary effort and a long time to build myself back up again to be genuinely competitive. I know and feel that this is it. I'm done.

It's time to build a future that's not about playing tennis and see what life is going to bring me now. After fighting so many things, especially in the last couple of years, I really don't have it in me for another long battle with my injuries.

⊖

Life is no longer a blur of airports and hotels. It's no longer exclusively about matches, points, rankings, wildcards, money and opponents. There are no screaming fans. I no longer get to feel the wonderful thrill that victory brings. There's no more adrenalin. I miss it all. I loved tennis, still do. I always will.

The years after my tennis career abruptly finishes are difficult. I have not finished on my terms. Injury forced me to retire. Consequently, life afterwards is a brutal adjustment, trying to figure out what I like and don't like when it comes to my career. Figuring out who I am outside of the tennis court. Soul-searching.

I want to stay close to the sport, so I dabble in coaching, writing and TV work. But I'm sometimes left confused and can't find which direction I really want to head in. Tennis life is not real life. It's a bubble that we tennis players live in. Ex-players have warned me about this and told me to prepare for the especially hard first few years after playing.

But after what I have been through, I try not to sweat the small stuff anymore. The important things are that I am healthy again, and I have two incredible relationships in my life – with Savo and Tin. As long as I have them, things will be fine.

Tin and I divide our time between Zagreb and Melbourne. We slowly settle into life away from tennis. Hoping the best is yet to come.

Epilogue

Everyone wants to know if I still talk to my father.

We sometimes talk, but what happened has left an everlasting bruise on my life.

I played my family out of poverty, but it wasn't enough for him. I couldn't draw a single word of praise from him, even when I reached world No. 4. Nothing was ever good enough in his eyes.

As much as he helped propel me to tremendous tennis heights, his destructive ways eventually crushed my spirit and almost destroyed me.

Did his mad, public drunken rantings – over the price of fish, WTA draw 'riggings', the Queen, the US president, Vladimir Putin, me being kidnapped, a whole host of conspiracies – cost me my career?

Definitely.

And the psychological torture he put me through when I left home was too much to deal with as well as trying to play tennis. The guilt of leaving my family, my shattered home life were too much for me to handle alone.

Could I have been a steady top 5, top 10 player? For sure; no doubt about it.

Could I have been the world No. 1? Won Wimbledon or the Australian Open? Who knows. A lot of people think I could have.

What I do know now is that I can survive any hell that life dishes up. The craziness, the physical and mental abuse, the public embarrassment, the way he destroyed our family unit – all of it almost killed me.

Yet today I am strong. I don't hate my father but I hate what he did. I am also very angry at him for breaking up our family. I get a bit why he did some of the things that he did. He's a son who was never truly loved by his mother. A man who carries psychological scars from the war in Serbia. A refugee who couldn't find his place, or acceptance.

The Australian tennis scene and Australia itself were no place for my dad.

He never would have left Serbia if it hadn't been for both the difficult circumstances brought on by the war and my hoped-for tennis career. I give him credit for having the guts to do what he did and relocate our family to Australia for a new opportunity.

As time has gone on I have experienced much of what he saw when we first arrived here. The racism, discrimination, exclusion. I understood why he was so angry when I experienced it first-hand, too; from the junior tennis trips to the whispering campaign against me when I returned in 2005. Having had a coach from Tennis Australia say I should not have been allowed back in this country stings me to this day.

But what hurts even more is that people on the tennis scene, especially in Australia, turned a blind eye to the physical and emotional abuse I suffered. From my childhood through to my late teens, and even into my early twenties, when it was obvious I was on the receiving end of constant abuse, individuals told themselves it wasn't their problem, chose to ignore it.

Some were quick to worry themselves about whether I was getting more of an opportunity than them or their kids. But not my emotional and physical welfare. I was being abused. Even though my father threatened my life thousands of times, and beat me, at least I know he would never have killed me, but victims of family violence don't always come out of it alive; we've all heard those tragic stories.

Women's rights, gay rights, call for equal prize money – these are all issues that I support and agree with – but we need more people to stick up for the men, women, boys and girls who are being physically and emotionally abused.

I know I was not the only one suffering on the tour.

I wonder if people would act differently if it were their brother, sister, mother, daughter who were being subjected to abuse? I hope so.

The tour can be a very difficult and lonely place for women, especially because most of us start to play professionally at a young age: fifteen, sixteen. You are very vulnerable. Most players travel without their parents, especially when they are starting out, because of lack of finances. They just take a coach for their tennis. That's why female tennis players should have support and protection. I was in a fragile state when Borna started coaching me. I wish I had chosen someone who had more concern for my welfare. Borna wasn't the right choice. I trusted him and in the end he really hurt me.

I don't condone the way my father reacted when he felt we were maligned and outcast. I hate how he reacted to pressure when I was rocketing up the tour rankings. In no way do I support his reckless actions and views towards Tennis Australia and the WTA. I would never in any way defend the abuse he subjected me to.

When I had finally wriggled from my father's grasp and regained faith in myself, recognised that I could play without him, my relationship with Borna drained me mentally. Coupled with my shoulder and wrist injury, in the end I couldn't get a clear run; I was always fighting something or someone. And after fighting for twenty-five years I was tired, mentally done, finished with tennis.

After I stopped playing, depression hit me hard again. My identity is tennis. Since the age of six, it's all I have really known. For some years after I retired I struggled with life away from the tour. While my father detested life on the road, I loved it. The buzz, the hectic lifestyle, the crowds, the adrenalin. When that buzz is not there life is quiet. I searched for answers and struggled to find them.

Now I am in a great place. I am finding and discovering new passions, discovering what I am good at outside of tennis, and learning new skills. I've enjoyed doing things such as commentating, which has shown me I have a knack for analysis – I can pick up a flaw or a strength in a player's game in a heartbeat. I draw on my tour life and tell the audience just what it feels like to be out there, in front of an excitable and loud grand slam crowd. I enjoy being in front of the camera.

Another thing I like very much is being a coach and mentor, advising and teaching junior and pro players about the game I love. I have so much experience and knowledge I can share and pass on. I'm also doing motivational speaking, which I find very rewarding: I can pass on my experiences and knowledge to help others. Charity work is something I look forward to doing more of.

My mum and I have a better relationship these days. We've had many conversations around whether she could have done things differently, if she could have done more to protect me. But she was in love with my father and, in a sense, under his spell. Also, she didn't want me to grow up in a broken home and without a father. Do I understand her fear of him and what would happen if she escaped? Yes, I do. Because of the hell I was put through when I left – and I know he made her life unbearable – I understand her fear and concerns, even if I have mixed feelings about her lack of support and protection during those awful, abusive years.

My brother, Savo, has brought me constant joy. Over the past years I have loved having him back in my life. He's lifted me up and made me smile when I have been down. It's a special relationship, the family relationship I most treasure. I wish he had been older when everything was happening. If he had been older than me maybe he could have protected me. At any rate, things would have been different – we could have been together in the tough times. And because I was young when I left home, and he was eight years younger, there was nothing I could do but leave him with my parents. But I never for one second abandoned him. I wish I could turn back time and watch him grow up. I missed too much of his childhood.

It's impossible to express just how important it is for me to be there for my brother. I believe that I didn't commit suicide because of my great love for him, and my need to protect him. The same goes for Tin.

Tin, my rock, who saved me. We've been together since we were twenty; as I write, that is going on fourteen years. He's been an unwavering force by my side through more bad times than good. He has never faltered. Never let me down. Over the years we have been together I have been overweight, depressed, bankrupt and on the verge of ending my life and he has never once said, 'This is too hard, I am leaving.'

He accepts me for who I am. He's my best friend and the love of my life.

Because of what we have been through, we want to parent our future children differently from how I was raised. It's very important to us to do it right. That is my biggest mission in life. Of course we want to have our own children, but we would also love to adopt a child in need.

As you now know, my story hasn't been a fairytale, but I don't want anyone to feel sorry for me – I am luckier than most. Healthy. No longer a victim. I am a survivor.

And I will always find a way.

Acknowledgements

Thank you to my fans in Australia and around the world for loving and supporting me and especially for giving me a second chance when I came back to Australia. I will never forget your great support during my matches; the incredible reception you gave me at the 2009 Australian Open will stay with me forever.

Thank you to my grandfather, Strahinja, who passed away when I was eight. I can hardly remember you, but I will never forget your love and kindness towards me. I did not get to say goodbye to you but thank you for loving me and making me feel so happy whenever I saw you.

Thank you to Tin's parents for your love, support and kindness no matter what. Thank you for being there for Tin and me.

Thank you to Tennis Australia for your time and investing in me when I was a kid. Without your help I would not have made it as far as I did.

Thank you to Craig Tiley for your support, advice and help; for giving me a chance and for your understanding and patience.

Thank you to Darren Pearce. You have been a wonderful supporter and friend to me, and helped me in some difficult times of my life.

Thank you to Todd Woodbridge for all your help and advice on and off the court. You gave me great direction when I stopped playing, and our conversations today continue to strengthen and inspire me.

Thank you to Roger Rasheed for your effort, time and help. Your tennis knowledge and advice has been of incredible value, your discipline and professionalism are attributes to learn from and admire. And I've enjoyed our fun conversations very much.

Thank you to Tony Roche for all your on-court help and for being so kind and understanding to me. You are not just one of the best coaches in the world but a fantastic person with such a kind heart and soul.

Thank you to Lesley Bowrey for all your hard work and for looking after me not just as a coach but as a person. I learnt so much from you. I am grateful for everything you have done for me and for having my back.

Thank you to Louise Pleming for working hard with me on the court and especially for everything you've done for me off the court. You helped in so many ways and your energy and positivity are wonderful to be around and learn from.

Thank you to Paul McNamee for your belief in me and for your constant support, patience and understanding. Especially thank you for all your help when I came back to Australia in 2005.

Thank you to coaches Drago Zorić, Milan Lacko, Josip Molnar, John Will, Chris Johnston, Glenn Schaap, Noel Callaghan,

Wally Masur, for your commitment and for making me the best player I can be.

Thank you to Aaron Kellett for your hard work and belief. You are the toughest fitness trainer I've ever had but you made each session as fun as possible and I'm so grateful for your friendship.

Thank you to Geoff Pollard for your patience and kindness; and to Patrick Mouratoglou for making us feel so welcome in your academy in France and your kindness to Tin and me.

Thank you to IMG and my managers Oliver van Lindonk and Marijn Bal for your hard work and for believing in me.

Thank you to Duje Kuvačić for being my hitting partner and for being a great friend to Tin and me.

Thank you to Namik Beganović for helping us in Australia and for welcoming us into your home.

Thank you to my manager Nick Fordham and The Fordham Agency for your support and having my back. I look forward to working with you for many years to come.

Thank you to Penguin Random House for publishing my book; to Alison Urquhart for giving me a chance to tell my story, for your support and care during difficult times and your tireless work on this book; to Catherine Hill for the exceptional edit and hard work; to David Chin for your advice, care and understanding.

Thank you to my writer Jessica Halloran for your incredible understanding, support and compassion. Thank you for your hard work and for all your trips down to Melbourne, long phone conversations and edits. Thank you for always making time for me and trying to help me, for your incredible patience, but most of all thank you for being a great friend.